Praise for Poe Ballantine

Love & Terror on the Howling Plains of Nowhere

Poe Ballantine is the most soulful, insightful, funny, and altogether luminous "under-known" writer in America. He knocks my socks off, even when I'm barefoot.

TOM ROBBINS, author of *Villa Incognito*

Ballantine's writing is secure insecurity at its best, muscular and minimal, self-deprecating on the one hand, full of the self's soul on the other.

LAUREN SLATER, author of *Lying*

Poe Ballantine is brilliant, sensitive, unique, and universal. Reading his work is inspiring, agitating, and invigorating. He is utterly transparent on the page, a rare thing. He's like a bird that's almost but not quite extinct. This is his best book ever.

CHERYL STRAYED, author of *Wild*.

If the delights of either Poe Ballantine or Chadron, Nebraska were a secret, that is over now. *Love & Terror on the Howling Plains of Nowhere* is an unprecedented combination of all of the following: true crime page-turner, violently funny portrait of a tiny Western town, field guide to saving a bilingual marriage and raising an autistic child, sutra on living with open mind and big heart. Many of the sentences start on earth and end somewhere in beat-poet heaven. Ballantine comes ever closer to being my favorite creative nonfiction writer and this is why.

MARION WINIK, NPR correspondent, author of *Above Us Only Sky* and *The Glen Rock Book of the Dead*

501 Minutes to Christ

Name an author we all need to read? Poe Ballantine's exquisitely funky *501 Minutes to Christ*.

TOM ROBBINS, Author of *Jitterbug Perfume*

Ballantine is never far from the trenches … the essays are readable and entertaining and contain occasional moments of startling beauty and insight. Still, the themes of addiction (to substances, people, new starts, the prospect of fame), dissatisfaction, and nihilism may limit the work's appeal; as with writers such as Chuck Palahniuk, some will become rabid devotees, while others will be turned off.

LIBRARY JOURNAL

Decline of the Lawrence Welk Empire

It's a downmarket version of Ben Kunkel's *Indecision*, with less surety but real vibrancy.

PUBLISHERS WEEKLY

Ballantine's genial, reckless narrator is part Huck Finn, part Hunter S. Thompson. And in a few pages he's charming you, more than any "pot-smoking, card-playing, music-loving, late night party hound" really should.

THE SEATTLE TIMES

This second novel from Ballantine initially conjures images of *Lord of the Flies*, but then you would have to add about ten years to the protagonists' ages and make them sex-crazed, gold-seeking alcoholics.

LIBRARY JOURNAL

Poe Ballantine, in this sequel to *God Clobbers Us All*, reveals that he is a writer with a keen ear and a blistering wit – it's a prime opportunity to observe a writer's joyful wallow in the decadence of words.

THE AUSTIN CHRONICLE

Edgar's supersize pal Mountain is the best of the author's creations: "He possesses a merry and absurd sweetness … combined with a body mass that can block out the sun."

BOOKLIST

Ballantine's second novel is … memorable … funny and smart.

PHILADELPHIA WEEKLY

Decline of the Lawrence Welk Empire has the same amped tone and sub-tropical setting as Hunter S. Thompson's *The Rum Diary* but less of the gonzo arrogance and more of that good ol' American angst. The prose is poised on the brink of perfection, and the plot twists into an unexpected yet perfect conclusion that makes scotch and roadkill seem almost palatable.

SAN FRANCISCO BAY GUARDIAN

God Clobbers Us All

It's impossible not to be charmed by the narrator of Poe Ballantine's comic and sparklingly intelligent *God Clobbers Us All*.

PUBLISHERS WEEKLY

Ballantine's novel is an entertaining coming-of-age story.

THE SAN FRANCISCO CHRONICLE

Calmer than Bukowski, less portentous than Kerouac, more hopeful than West, Poe Ballantine may not be sitting at the table of his mentors, but perhaps he deserves his own after all.

THE SAN DIEGO UNION-TRIBUNE

It's a compelling, quirky read.

THE OREGONIAN

Poe Ballantine has created an extremely fast page-turner. Edgar, in first-person narrative, is instantly likeable, and his constant misadventures flow seamlessly. Ballantine paints southern California with voluptuous detail.

WILLAMETTE WEEK

God Clobbers Us All succeed[s] on the strength of its characterization and Ballantine's appreciation for the true-life denizens of the Lemon Acres rest home. The gritty daily details of occupants of a home for the dying have a stark vibrancy that cannot help but grab one's attention, and the off-hours drug, surf, and screw obsessions of its young narrator, Edgar Donahoe, and his coworkers have a genuine sheen that captivates almost as effectively.

THE ABSINTHE LITERARY REVIEW

A wry and ergoty experience.

GOBSHITE QUARTERLY

Things I Like About America

Ballantine never shrinks from taking us along for the drunken, drug-infested ride he braves in most of his travels. The payoff – and there is one – lies in his self-deprecating humor and acerbic social commentary, which he leaves us with before heading further up the dark highway.

THE INDY BOOKSHELF

Part social commentary, part collective biography, this guided tour may not be comfortable, but one thing's for sure: You will be at home.

WILLAMETTE WEEK

Meet the new guide on the lonesome highway. Poe Ballantine's wry voice, clear eye, hilarious accounts and lyrical language bring us up short by reminding us that America has always been about flight, and for most of its citizens it has been about defeat. His wanderings, drifters, bad motels, cheap wine, dead-end jobs and drugs take us home, the home Betty Crocker never lived in. We're on the road again, but this time we know better than to hope for a rumbling V-8 and any answers blowing in the wind. The bus has been a long time coming, but thank God it has arrived with Mr. Ballantine aboard. Sit down, give him a listen and make your own list of *Things I Like About America*.

CHARLES BOWDEN, author of *Blues for Cannibals* and *Blood Orchid*

Poe Ballantine reminds us that in a country full of identical strip malls and chain restaurants, there's still room for adventure. He finds the humor in situations most would find unbearable and flourishes like a modern-day Kerouac. It's a book to cherish and pass on to friends.

MARK JUDE POIRIER, author of *Unsung Heroes of American Industry* and *Goats*

Poe Ballantine makes writing really well seem effortless, even as he's telling us how painful writing is. He knows that life is the most funny when it shouldn't be, and that the heart breaks the most during small moments. These stories are shining gems. He kills me, this guy.

MIMI POND, author of *Splitting Hairs: The Bald Truth About Bad Hair Days*

In his search for the real America, Poe Ballantine reminds me of the legendary musk deer, who wanders from valley to valley and hilltop to hilltop searching for the source of the intoxicating musk fragrance that actually comes from him. Along the way, he writes some of the best prose I've ever read.

SY SAFRANSKY, Publisher, *The Sun*

Copyright © 2013
Poe Ballantine

Library of Congress
Cataloging-in-Publication Data

Ballantine, Poe, 1955–
Love and terror on the howling
plains of nowhere / Poe Ballantine.
pages cm
ISBN 978-0-9834775-4-9

1. Ballantine, Poe, 1955–
2. Authors, American–20th
    century–Biography.
3. Chadron (Neb.)–Biography

I. Title.
PS3602.A599Z46 2013
814'.6–dc23
[B]
2013000038

Hawthorne Books
& Literary Arts

9 2201 Northeast 23rd Avenue
8 3rd Floor
7 Portland, Oregon 97212
6 hawthornebooks.com
5 *Form:*
4 Adam McIsaac, Bklyn, NY
3
2 Printed in China
1 Set in Paperback

For Sy "Saffron Sky" Safransky

Love & Terror on the Howling Plains of Nowhere

A Memoir
Poe Ballantine

HAWTHORNE BOOKS & LITERARY ARTS
Portland, Oregon | MMXIII

Introduction
by Cheryl Strayed

THERE'S A SECRET SOCIETY OF US: THE PEOPLE WHO love Poe Ballantine. I don't mean love him personally. I mean love his work. His smart, funny, perceptive, crack-your-head-and-heart-open and holy-smokes-I-have-to-pause-so-I-can-read-that-paragraph-again-because-it-was-so-damn-good work. When we find each other we say, *Oh my god, don't you just LOVE HIM?* And we do. We love Poe Ballantine.

No, but I mean really.

And then there's a whole conversation we have about the nature of our love for him and the conversation kind of hurts because the way we love him is so genuine and gigantic it's essentially inexpressible – ours being the unrequited passion of a reader who can only truly inhabit his or her love in the solitary and entirely particular act of reading itself, in the private bedazzlement of words on a page or computer screen – so of him we are left to simply say to each other: *Wow. Yes. Jesus. Poe!*

I've met him in real life twice. The first time was in a thundering echo chamber of a convention center hall in Portland, Oregon in 2006. The second was in the company of a gaggle of writers in the back of a white stretch limousine with groovy interior lighting in Chicago in 2012. Both times I attempted to fully express my admiration for his work. Both times I failed, able to do little more than utter: *Wow. Yes. Jesus. Poe!*

So when I learned that he had a new book coming out and his editor, Rhonda Hughes, asked me to write the introduction to it, I immediately said yes. Finally, I had the opportunity to say what I've always wanted to say about Poe Ballantine – not only to the secret society of those who already love him – but to the jillions of people who have not yet become members of what I'll just go ahead and call the *Wow. Yes. Jesus. Poe!* Club for reasons that have nothing to do with his inspiring, agitating, hilarious, invigorating, big-hearted writing and everything to do with the complexities and challenges of getting ass-kickingly good books into the hands of readers.

Poe Ballantine is an original. He comes from the place all great artists do – the gloriously singular hell pot of everything that made him – and like all great artists, he brings all of himself to the page. The odd-job drifter. The committed and loving father. The drug-addled mooch. The self-loathing writer. The ambivalent but deeply moral spouse. The train-hopping world traveller. The best friend you'd ever hope to have. The half-in-love but mostly just horny jackass. The uncommonly kind neighbor. The line cook with stunning punctuality. The insecure kid with the zits on his face. The smitten student of Spanish. The why'd-you-go-and-do that punk. The hysterically frank middle-aged ranter-and-raver.

He's all of these things and more in his work. You know who Ballantine is in every sentence he writes because in his mastery he makes himself known. He's bold and perceptive and utterly transparent. He writes like every word is his last. Like the whole place is about to burn up. He's like a bird that's not quite but almost extinct: when you see him, you can't help but look.

I love every book he's written, but I love this one most. In *Love and Terror on the Howling Plains of Nowhere*, Ballantine gives us everything he's got. It's a spellbinding story of a good man who died mysteriously and a moving memoir of uncommon grace, intelligence, and generosity. As I read it, the book seemed to glue itself to my hands. I never wanted to put it down. When I did, finally, after reading the last page, I said what I always say about Ballantine: *Wow. Yes. Jesus. Poe!*

Welcome to the Club.

LOVE & TERROR
ON THE HOWLING PLAINS
OF NOWHERE

Prologue

JEANNE (PRONOUNCED GEE-KNEE) GOETZINGER, MY EM-
ployer for close to four years, called me on the phone on March
9, 2006, with news that our missing math professor had finally
been found. Jeanne's hotel, The Olde Main Street Inn, is right
next to police headquarters and because you can cross-reference
or background check any resident of this rumorous rural town
at her Longbranch Saloon, I call it Grapevine Substation #1.

I lived just three blocks east of the Olde Main Street Inn,
on First Street, right along the railroad tracks. I was looking
out the window when Jeanne called. A train carrying lumber was
passing slowly by. Jeanne told me in a thrilled hush she'd just
received word that Professor Steven Haataja (pronounced *Hah-
de-ya*) had been found bound and dead in a ditch. That was all
the information she had but she would call me back when there
was more.

Two hours later she called again. The body was burned
and bound, not recognizable as a man or woman, she amended,
and they were doing some tests to determine its identity.

Fascinated by, and sympathetic to, the unusual details of
Steven's baffling disappearance more than three months before,
I had undertaken a book on the subject, which had also afforded
me the opportunity to discuss my very quiet but quirky Western
Nebraska town and some of its exotic characters. I had no idea the
story would turn out like this.

"Who else could it be?" I said, unable to imagine how such a thing might have happened.

When I learned that the burned and bound body was indeed Steven Haataja, that the circumstances surrounding his death had no explanation, that the police themselves had thrown up their hands, I thought innocently: I will solve this mystery and bring to Steven and his family justice.

But let's begin at the beginning.

1.

Last stop: Chadron, Nebraska

I FIRST CAME ACROSS CHADRON, NEBRASKA, BY ACCIDENT, in 1994. I had borrowed a car, thrown all my meager belongings in the back, and driven west, the direction of escape after disaster, the direction of decline and the setting sun. I intended to kill myself. The farther you go west, the higher the suicide rate gets, and I thought perhaps that would give me the momentum I needed. In America we remake ourselves, though it rarely works out.

I was 38, $5,000 in debt from a school loan that I'd wasted by dropping out of school (an aborted attempt at becoming a drug counselor). All my beliefs about sacrificing everything to become a novelist had amounted to nothing. To top it off I had just come off a dizzying romantic flop with a Spanish professor I had no business being with in the first place. I had been drifting for some time, starting all over freshly unknown in a new town – 15 states in the last 10 years, without any measurable results. The road had long lost its savor. I was not in the best state of mind. It was no coincidence that I was about as far away as I could get from the people I loved.

A funny thing happened when I arrived in Chadron, however; a bucolic, hardscrabble, sandblasted prairie town of 5,000 in the northwest corner of the state, the panhandle as it's called, elevation 3,400 feet, a quaint, forested, friendly old snow-still-on-the-ground-in-May town. Chadron had a water tower, grain elevators, a tanning salon, a video rental store, a small liberal arts college, a Hardee's, a stoplight, and a curling yellow sign in the pet store window that read: "Hamsters and Tarantulas Featured Today." There were abandoned houses everywhere. It felt like a dying town, politely hanging on. I felt akin. I felt indebted. I thought, you know, we can't all win the game. So why not just shut up for a change and be satisfied with what you have? Why not just be a good neighbor and live an honorable life and take out the trash? Why not stop torturing yourself about fame and art? Why not relent, marry a reformed hooker, buy some old furniture and a ping-pong table, become a Cornhusker fan, open a dusty bottle of Kentucky straight, turn on the Rockies game, and enjoy the brief time you have left on this weird planet of sorrow?

Most people would live in an outhouse in Bangladesh before they would voluntarily move to Nebraska. They drive through the state on I-80 and think of it in a vague, resentful way as a flat expanse of interminable boredom sparsely populated with pigs, rednecks, and blue-eyed howdies juggling their nuts among the deep rows of sweet corn. Nebraska? Are you kidding me? I heard the same Nebraska joke twice before I got here: "Custer says to his men, got good news and bad. Good news is that we're all going to be massacred at Little Big Horn. Bad news is that we have to cross Nebraska to get there." The panhandle of Nebraska is actually more like Colorado in flavor, with topo-graphical variation, forest, buttes, bluffs, black cowboy hats, gun racks in the pickup trucks, craggy, sinewy faces, cloud formations like lost civilizations, not much corn except for the ethanol-fortune-seekers fouling up the water table, and the insistent mes-sage of self-reliance.

This town has been poor since it can remember, one reason people are so inclined to cooperate. The land is dominated by wheat, cows, and education. Unlike the rest of Nebraska, Chadron doesn't quite sit on the great Ogallala aquifer, so there isn't much water here. The closest lake is 20 miles. It rains about 16 inches a year. Western Nebraska is the only place in all my travels where I have seen the dust blowing and the rain falling at the same time.

2.

City of barking dogs

I RENTED A ROOM AT THE ROUNDUP MOTEL OUT ON THE highway, right across from the Chuck Wagon restaurant, for $16 a night. The room was solid with homey touches, doilies, and a real quilted counterpane and pine wainscoting. The small phone book listed the businesses and residences of four states. In the weekly paper, *The Chadron Record*, amid the softball scores, the courthouse news, the sermon of the week, the super cheap houses, and the very few jobs available, I found a textual antidepressant called *Police Beat*, a log of the latest week's calls to the Chadron Police Department:

> 5:24 P.M. Caller from the 400 block of Chapin St. stated that the dog across the street is not supposed to be outside because it is so small. She stated that the dog should be inside and if the owners didn't want it she would buy it from them. Officer told caller that he could not require the owner to sell the dog, officer then inspected the dog and it was not lacking anything. Officer informed caller that just because the dog is not played with does not make it abused.

> 7:13 P.M. Caller from the 500 block of King St. advised that somebody cut his clothesline in his backyard and hung a scarecrow on it. He advised he just wanted it on record. He also advised that he was going to keep the scarecrow if nobody claimed it.

> 1:26 A.M. Caller from the 300 block of Lake St. advised he just got home from the bar and his truck had been wrecked. Caller stated he didn't drive tonight because he knew he'd be drunk.

In *The Chadron Record* I also found a shack for $150 per month in the alley off of Mears Street, not far from the Native American Center, one block north of the railroad tracks. This had once been a railroad town. There had also been a Swedish-tooled flour mill along the tracks that had burned down long ago. Any hopes of rebuilding the flour mill had been dashed by the cost of the new parts required from Sweden.

My new home was two rooms, furnished, bathtub and toilet, a small yard with two tall Siberian elms, a bit "rough," as the agent described it, with a small Smithsonian refrigerator that froze all my vegetables, giving new meaning to the word "crisper." In the bedroom was Betsy Ross's original mattress, the broken springs of which stuck up through the fabric like the tails of welded pigs, the whole nightly experience rather like lying on a bed of nails, though you could arrange your body on the mattress the way a river arranges itself through a forest, and it was better any day than a hard chair in a bus terminal or the front seat of a borrowed car at a rest stop.

My life was settled: one cup, one plate, one fork, one knife, a spoon, a Bible, fingernail clippers, radio, scissors, hydrogen peroxide, toothpaste, notebooks, grease-stained raiment, pots and pans and pens all in their proper places. A hamburger in a Styrofoam container. A dead grasshopper. An emaciated spider. A gallon of red wine. Three packages of Old Golds. How many times have I done this, vowed to end my days, started over, lied to myself about settling down, believed that something essential in me had changed, when nothing of the kind had happened? And how long would it be before I was packing up all my crap and running off again?

Though Chadron is a Lakota word for "city of barking dogs," and each resident is required to tie his dog up in the yard until it barks itself unconscious, presumably to frighten off coyotes, there are times when the peace of this town, the quiet of inaction, is so thick that you have to get up and check out the window to see if the world has not come to an end. Time here is as big as the sky, especially when you don't know anyone, so I would take long walks through town, past the abandoned homes, the rows of trailers and prefabs, the original 19th century log cabins, the classic Puritan boxes, the Dutch bungalows, the Georgian mansionettes with their wide porticoed verandas and weeping birch trees out front. Sometimes I walked up into the hills south of campus. There were trails that led back into the hinterland. If you walked far enough south the pine forest resumed. Standing up here you could see the curve of the earth and great floating rafts of rain, like islands made out of iron and whipped cream.

The year before, when I'd quit school midsemester, it was curious that the professor who had taught *Beowulf* would be the one to insist I see him in his office. I called him from a pay phone instead. He urged me to stay in school. He insisted that I had much to offer. My grades were good enough to make me eligible for many privileges, including an assistant teaching position and the probability of a handsome fellowship. He wondered what I would do if I quit school without a degree. I told him I did not know what I would do, but I wanted something more for my life's work than a bench named after me or a memorial tree. I didn't want to be comfortable in the cafeteria with the vents blowing Alzheimer's spores all around and an unopened volume of Henry Wadsworth Longfellow in my lap. "Do you remember where the glory in *Beowulf* is?" I asked him. "It is out amid peril in strange lands pitted against monsters and the mothers of monsters. It isn't in the warm mead hall with roasted meats and the comfort of jesters and wenches." Sometimes you can hear a nod on the other end of the line. He was silent for a time. I don't think he ever dreamed that anything he taught would have this kind of effect on a student. He let me go after that, even wished me luck.

In spite of the fact that I'd already laboriously composed 14 complete novels unfit to print, the recollection of this adolescent fantasy, and also the fact that I had nothing else really to do, made me want to write another. If the horse throws you off, get back on, even if it kicks you in the head and you suffer irreversible brain damage. Who's going to notice? Wasn't Thomas Pynchon kicked by a horse?

My trusty 286 word processor had burned up in the Iowa

summer heat the year before and I didn't have the cash to replace it, but I had never been able to write anything worthwhile on a machine anyway, so I decided to write my next novel longhand. Name all the great novels written on word processors. If Dickens had a word processor *Great Expectations* would've been the first novel to circumnavigate the globe.

My new novel sustained me. It was my psychological Jesus: comfort, purpose, magic, spirit, transformation, companion-ship, salvation, sacrifice. I jotted down gems on napkins, chanted sage insights *sotto voce* until memorized, remarked on an angle of light or a gesture. I snatched up my 110-sheet Mead notebook and scrawled epiphanies into the margins. The novel was my mad lover and my only faithful friend. It sang to me its sea-nymph song as the alley dogs yapped and the homeless Indians combed through the dumpsters for aluminum cans, as I shopped for green discount meat at Safeway, as the grasshoppers munched through the blasted verdure and the tumbleweeds bounced along on their way east or south. Now and then I would lean back in my chair and think of my academic debt, my enforced jack-off solitude, the stubborn lifetime of menial jobs that awaited me. No wonder I was so depressed.

3.

Olde Main Street Inn

WHEREVER I'VE TRAVELED, NO MATTER THE SEASON OR circumstances – except in Las Vegas, a fluorescent strip of flypaper for the lost, desperate, and insane – I've never had much trouble finding work. I put in my application at all six (non fast-food) Chadron area restaurants, the truck stop, Valentino's, the 120, the South Forty, the Chuck Wagon, Helen's out on the highway. Since no one else wants them, cooking jobs are the easiest to get when you land in a new town. There is a culinary revolution happening in this country, but that's mostly on television. The real life of short-order cooking is not about shallots, white truffle oil, and foie gras, but about instant mashed potatoes, frozen burger patties, and Pan 'n Grill. It's about low pay, high heat, high pressure, injury, the guy who doesn't show up for work, a short lifespan, and working with jailbirds, junkies, drifters, and drunks.

But no positions were open. The Chadron economy had been a little slow since about 1897. What was the hurry? Sometimes you'd see drivers sitting for hours at the four-way stops, tires flat, birds building nests in their hair. I filed at Job Service (unemployment). I was in no hurry either. I had 400 bucks and the rent was paid. The fierce pink sunsets and the magnificent storms with their purple splits of lightning did their best to entertain me, though I have never found much solace in the grandeur of nature.

THE CONVALESCENT HOSPITAL had an ad in the paper for a breakfast cook and the dull pressure of institutional cooking appealed to me over the hellion lunacy of short order. But Will, the captain of the old folks' kitchen, who would go on to work with mentally retarded people and Nebraskaland Tires before he finally settled into a cool landscape job with the city schools, thought I was overqualified.

I had cooked in several restaurants in San Diego, at the Broadmoor Hotel in Colorado Springs, at the Caneel Bay Plantation in the U.S. Virgin Islands, a diner in Iowa, two hotels in Las Vegas, a dinner house in Vermont, a vegetarian place in Northern California, my own kitchen in a bar and another restaurant in Niagara Falls, and so on. So he sent me across town to a bed and breakfast on Main Street, which I had not applied to because of its name, where I was immediately hired as a full-time dinner cook at $4.25 an hour.

Jeanne, the owner of the Olde Main Street Inn, a hotel/restaurant/saloon, was a fiery orange-haired German divorcée, a Harley enthusiast, a hunter, and a jolly member of the National Rifle Association. She did not trust me at first (that's all right, I'm used to it). "Where are you from?" she demanded.

"Born in Denver, raised in San Diego."

"I mean, how did you end up here?" she asked, the question without fail, wherever I go.

"I move every few months," I said, "remote and unlikely places." Listeners are usually interested in my life in a skeptical yet vicarious way. Most people want to travel from town to town, though they don't trust those who do, employers especially. I was reluctant to say that I wrote and that since I was philosophically abstract and romantically inept, that travail and travelogue were the only adventure I could really offer. I presented a cliché about restlessness and travel being the best education, which satisfied her.

She could not believe that someone with my qualifications would walk through her door and accede to four and a quarter an hour. She thought I was one of the dozens of frauds, hustlers, bounders, and thieves that had paraded through her kitchen the last few years and by now had moved on to Las Vegas. For a week or so she wouldn't even let me take my tool bag down into the kitchen for fear that I would haul out a prime rib. The moment she realized that I had talent, however, that I came as advertised, she expanded her menu to include a fresh soup du jour, a daily pasta special, and locally dressed lamb, which I marinated in oil, rosemary, garlic, and thyme, and grilled to order. I sharpened all her knives and added a pecan-butter-brown sugar-Tabasco sauce option for the salmon. Fresh chopped parsley replaced dried. The lettuce out on the salad bar went from bagged oxidized iceberg with grated carrots and red cabbage, to fresh romaine. The frozen corn on the cob eventually gave way to snap peas in olive oil with red onions. Fresh trout arrived. I was given a 50 cent an hour raise. And so on.

Jeanne's hotel was reputedly haunted. How else do you explain the staircase apparitions, the green beer from the tap when it wasn't St. Patrick's Day, the glass that cracked audibly on the bar of its own volition, the call from room 207 when the hotel was empty (on a ring-down system where the call could not have come from outside the hotel), the time an Australian guest had come flying in terror down the stairs after being touched by an invisible hand, the peculiar evening when Lorri, Jeanne's daughter, was spattered with mint jelly all alone in the dish room shortly after declaring her dislike for mint jelly (she thought I flipped it at her, but I was upstairs)?

Jeanne liked to call herself "Madam" after the possibility of her illustrious old hotel once entertaining hired ladies in the rooms upstairs. Her saloon downstairs is one of the most unusual I have ever encountered, open to all, but particularly inhabited by cowboys, Indians (who are *persona non grata* in most other drinking establishments around town), police officers, bikers, and gays. A Cowboy-Indian-Biker-Police-Gay bar, tell me the last time you walked into one of those. Artists, like the mad potter, Bob Zelig, also liked the Olde Main. The frowzy-headed Bob usually sold out his ceramics and paintings early whenever he got the energy to attend a show. Bob was the most talented and prolific artist in town, even when he was messed up on drugs, and could've made his living solely as an artist if he cared to travel, but he preferred to stay home, experimenting in his basement lab and keeping his job as a maintenance man at the local college.

I became fast friends with Jeanne's daughter, Lorri, who ran her mother's kitchen but conceded the broiler to me. Lorri was and still is a remarkable pastel painter, who sells her paintings for thousands of dollars. She is a wine snob, and remains to this day a skeptic on all things spiritual, especially ghosts, even in the face of flying mint jelly (or was it really ectoplasm?). We stayed up late many nights after the shift smoking menthols, drinking wine, and jabbering about art, God, sex, music, and the unusual characters who passed all night through her mother's barroom doors.

After painting, Lorri would sometimes come over to my place, always late with a bottle of good wine, her vision skewed, her brain crackling like an electric frying pan. "I can't even see straight. I could barely drive over here."

"What are you working on?"

"Oh, it's a portrait of that girl I was telling you about from Hay Springs. Her boyfriend just dumped her.

"The Satan-worshiping dwarf?"

"That's the one. It's in the car, do you want to see it?"

Portraits were her specialty. She had the uncanny ability to draw out the scary, vulnerable, lost, and shattered parts of her subjects, which didn't always please them. She painted me once. I looked intently confused and appeared to be dressed in a straitjacket. I thought it a good likeness.

A more compatible woman I had not met in a while. Something would've surely happened between us (wouldn't it?) if she hadn't already had a boyfriend, George, a drummer in a band, the best thing that had ever happened to her, the man who had made all the bad dreams finally stop, and isn't that the way it always works?

4.

Wyoming!

SHORT-ORDER COOKING REQUIRES THAT ONE PERFORM a countless sequence of overlapping 45-second tasks that all must be executed in 30. Short order is spinning in circles with a smoking spatula while waitresses shout, a bell rings constantly, and a broken egg dries on your shoe. My nerves would be barking and I would still be whirling spastically with the bell ringing in my ear and I'd have a steam burn on my wrist when I got home. Dear Coroner: No need for an examination. Just please write in "Short-Order Cooking" as cause of death.

A short wet spring soon gave way to a murderously hot summer. The days were as long as medieval dragons and even harder to kill. It was so hot the squirrels took off their jackets, dredged themselves in cornmeal, and arranged themselves with pearl onions in buttered pans. The cicadas screamed from the trees and the wild rhubarb wilted, the sky turned white, and the town melted into a puddle of molten lava-colored sunlight. The creeks pooped out and turned belly-up in their dusty beds. Even the mosquitoes and the weeds seemed to long for winter. My little shack was sweltering.

One night late a giant, trembling, cockeyed simpleton, shoulders wide as a snowplow, knocked on my door. "I'm Byron," he announced in a voice trilling with insane cheer, his boot up in my doorway. "I live right next door there. I'm your neighbor. They call me Lord Byron of Windsor," he said, the iris of his right eye banging against the bridge of his nose. "Hell, I'm your neighbor."

I shook the giant's rough hand. With his great beak of a nose, mismatched eyes, and fast, high, ecstatic way of talking, Byron reminded me of an enormous cuckoo bird. "We're havin' a party over at my house," he explained, indicating with elated eastward thumb jabs. "A party, me and Hazel." He was so happy to see me I felt I might be his long-lost brother. "You wanna come over for a beer?"

BYRON'S SHACK, THOUGH a bit roomier than mine, had the same thin walls, ancient floor heater, and starved daddy long-legs shriveled in the corners. There were biker and naked-women tapestries covering his walls. On one of the tapestries the naked women had begun to turn into serpents. Byron also had cable TV, a swiveling three-speed fan, and an armless man with just one finger extending from his right shoulder and a huge, red pock-marked head sitting on a barstool at the counter between the kitchen and the living room. "This is Hazel," said Byron, as if he were showing me the Hope Diamond. "Hazel Devine. We're best buds."

Hazel Devine wore big Dave Garroway plastic-framed glasses, white corduroy shorts, and a crisp white polo shirt. A purple bruise around his red-streaked left eye had spread up into his temple. His right sleeve was carefully cuffed back to allow for the free play of that lone finger, which he wiggled at me. I accepted the finger and gave it a firm shake.

"Sit on down, Poe. Get 'im a beer, Clown," he said. "We been wanting to invite you over for some time. Where you from anyway?"

I told them Iowa last, Mississippi before that. I'd been moving for some time and all the rest of that Dion song, round and round and round and round.

"What do you do?" Hazel said, hunching down to suck at the beer in front of him through a bent straw.

"I'm a cook over at the Olde Main."

He pressed the ball of his bare foot to his face and took a

thoughtful drag from the cigarette propped between his big and middle toes. The grin on his face was mostly a muscle configuration to keep his glasses from sliding off. "I sell cars," he said. "What kind of car you drive?"

"I don't have a car."

"What?" he said, teetering back on his stool so far that my instinct was to lunge to keep him from going over.

"Haven't had a car for years," I said. "Too expensive."

Byron fished a Busch Light out of the fridge, cracked it for me, and handed it shyly across, his funny eye shivering in his head. "I don't have a car either," he said.

"Jesus Christ," said Hazel. "The Clown can't drive because he's had so many DUIs. Went to prison on account of all the DUIs."

"Idaho," said Byron with a sentimental mist forming on his eyes. "I miss them days. You could get a job at Simplot, just go in there and get a good-paying job. One time I stood in a room with a bucket of glue and every time a box went by with a flap up I'd slap on some glue and seal the flap on it. I was married in Idaho, too, and had some nice furniture and worked at Simplot."

"Hell, Byron, you went to *prison* in Idaho," Hazel interrupted.

"What do you do now, Byron?" I asked.

"Work at the sawmill," he said. "I oil the chain and sweep."

"That won't last," Hazel said, pushing his spectacles back against his battered face with the ball of his foot. "They don't pay. Oughta get you a real job. Then you could pay your bills. He's two months behind on his cable and they're gonna shut off his heat," he explained to me, taking a peck from his smoke. "Gonna be snow ass-high to an Indian in three months and you aren't gonna have any heat."

I'd already grown used to Hazel's legs on the table, moving about like wondrously shaped arms with long stumpy-toed hands. He shook his head. "God, I'm half plowed-under. Give Poe here another one. You're probably wondering how I got this black eye," he said. "Well, tried to take a piss by myself, slipped in the bathroom and fell flat on my face." Hazel said. "How long was I out, Byron?"

"'Bout five minutes," Byron answered.

"I'm lucky I didn't *drown*. Byron, help me down here. I gotta pee."

I stayed late that night. I liked the fan and the cold beer and the cable TV. Being with these two convivial men was like a merge of *Of Mice and Men* and *A Farewell to Arms*. I learned that Byron's parents had abandoned him when he was 14. Byron had come home from school one day and his parents had simply left town without him. "The Clown is slow," Hazel said when Byron was out of the room. "Do you know what I mean? Re-TAR-ded. He don't understand work. He don't understand money. I been taking care of him for 37 years. Ever since his folks left him high and dry."

But "the Clown," or "Lord Byron of Windsor" (a nickname he earned in detox), as he was sometimes called, would've much rather been in Idaho, or Wyoming would've been all right too. "I was in Rawlings once," he said. "A job laying cable. That's a nice town, Rawlings. We laid cable right up into the winter."

Except for a year in Kansas City working for the Department of Transportation, Hazel had lived all of his life in Chadron. He had attended the Catholic high school and married the same woman he went to the prom with. He was proud to recount the pugilistic exploits of his two healthy-armed sons. From what I could gather, Hazel was very good at selling cars. He'd sold Byron two or three different cars over the years, but Byron had had so much trouble with drinking and driving that he'd finally just given up the driving part.

At least two evenings a week I found myself perched on a stool at that island between Lord Byron's kitchen and the living room, drinking cold light beer and watching Byron play valet to his devoted companion. Hazel did most of the talking. Byron laughed in all the right places. Hazel crouched over his cigarettes like a starving man on a fried chicken wing. His wife wouldn't let him smoke, he explained, and he couldn't smoke down at the lot because it was just bad form when your customers saw you smoking with your feet.

On Tuesdays, Hazel's day off from the lot, Byron and Hazel often took what they called "tiny trips," which were actually daylong, meandering, beer-propelled, Odyssean expeditions along the cattle trails and barbed-wire ridges of Willa Cather consciousness. Since I had lost all fear of dying and had Tuesdays off, too, I went with them when invited, rode in the back of Hazel's burnt-orange '76 convertible Impala, distributed the cans of warm beer, scouted for cops, marveled at the massive cloud structures, and let come what may out of the Grendel darkness, even if the armless man, "half plowed-under," as he was fond of saying, always drove.

The whole purpose of a tiny trip was to land yourself in some unaccountable condition as far away from home as possible; Wyoming, for example, or the Pine Ridge Indian Reservation in South Dakota at midnight, probably the most dangerous place you could put yourself after dark, but these forays were easy for me to understand. They were miniature versions of what I had done all my life: escapes from dreariness and decrepitude, or if you prefer: peril in strange lands pitted against monsters and the mothers of monsters. Hazel was an exceptional driver, one bare foot on the wheel, the other foot planted on the gas, chin mashed down on his chest, the lone finger twirling a friendly greeting to all those who passed us openmouthed.

Toward the end of one of these tiny trips, a drunken Hazel was avoiding law enforcement by taking the back roads across the ranch-dotted grassland. He knew that network of rural, mostly unpaved roads well, but one time we did end up in Wyoming. The moon was full. The spiral of Andromeda was bright. Hazel slammed on the brakes when he saw the sign. To the right was a familiar sight, a farm failed long ago, an old rust-ravaged harvester with the door fallen off, a singlewide trailer with its windows blasted out, a crumbling paintless barn, the privy blown down.

"Wyoming!" Hazel bellowed, kicking his door open and waddling out to survey the distance from the top of a berm. He seemed deeply offended. "By God!" he said in amazement several more times. "We're in Wy-O-ming." He was secretly pleased, however.

As was Byron, drunk and slumped in his seat. Those summer nights were usually cool, a dry high-plains cool, the stars a glittering powder across the sky.

5.
Mexico

THAT SEPTEMBER I WAS SO SICK OF LIVING IN A HOT box and working in a greasy hole and being shouted at for $4.75 an hour and having novels blow up on me that I took several tiny trips in the hopes that I would be killed in a car wreck. This brand of recklessness often backfires, working instead by the humor of the gods like a talisman in your favor – but on one of these trips, at Sioux Sundries in Harrison, Nebraska, the last town west before Wyoming, I did have the pleasure of witnessing Byron finish what was billed at the time as the largest hamburger in the world (the patty alone weighed in at nearly two pounds), an extraordinary feat. The 51-year-old Byron had never graduated from high school, but he paraded around that day clutching his Official Completion of Burger Certificate as if he were up on a platform in a gown and pasteboard cap accepting his diploma. "That was easy like a regular hamburger," he said every few minutes, his face flushing. "Like a little old cheeseburger. I might just have me a fudge sundae. Extra fudge on it. Shee-ut." I took unusual satisfaction from Byron's late-life achievement. Raymond Chandler, recall, did not publish his first novel until his early 50s. Colonel Sanders didn't begin franchising Kentucky Fried Chicken until he was 62. Noah did not invent wine until he was 600 years old. Maybe by the time I had my moment in the sun, I would be an old man, too.

In spite of all the friends I'd made and the pleasant eccentricity of my surroundings, I struggled as usual with restlessness, self-loathing, and not making a dent in the world of literature. Wanting to head south again before the first big snow, I only stayed in Chadron for six months. Lorri gave me a ride to the bus terminal in Rapid City, an hour and a half north, and I bought a one-way ticket to Hot Springs, Arkansas, where I planned to hole up for the winter. It was Halloween and I had $600. It snowed all the way across South Dakota, but as the bus turned south through Iowa and Illinois the snow began to turn to rain. I rarely travel on the brink of winter. It isn't smart. People are settled, jobs are taken, rentals are filled, the weather is rarely an ally.

I continued to travel for the next few years, California, Texas, Kansas, Ohio, Wisconsin, Mexico, picking up odd jobs and composing novels with special internal mechanisms that would make them explode like trick cigars. I kept telling myself the next place I'd stop, the next place I'd stay (the dream is dead, just admit it). But I could not quit my dream (it was all I had) and I could not escape that cycle of failure and flight, failure and flight. Hard as I tried to stick it out in each new place, there was never any reason to stay. I'd always thought as I got older I would slow down, eventually settle and have a family (that notion of companionship dies pretty hard, too), but I was only moving faster and faster, like an escaped electron in a particle smasher.

While living in Kansas in a residential motel and working at a radio antenna factory, a story I'd compressed from that failed longhand novel in Chadron won me a prize and then a book contract with Houghton Mifflin. It was a fluke and most of the people I knew, including me, had trouble digesting its meaning. A fat granite Cheerio had already been inscribed in the pantheon above my name. How could I achieve anything now? Nevertheless, my dream had come true at last. I was 41 years old. Finally, I thought, with more relief than joy, I can settle down, find a girl, be normal, be satisfied, be myself, stop starting over, stop working in factories, warehouses, and kitchens, stop running. A few months later, bored with myself and alone, I took off for Mexico.

6.
Cristinaland

IN THE SUMMER OF 1999, CRISTINA GOT FLATTENED
BY a drunk driver as she was crossing a busy street in the capital
city of Zacatecas, Mexico. Her head hit the pavement and she
was knocked unconscious. Her pelvis was fractured. She was told
she might not ever walk again. She spent a month in bed, much
longer learning to walk again. Her 20/20 vision would continue
to deteriorate. I met her two years after the accident in her
hometown of Jerez, Zacatecas. She was a student of English at the
instituto where I was teaching for two dollars an hour after my
advance from Houghton Mifflin had run out and my contract with
them had fizzled because I could not get along with my editor.
Cristina was a quiet, serious young dentist who lived with her
parents. Her English was terrible. At 27 she had no boyfriend and
was inclined to stay in during the evenings drinking tea with
her mother. I was 44 and I had been alone for a chewy long time
myself. Despite our age and cultural differences, we were *simpa-
tico*. We were both wallflowers, indoor coffee drinkers. She liked
American football and Echo and the Bunnymen. In the evenings
we would sit in the cafés and eat cake and smoke cigarettes.
Neither of us had ever been married or dreamt of obtaining a real
estate license. I found her pleasing, attractive company, though
because of the head injury she often drifted off to a place I came
to call Cristinaland.

"Cristina?"

"Eh?"

"Where are you, baby?"

"What?"

"Tell me what it's like. Tell me about Cristinaland."

Slow sweet smile.

We went out on several dates. I had never really dated when I was young, unless you define dates as "drinking arrangements with women for the eventual purpose of sex." But these were sober, proper, painstakingly old-fashioned dates. On our third date we were sitting on a park bench in the Jardin, the central plaza, waiting until it was time to stroll down to the theater, and she turned to me and said earnestly in Spanish, "Can I ask you a question?"

"Yes, of course," I replied.

She knit her brow. "What is your *name*?"

I decided to bring Cristina back to America with me. She had only three big dreams: to see America, to learn to speak English, and to make enough money to open her own Mexican dental practice, maybe $5,000. I thought I could grant all three of these wishes with one wave of my magic gringo wand.

7.

Chadron the second time

I RARELY RETURN TO A PLACE I HAVE LIVED, BUT CHAD-
ron, for its safety, affordability, lack of Spanish speakers, and
friendly residents seemed the best option for Cristina. After a
seven-and-a-half-hour trip the Denver Shuttle dropped us off in
front of the Olde Main. It was April and cold, and even those
who love Chadron have to admit it is an isolated town with few
prospects. Cristina shook her head. I took her into the hotel to
meet Jeanne.

Lorri, married (to George the drummer) and pregnant now
for the third time and unable to work in the kitchen through
the summer, offered Cristina and me a house rent-free for a few
months, employment for Cristina, and my old job back for eight
dollars an hour. Cristina, who'd just gotten her six-month tourist
visa, approved the plan. She would have to be demoted from
dentist to maid, but she understood that this was how the game
worked in America.

Though Chadron was new-and-improved, with a Walmart,
a McDonald's, a Subway, a second video rental store, a Dollar
General, a pseudo-Mexican restaurant (like food you'd get in a
Mexican hospital, one of my friends quipped), and a Chinese
restaurant (run by real Chinese people!) where the old truck stop
had been, the same houses and ranches were still abandoned.
The population had not changed. The general attitude toward
Nebraska had not changed. The Police Beats were as good as ever:

9:36 A.M. Caller from the 200 block of West Third St. advised that John Lennon was at the bank yesterday three times and he's already came once this morning. Caller stated he told her today that he's the ruler of the world.

4:28 P.M. Caller from the 500 block of King St. advised it appears someone broke into the above location through a window. Caller was unsure if anyone took anything but appears unknown subjects used the coffee pot.

11:49 P.M. A rescue unit was asked to respond to the 100 block of Main St. for a woman who had one drink and then went down.

Before we left Mexico I found a doctor who agreed with some urging to prescribe me Valium and another milder tranquilizer so I could get through six months of short-order cooking. My back was also quanked and I was often inclined to scuttle across the land like a hermit crab. As we'd traveled across America, Cristina had not been very impressed. Johnny Depp was nowhere in sight. There were no streets paved with gold and very few palm trees. The oceans were neither warm nor very blue. The churches had been sabotaged and Americans were zombies ("zombie" being the same word in both languages). Americans were cold. Americans were like robots ("robot" is also the same word, see how easy it is to speak another language?). I was offended and leaped to the defense of my countrymen. I could make fun of them, they were my people, but we're lining you up the number-one blue plate special, American Dream with fries on the side, so think twice, child, about these cavalier remarks. Also consider how distant people might seem when you can't understand what they are saying. Also realize that several tens of millions of the people who live in this zombie nation have recently come (many at the risk of jail and death) from your country. And it wouldn't be long, I warned her, if things worked according to plan, before you're attached to a cell phone, butterfly-tattooed ankle laid up on knee, Xanax kicking in, bargaining with the newest credit card company over that sudden outlandish jump in your APR.

Compounding her culture shock, Cristina had to learn about the real me, not a tall rich *gringo pacifico* salvaging her humdrum life, but a guy with very little money who had never stayed anywhere with anyone for very long. Along with the forfeiture of my contract with Houghton Mifflin, I had given up the second half of my advance, and my chances of ever playing in a big-time pool hall again seemed pretty small. Whenever I told her one of my crazy beach, drug, or traveling-with-no-money stories, it only made her frown as if the sun were in her eyes. My past was so wild it appeared to have been lived by Peter Pan sniffing airplane glue. I told her she could go home whenever she wanted, no hard feelings.

8.

Culture shock

ONE MINUTE CRISTINA WAS A LICENSED DENTIST MAKING top Mexican wages and addressed as *doctora*, the next minute she was trying to figure out how to turn on a vacuum cleaner and one of the guests she had to clean up after had thrown a used condom on the floor. Enter America, become reborn, and here is your cotton hat and feather duster. It was all very different from the legend that had been told. For the first time in her life, she confessed to me, she feared that she would lose her identity.

She was also certain she was working with ghosts. Was that a child running down the hall? Who played the piano when there was no one else upstairs? She had been touched on the shoulder by an icy hand in room 207. In room 202, the Mari Sandoz Suite, she had seen the impression of someone sitting on a bed that she had just made, a common report from that room. She talked with the ghosts, made firm pleas, tried to strike bargains. Jeanne explained that the ghosts were Jack and Anna O'Hanlon, two children of long-ago owners when the original hotel had burned down. Jack and Anna had carved their names in the brick wall out in the front of what was then their new hotel. Anna was dyslexic so her Ns were backwards. They were mischievous, not malevolent, Jeanne assured Cristina, even if they manifested as grown-ups.

Cristina was nevertheless unnerved being all alone upstairs with Jack and Anna and God knows who else. "Please, I'm just here to clean the rooms," she would tell them. "I don't want to bother you. It wasn't my idea to come here." And even if Jack or Anna could've understood Spanish, they weren't at all ready to let a silly thing like death get in the way of having a lark.

9.

The Clown is dead

THE BLUE VALIUM TABS, EVEN MIXED WITH RED WINE,
did little to appease my short-order aggravation. Cristina, with
not much maid work to occupy her until the narrow tourist season
began mid-June, was miserable too. I was gone all night and she
was left alone. The wind howled and shivered the windowpanes.
The snow fell. Far from home and away from her family for the
very first time, unable to understand the simplest phrases, thrown
into a haunted hotel as a maid, living with a man she idealized
who smoked and drank and cursed and came home smelling of
french fries and beer, she cried many nights, longed for home,
and was plagued with weird recurring nightmares about lavishly
strange houses full of the walking dead.

So she asked for Valiums, though they didn't have much
effect on her, even a whole 10-milligram tab, a dosage that sent
me to a cool oasis. One time she took 20 milligrams and just went
to bed. I was worried. My girl would not be able to make the
transition. America was not a storybook land.

I introduced her all around and everyone dazzled her with
their rapid and incomprehensible tongues. Friday nights I'd try
to drag her to the President's Table with the artists and bohemians
at the Olde Main, where she was always swooped on with kind
if not solicitous attention, which she endured as everyone had to
practice their rudimentary Spanish on her.

We found Hazel Devine at the corner of the Olde Main
tavern one afternoon, feet up on the bar, sucking from a straw

stuck into his mixed drink. It was the first time I'd seen him in seven years. I knew that he would be pleased to see that I finally had a girl. I presented Cristina. He whirled his finger in approval.

"You got yourself a pretty one," he said with a chuckle and a finger shake that I took to mean an appreciative slap on the bar. "About time."

"I've always been slow."

Hazel took a long pull from his straw, then began to hunch his shoulder up and down until his pack of Marlboro Lights rose from his pocket. The extant finger hooked the package, Hazel knocked the top with his chin, and he seized triumphantly with his teeth the first cigarette that appeared. "Gimme a light," he said.

I lit him up.

"The Clown is dead," he said, blinking away the smoke. "Heart attack. He was 58."

"I'm sorry," I said. "He was a sweetheart."

"He died in the saddle. Black Betty," he added with solemn pride. I remembered seeing Byron several times with Betty, who was called "Black Betty" because so many of her lovers died unexpectedly including her husband, who had drowned trying to save one of her children.

"No more tiny trips." Hazel shook his head for a long time, puffing on the cigarette between his toes. "You got a car yet?"

"Not yet."

"Jesus Christ," he said.

"Probably get one soon," I said.

"You'll have to," he said, glancing at Cristina. "I got a couple of good ones for you. Very low mileage. You like Escorts?" He worked his eyebrows, indicating that I should extinguish his cigarette and light him another.

"I'll let you know," I said, shaking out the match.

"Gimme a little pat," he said, leaning down.

I rubbed his shoulders the way Lord Byron of Windsor used to do it, half scratch, half massage.

"Oh, I like that," he said, scrunching down like a cat getting a tickle behind the ears. "A little over to the right there."

With an exotic young woman in tow, many of the men of Chadron had to stop me, grab my shoulder, grip my bicep, and stare at my girl for a while as if to determine if some alien force had taken over my body. At the Olde Main one night I was introduced to Sam Killinoy, a handsome and argumentative perfectionist with meticulous snow-white hair, who had lived all over the country and been married many times and had finally returned to Chadron because in all the cities he'd lived this one felt the most like home. He had not been able to find a job for a year, Jeanne explained, and pride had made him hard to take. He looked Cristina over with thorough appreciation. I'd forgotten all the extra work it takes when you have a pretty companion, though the fact that she couldn't speak English usually threw a wrench in the charmer's machinery. "*Muy bonita,*" he said at last, exhausting his Spanish arsenal.

"*Gracias,*" Cristina said, lowering her head.

"What do you think about those Rockies?" he said, reluctantly returning his attention to me.

"Looks like the pitching won't hold up again."

"You nuts? They're going to put the balls in a humidor this year."

CHADRON POLICE SERGEANT Charles Chaffwick, Chuck as we called him, an easy-moving bear of a man with an extra-droopy Teddy Roosevelt mustache, seemed to like me better with a pretty young woman on my arm, too. Even though I'd grilled him dozens of cheeseless buffalo burgers, which I hand-delivered from the kitchen (he always ate at the bar), he still wouldn't call me by my name. I was always "the cook," or "chief," or "well hello there." "Well hello there," he said in his dry baritone, the heavy mustache twitching, his head darting around a bit as he processed his perceptions of this young dark creature at my side. "She's legal," I said.

He hooked his thumbs into his belt and smirked. He was broader at the waist than the shoulders, though he was still considerably taller than your average policeman. "You gonna marry her?"

"Good chance of it."

He nodded. "Heard you're a writer now."

"Getting there."

"You going to put me in one of your books?"

I was tempted to quote the famous line from the preface of *Slouching Towards Bethlehem*, Joan Didion's sterling indictment of the counterculture era: "Writers are always selling somebody out."

Instead I said, "As soon as you do something interesting."

10.

Fish bisques and black barley burgoos

I'D HOPED THAT AS CRISTINA'S ENGLISH IMPROVED SO would her sense of alienation. Unfortunately, we didn't have that much time. It had taken me a good year and a half living in Mexico before I was able to have a functional conversation in Spanish, and this is probably an average immersion timetable for foreign language acquisition. You can understand all the grammar in the world and possess a massive vocabulary, but it simply takes time for your brain to accommodate idiom and speed.

The experiment was a failure. Cristina's tourist visa was up. We sat at the kitchen table. I felt like a manager about to fire an employee. I wished that I had been able to make at least one of her dreams come true. But I had very little power in America. I could not get her a great job, introduce her to Johnny Depp, or put her on an inside track. I couldn't even raise $5,000 in six months. And she was so unhappy I felt I would be doing her a favor sending her back home.

When I told Cristina this she cried and said, "I will go home with nothing." I calculated the relative unimportance of the few years I had left on earth and decided to do whatever I could to help her. When we returned to Mexico, Cristina would not have to be ashamed. She would be proud to have an American husband who took good care of her. There was something in the deal for me too: companionship and a reason to stop traveling. Marriage will work, I thought. She will learn English. We will take long walks among the skipping tumbleweeds. I will bake her cinnamon banana cakes with citrus frosting, fish bisques, and black barley burgoos, chelada with boiled shrimp and garlic olives, and red beans with bacon and cornmeal dumplings.

Before her tourist visa could expire, Cristina and I had a civil wedding at City Hall. Not being Catholic or inclined to hypocrisy, it was the best I could do. The diamond on her ring was pretty small, but show me a big stone and I'll show you a short marriage. Cristina, unable to understand anything said to her on one of the most important days of her life, was overwhelmed.

11.

Rise of the ruined city

I HAD BEEN INGENUOUS ENOUGH TO THINK THAT ONCE I got Cristina across the border and married that she would become an instant citizen, but we'd been preceded by a long tradition of marriage fraud, American citizens paid handsome sums to wed aliens, follow naturalization procedures, and then discard their spouses for free rein upon the American Dream, or prostitution, whichever came first. Thousands of dollars in fees, dozens of forms that could not be correctly filled out even by INS (Immigration and Naturalization Service) personnel, fingerprints, medical examinations, resurrection of ancient Mexican documents, and several long-distance trips to INS headquarters on the other side of the state waited for us. I began to fill out the forms, to make the frequent long-distance calls where I was put on hold for hours and each time I talked to an agent I was given a different answer.

After my unpleasant experience with Houghton Mifflin I vowed never to do business with a big publishing house again. I continued to sell stories and essays to various magazines. It seemed to me that if I was good enough someone would come along eventually and ask if I was interested in a larger project, which is exactly what happened during my first few months back in Chadron. A small press called Hawthorne Books was just starting up, and Rhonda Hughes, the publisher, had seen some of my stories and essays in *The Sun Magazine*. Would I be interested in doing a book?

One minute I was wandering stunned and defeated amid the smoldering columns of the ruined city, staring perplexedly at the sunset with wrinkles at the corners of my eyes. The next minute I was selling a book, married to an attractive young immigrant Hispanic, and getting a prescription for Viagra. My life kept ending and then it would start again, like some old pull-string garage-sale doll picked up and yanked on the whim of a stray child. Everyone kept looking at me as if I had planned the whole thing all along.

12.

That old guy yelling at your high school graduation

WHEN LORRI AND GEORGE MOVED TO GORDON, 45 MILES east, they offered us their house, a real ranch home (dragged in from the country, circa 1920) with good ghosts and tulips and clean drains and a dishwasher and a crabapple tree and a gorgeous view of the railroad tracks and the prairie across the street. The house had three bedrooms, a skylight in the dining room, a large backyard, and two enclosed porches. The price was $33,000, the only price at which I would have ever become a homeowner.

The next summer Cristina began to work with me down in the kitchen. The hours were more reliable, it was a much better environment to practice her English, and we could spend more time together. We'd get off late and go home to our new house, wash off the grease, salve our burns, open a beer or two, and watch movies that for the most part she did not understand. A friend had given us a television and we had cable, a must for young newlyweds who don't speak each other's language well. She liked movies. I had quit watching movies long ago because it wasn't worth the trouble anymore. Nevertheless, movies, even weak cable movies, are one good way to learn a foreign language.

Cristina: I must have a baby.

Me: I'm not ready to have a baby.

I'll take care of him.

I'm sure you will. But give me a chance to publish this book first. When I have two books published we can have a child.

She expressed doubt about my ability to publish a book.

And even if I got it published, she didn't believe it would make any money. Had the head injury made her *clairvoyant*?

Cristina had no faith whatsoever in literature as a means of income. She thought I should go back to college. Why had I quit school? Why was I 47 years old and still a cook? She thought I needed a job with benefits. Pragmatic as her arguments might've been, it was too late for me to turn back. I was just getting started. A lifetime of work and sacrifice had finally hatched. Just let me finish this book, dear, and then we'll have the child.

Viagra is an embarrassing and expensive drug that gives you a giant headache and an all-night boner like a moose antler in your shorts. Whenever I could, I tried to ride without it. Then one night without Viagra, a bit of magic, and wham! (as the obstetric saying goes). A month later she began feeling nauseated. I knew immediately that she was pregnant. We got a kit and confirmed. My friends and neighbors went wild at the news. I was realistic, accepting, dismayed. I thought I was too old to be a father. I was pushing 50 and I was going to have a child? Well, that's all right. I liked children. And I'm not afraid of reality. Of course, I'll be slobbering in a wheelchair at his high school graduation and all his friends will be saying, "So nice your grandfather could attend," while I yell in a cracked and senile voice, "Which one is he? Why don't they let him play third base?"

But I vowed to do my best. Maybe the greatest opportunity to learn, better than traveling, odd jobs, or hardship, is raising a child. It's another try at growing up, a fresh shot at love. I needed to know all about the world in order to write about the world and here I was. The fates had handed across one more silver platter. And I'd write as many books as I could so that there would be some trickle of pennies beyond my days and my child could say yes, he was an author (that old guy yelling at your high school graduation?), so what if you never heard of him?

We bought a car from Hazel, an old Subaru that had been in a wreck but ran pretty well anyway. I had not owned a car in 20 years. I did not believe in cars. They were ship anchors with wheels.

Hazel Devine nevertheless was delighted. Hazel Devine was at peace. I was married, my wife was pregnant, I had a car. I had finally achieved manhood under his watchful eye. "I think the clutch is going out, Hazel. How much is that going to cost me?"

"It's not your clutch," he said. "It's probably your synchronizer."

Everyone said our child would be a girl. They knew by a number of factors, the way Cristina carried, her craving for sweets, the tilt of her eyebrows, my reluctance to purchase an automobile, and so on, but mostly, I suspect, because I seemed like the sort of man who would father a girl. My wife and I believed them too. We'd even named the child Isabela. Then it occurred to me about three days before Cristina was to be induced that most people are wrong. They invest in the wrong stock, bet the wrong football team, make the wrong career choice, move to the wrong city, pick the wrong suspect in the police lineup, vote for the wrong president. They are afraid to take a chance; they prefer the straightforwardness of ignorance, the smoothness and the reliable landmarks of the road most traveled, the ease of conformity; they rely on experts (who you can make a living betting against); they imagine the past as an orderly event; they possess the will to believe what should be true.

I also realized that a girl would be too easy for me to raise. If I had a boy I would be under obligation to provide a masculine role model. I was the only one by the day Cristina delivered who knew that my child would be a boy. My wife was astounded when she saw the baby slip out and was raised slippery red into the air with the doodlebug hanging. The doctor handed me the scissors to cut the umbilical cord and I could see by the crafty glint in his eyes that he expected me to faint. A little blood spurted onto my smock and I stared at my son. He was not much of an Isabela, so we decided to name him after both of our fathers, Thomas Francisco.

Cristina focused on her English skills when she realized that soon her son would be speaking and she could not bear the thought of him surpassing her linguistically at say, age three. The combination of working in a kitchen, watching vulgar American movies, the fact that there were few Spanish speakers around to support her, and the imperative of understanding what was said to her, especially as her child was in a completely helpless state, all served as strong learning incentives.

And I can't say that at any time our marriage was a picnic on a sea cliff with a roasted duck and a frosty bottle of Pouilly-Fuissé. We fought a lot. Cristina was preposterously jealous and refused to teach her son Spanish. She worried, dreamt of zombies, and sailed away to Cristinaland. I shut myself away for hours at a time and slaved away on my books, which she had no appreciation for. But we did have enough in common to hold it together. I did my best to cook the traditional dishes that eased Cristina's nostalgia. You can't very well make an authentic *birria* without maguey leaves and a clay oven. And that lamb shoulder at Safeway will originally be priced at around $35. However, no one will buy it, because it's half gristle, fat, and bone and fit for little better than boiling. And since no one around these parts eats lamb much anyway (note the natural bias in beef country against sheep interests) eventually the shoulder will be marked down at least 50%. It's then that it can be boiled in beer and *mirepoix*, pulled, and reintroduced into a *salsa roja* and *refritos* base and folded into flour tortillas with *queso fresco* and onions.

My wife was accustomed to having her popcorn *picante*. In the shops in the town where Cristina grew up you could buy your quantity of popcorn by the peso and the vendor would ladle over it a quantity of vinegar straight from the jalapeño can. Tasty as this might be, it renders the popcorn *soggy*. I like my popcorn popped in olive oil and butter and sprinkled with Parmesan. I make it in a Dutch oven on the stove and throw the kernels in just as the butter begins to smoke. After popping, I shake on the Tabasco and cheese. It's picante this way, not soggy, with a nutty brown-butter flavor.

I never did anything quite the way it was supposed to be

done. I always thickened the enchilada sauce with a roux, sometimes I put fresh spinach in the *rellenos*, once I mixed Cristina's
papas rajas with collard greens and salmon. Nevertheless, her
misgivings usually gave way to acceptance, if not pleasure. Food,
like "nature," rarely makes me happy, but it could make my wife
happy. She especially liked my *gringo*-style *chile verde*. "We
must have this again soon," she would say, licking her spoon.

But it was our marvelous son who really kept our marriage
intact. Tom walked like a little sailor, erect, chest out, arms
swinging freely. He was cheerful, quick with a smile, and when
the music came on, he danced. He feared nothing, not dogs nor
darkness nor perfect strangers. He had clear eyes and a steady
gaze. He was curious, alert, and independent. He preferred adult
music to nursery rhymes, and would listen to certain songs over
and over: "The Rockefeller Skank" (extended dance remix) by
Fatboy Slim, "Mr. E's Beautiful Blues" by the Eels, "Mexican Radio"
by Wall of Voodoo, "Everybody Knows" by Leonard Cohen,
"Always the Sun" by the Stranglers. He had an extraordinary memory and could count to 124 at age three and a half. He talked
and asked a great deal of questions about the wind, the moon,
and storms. When he grew up, he told us, he was going to collect
spoons. Tom was the sort of child, as all parents will tell you about
their children, who was truly exceptional.

13.

My publisher and her homicide cop fiancé come to Chadron

ON A SNOWY DAY IN LATE NOVEMBER, FIVE-YEAR-OLD Tom and I drove out to the two-flights-a-day airport four miles west of town to pick up my publisher, Rhonda Hughes, and her fiancé, Kevin Warren, a homicide detective for the Portland, Oregon, Police Department. My son loved the Chadron Municipal Airport, loved taking planes and traveling, and even though he disliked children and had no friends, he loved having guests. Just weeks after starting kindergarten, Tom had been red-flagged as autistic. The symptomatology went something like: slow verbal development, poor social development, repetitive and ritual behaviors (especially rocking and foot bouncing), tactile obsessions, fixations, advanced facility with numbers and numerical concepts, wandering attention. Because Tom met your gaze, smiled readily, pointed to indicate, drank water from a martini glass, owned two rubber skeletons he'd named "Thing" and "Baby Love," refused to eat anything that might be healthy for him, claimed he would be an alligator when he grew up, and was never once tempted by Barney the purple dinosaur, I didn't think he was any more autistic than I was. (*The father, like his son, is nonstandard, a bit slow, has trouble focusing on things that don't interest him, is taking longer than the usual time to develop. He is hypersensitive to stimuli, especially loud sounds and nonsense. He is inclined to withdraw, a constructor of secret worlds, seems narrow in affect, and can listen to that Paul Simon song "Mother and Child Reunion" over and over.*)

Nevertheless, on recommendation of school staff (an occupational therapist, a special education teacher, the school counselor, the principal, and Tom's teacher), Tom began seeing a pediatrician who eventually referred us to a psychologist, an autism expert in Casper, Wyoming, about three hours away. Tom liked the long monthly drives to the place he called "Casper, Yie-Yoming," and he enjoyed the testing and interviews and remembers all his doctors to this day. He could recall the names of his entire extended family in Mexico two years after having only seen them once. But exceptional memory is another red flag of autism, isn't it?

The plane was late. Tom washed his hands twice, studied the buttons on the coffee maker, pressed his nose against the glass to watch the snow, and announced that in the year 3000 everyone would have four eyes. At last the small, single-engine craft landed and Rhonda and Kevin, ducking whirling flurries, came through the doors.

Rhonda, a slim, urbane, and successful woman of 39 years, hugged me one-armed around the waist and kissed my cheek. Rhonda made her living as a print broker, but had started up a small-publishing outfit seven years before. So far I'd published four books with her, and Rhonda and I had become good friends. Whenever I went to Portland on a book tour I bunked at her ninth-story loft downtown and we stayed up drinking and confessing long into the night. We'd both grown up stoner beach children in San Diego and Rhonda had rescued me editorially numerous times. She'd also taught me how to tell if a woman has had a boob job or not.

Rhonda was also an admirer of *The Chadron Record*'s weekly published Police Beats, the local-color gems culled from the Chadron Police Department blotter, which she believed would somehow provide the key to a full-fledged literary project about Chadron, Nebraska, though a narrative built around an item such as "7:09 p.m. Caller from North Main St. advised she thought she needed to go to the loony bin" had thoroughly escaped me so far.

Kevin, 40, a liberal policeman with a wry sense of humor, brushed the snowflakes from the sleeves of his coat and said, "Do you think you've gotten far enough away from civilization yet?"

I admitted that I hadn't, and shook his hand. Kevin's father died when he was young, and he had the saturnine bearing of a child looking out the window all alone at the falling autumn leaves. His hair was thinning. He wore a neat goatee. An Oregon native, he went to Atlantic City once in the folly of his youth pursuing a woman who had no interest in him and spent a year or so as a paramedic there, mostly hauling fat guys with heart attacks out of Trump casinos. Though Rhonda and Kevin had only been dating for a year (they'd met on Match.com) Kevin and I had already become good friends, too. He'd picked me up on my last book tour at the Portland Airport in a police cruiser and later that trip we had sojourned together to Seattle, where I'd read at Elliott Bay Book Company to an audience of 16 then spent the rest of the evening at various bars watching college football games.

Lifelong city dwellers both, Rhonda and Kevin had never seen the Great Plains of Western Nebraska.

Tom was enchanted by his new guests and the stuffed toy beaver they brought him, a mini-mascot of Kevin's favorite college team, the Oregon State Beavers. "Don't ya know what?" he asked Rhonda, who had slid into the backseat next to him.

"What?"

"That snowstorm is coming from the north*west*."

Rhonda rubbed his head. "And when we get home we can have Easter eggs," he told her. "*White* Easter eggs," he said. He meant hard-boiled eggs, which he had just learned to like. He liked them plain, without salt, any time of the day.

"Easter eggs are *Italian* eggs," he said.

Tom delighted most people with his diamond brightness of smile, his mother's good looks, and that natural child directness of emotion and vulnerable purity of innocence. But he could also be remote. I watched him once for a few hours through a one-way mirror in his class at the Child Development Center and he treated his mates as if they were ghosts. When he encountered another child, he would simply ice him with indifference. And though he was warm to his teachers and caregivers, he could detach from us as well. He'd go into himself for long periods alone, oblivious as a cosmonaut to the outside world, composing on his dry erase board or rummaging through his toys in the closet. No doubt he had a distinct and winning personality, but sometimes it would recede, leaving in its wake a dark-eyed boy who merely resembled our son.

On the drive home, I showed Rhonda and Kevin around the little haven I had stumbled upon in the darkest days of my life a dozen years ago. One of the big appeals of Chadron, in spite of its viral plastic enfranchisement along the highway, is the agreeable lethargy that presides over all. What in heaven's name are you doing in this Godforsaken place, I'm often asked. Well, I like it here, is all I can say, and so do my wife and son.

"What keeps this town from drying up and blowing away?" Kevin wanted to know.

"Walmart," I replied, "and the state college to the south."

"You've got Daylight Donuts, too," he observed, his hands beginning to tremble. "Do they have savannahs?"

The snowflakes grew larger, zigzagging down like lacy tissue-paper patterns cut by exceptional children with scissors, and Tom had begun to laugh at some private reflection. He was more of a daydreamer than a thinker, I suspected, though he never told his mother and me what he might be dreaming or thinking about.

Steven Haataja (*hah-de-yah*), Chadron's new math professor, with his outsized wire specs sliding down his nose, shuffled heedlessly through the drifts in his Birkenstocks in front of us. Fresh from the University of Nebraska in Lincoln, where he'd just earned his PhD, he'd slipped into town without most noticing, the same way he would leave us, and even though his body would

be eventually discovered, the reasons for his death and disappearance would not. All I knew about him then was from what
two mutual friends, Deane Tucker, a philosophy professor, and
Kathy Bahr, a literature professor, had told me: he had perfect
pitch, he was compulsively neat, he was a brilliant theoretician,
and he possessed a fine and subtle wit. His strides were long and
he limped slightly from a recently broken hip. If I'd known
what was going to happen to him, I would have run him over then
and there, hit him hard enough to break his other hip, put him
back in a wheelchair to sing in his office and cipher semicubical
parabola and quadratic equations for another 10 or 20 years.

14.

Go-go girls all around

RHONDA AND KEVIN HAD RESERVED THE GENERAL MILES Suite on the second floor of the Olde Main Street Inn. General Nelson Miles was a famous Indian fighter and Civil and Spanish War figure who stationed himself at this very hotel in his suppression of the Lakota Sioux and their ill-fated Ghost Dance in the early 1890s. Most of the rooms had Western themes, the General Miles Suite, the Mari Sandoz Suite, the Cowboy Room, the Railroad Room. Long ago the railroad was the prime economic mover in Chadron. Back in 1943, you could catch a westbound train for Newell or one headed east for Long Pine every half an hour or so.

After four years of running the kitchen at the Olde Main Street Inn, I'd burned out finally and found a position cleaning the floors at Safeway. My first two bosses were undocumented workers from Mexico City who did not speak English. One had a criminal record, both had wives and children in both countries. The Stateside wives, big homely American girls, acted as translators. This was nothing startling or new to me. My position as the floorman at Safeway was simply another descent into a class so low as to be invisible, though I saw it as a good chance to practice my Spanish with people other than my wife.

Now, my old employer, Jeanne Goetzinger, was waiting for us with her guest book open. "Hello, hello, and welcome to Chadron," she said, arms outstretched. We all got hugs, then Tom dashed off to explore. He adored the Olde Main Street Inn.

Over the years we've held dozens of impromptu tornado parties here, notable for their bawling sirens and chicken-liver-colored skies.

"Let's have an unwinder before we drag everything up," said Kevin, parking himself at the bar. "I haven't flown in anything that small since the Dumbo ride when I was five."

Jeanne guffawed and poured us all strong ones. Jeanne had that special weakness for cowboys and bikers, not Village People poseurs dressed as cowboys and bikers (even if the Olde Main was once a YMCA), but real men, surly and terse with sunburned necks, facial scars, and crooked spines. When real bikers or cowboys strolled in to flip up their eye patches, dust off their chaps, and cut their thirst at her Longbranch Saloon, Jeanne's eyes got fuzzy, her long red hair kinked up a notch, and she pranced all about as if the crowned heads of Europe had called. The free drinks usually flowed. Sometimes she brought down her hunting rifles and old muskets to show off. Among her collection was an old Indian flintlock. The Indians used to paint their flintlocks. Jeanne's flintlock was painted ochre and green.

She liked policemen, too, especially big-city homicide detectives, and she showed Detective Kevin the loaded .38 that she kept behind the bar.

"That will keep them polite," Kevin said, sliding it back. "All of them in range at least."

Jeanne's hotel was right next to police headquarters, and because she often played host to members of that force and many other law enforcement officers, federal and state, who rented her rooms upstairs or tarried in her saloon and restaurant or admired her firearms below, her establishment was one of five or six small-town grapevine substations worthy of consultation, especially, as we would soon learn, in the area of crime.

Long ago, I explained to Rhonda and Kevin, when Jeanne's mom, Evva, owned the Olde Main, before it was a bed and breakfast or a dining establishment, there used to be go-go girls dancing in bikinis down in what was then called "The Cave."

That was the extent of the business, drinks and go-go girls in a cave. Evva did fabulously well. What do men really want? It isn't complicated. But if you wanted a seat in the Cave you had to get there by 5 p.m. "There were a lot of fights in those days," I recounted. "Nightly brawls as you might expect with cowboys and Indians and go-go girls all running around higgledy-piggledy with booze in a cave."

"That's why we like Poe," said Rhonda, "because he says things like higgledy-piggledy."

"I took Latin in high school," I said.

"Let's have a couple more," said Kevin, digging for his wallet. "Why are the drinks so cheap here?"

"Everything is cheap here," Jeanne replied. "It's the only way to keep people from leaving town."

"An anti-ghost town measure," he said. "Well, I'd move here if they had an opera house."

"They do have a college football team," I put in.

"Do they?"

"Yes, this was the home of Don Beebe, Green Bay Packer and six-time Super Bowl participant, stadium named after him, and Danny Woodhead, all-time Division II yard record whatever-you-call-it (and soon to be NFL star)."

"You don't say?"

The effervescent Abner Violette, who was partial to ball caps and loose Hawaiian shirts, came tromping backward at this point down the stairs, a camera around his neck and an EMF meter in his right hand, its needle bouncing splendidly. A tall, curly-headed fellow with the kind of dorky Buddy Holly horn-rims I'd worn in fifth grade but were now fashionable again, Violette had a gaussmeter attached to his belt along with a few other gadgets he used to measure temperature gradients and terahertz waves and whatnot. All I knew about ghost hunting was the little I'd seen on TV and what Violette, an avid tracker of supernatural phenomena, endlessly and enthusiastically told me at the bar as he ate his rattlesnake pizza and drank his pitcher of draft.

Violette was a retired NASA aerospace engineer, Kentucky-born, but most recently from Huntsville, Alabama, where he owned two houses he was trying to sell. Never married, he was still on the lookout for his ideal mate. An inventor with a number of patents both issued and pending, a pilot of his own Cessna 172, he was starting up four classic rock and alternative radio stations across Western Nebraska and Colorado, one already operating in Chadron. He planned eventually to buy a house in Chadron and settle here, the town he thought was so refreshingly kooky, and never until Chadron had he lived in a place so dry that you could set a cold beverage down on a summer's eve without the glass sweating. In the interim, he was living in Jeanne's hotel, as you might expect, in the Terribly Haunted Room: number 207.

"You seen my son?" I asked Violette, who adjusted the strap on his shoulder, looked up the stairs and said, "He's up on third, looking out at the snow. Where's your beautiful wife?"

"She's at work," I said.

"Got her dental degree yet?"

"Not yet," I said. "She's still a janitor at the college."

"Pity," he said. "She needs to pass her boards so you can be a millionaire."

"What would I do with a million dollars?"

"Buy me a full-spectrum camera, for one thing. Hold still." He snapped our picture.

"Are we ghosts now?" said Rhonda.

15.

Big dick omelets

DOWN IN THE SUNKEN DINING ROOM AMID THE INDIAN oil paintings and massive antlered head of a bull elk mounted on the wall, and the glass cases full of Old West souvenirs and alpaca items that Jeanne has spun off a wheel and carded and knitted herself, Rhonda, Kevin, Tom, and I sat in a booth below the 55-gallon aquarium full of tropical fish, just a few feet from the bubbling open well, and ordered at my recommendation Jimmy Dick omelets, which have grits, sausage, and green onions in them. That meat in your Dick omelet? Relax, it's only sausage.

In the four years I had cooked here, many rogue dishes had passed through these rooms, among them: buttermilk biscuits with smoked chicken and tomato gravy better than sex, wild goose gumbo, ham and alligator chowder (though I never could determine the best stock to use for this dish, chicken, seafood, or reptile), grilled *arrachera* (marinated flank steak) *con limón*, chicken thighs braised in beer and wild fennel and onions, peach-pecan-pork pancakes, scalloped potatoes with roasted anchos, mushrooms sopped in garlic with pesto, and provolone pasta al ceppo. Black beans with gizzards and red wine. It was all peasant food since that is where all the good food comes from. My *Bon Marché* influence removed, the menu had returned to convention, as the town preferred: prime rib, steaks, grilled salmon, mesquite chicken, buffalo burgers, and the Dick omelets. I always recommend a big Dick omelet if you have room. Tom, as usual, had french fries.

I pointed out Chadron Police Officer Joni Behrends dining over by the fireplace with her husband, Steve. Joni was the youngest, friendliest, most outgoing, and best-looking police officer on the force, earning her the nickname "Hot Cop." Her specialties were homeless Indians and domestic and child abuse, and when she talked to you she'd swat you good-naturedly across the arm.

Chadron Police Department Sergeant Charles Chaffwick owned a Chihuahua named Red, had a Green Bay Packer banner hanging over his porch, and who could be found once a week dressed up and rumbling with his Harley crew in their motorcycle colors, was proof that you can live a double life even in a small town, wandered over to our table.

Well over six feet, the picture of tranquil complacency, Sergeant Chuck was originally from Oconomowoc, Wisconsin, affectionately regarded by its fellow officers as Wisconsin 5-0 (for the five Os in Oconomowoc). He'd worked 12 years for Wisconsin 5-0 before joining the Chadron Police Department, and upon arrival had purchased the Daylight Donuts from Ted Vastine, our last good police chief.

Chuck had just recovered from prostate cancer and was thinner and more pallid than usual. He was a master of the double take, and a shrugger as well, part of his Dangerfield shtick, along with that deadpan look of offended disbelief.

"How come you're not cooking tonight?" he wanted to know.

"I quit a year ago, Chuck," I said. "I'm cleaning floors now over at Safeway until we come up with a best-seller. This is my publisher, Rhonda Hughes, and her fiancé, Kevin Warren. He's a Portland homicide detective."

"How's it going?" said Kevin, reaching across to shake Chuck's hand.

Kevin was never reluctant to express his lack of appreciation for anyone who didn't impress him, though I don't think Sergeant Chuck noticed. Kevin endured Rhonda's constant traffic of "artists," the majority of whom he considered charlatans.

Rhonda's only complaint about Kevin, besides him throwing his handgun on the bed when he came home from work in the evenings, was that she couldn't discuss with him her favorite subject, art. Kevin had run a restaurant with his ex-wife, so he knew about food and wine, and he was up on politics and far above the average intelligence, so he was by no means un-qualified to pontificate upon Proust or sight a watercolor down his thumb. He simply didn't care about art.

Chuck rocked back on his heels and regarded me in a new light. "So you're publishing books now."

"It's been going on for a while," I said. "I try to be as low-profile as possible, keep my sales down so I'm not wrecked by fame. So far it's working perfectly. I have four books out. Number five coming soon."

He asked me again if I was going to put him in one. "Only if you do something interesting," I said, which didn't seem likely, but how could we have known?

"I've got it," said Rhonda after Chuck had strolled off. "We'll do a graphic novel of all the characters in your town."

"And then I'll have to move," I said

"What about a cookbook, with ghosts? People love cook-books and people love ghosts. I'm just throwing out ideas here."

Elbow planted on table, Kevin laid his cheek in his palm and rolled his eyes.

"Cookbooks sell," she said defensively.

"Yeah," I said. "A cookbook."

Kevin signaled the waitress for another bottle of beer.

16.

Autism cookbook

THE NEXT MORNING, A COLD THURSDAY, THE LAST DAY of November, Rhonda and Kevin came over for breakfast and to meet Cristina. Everyone liked Cristina, her good looks, adorable accent, and the impression she gave of regal self-possession. People liked our house, too, and were always surprised by how roomy it was inside. It didn't hurt that Jeanne had burned sage throughout the rooms to rid the air of evil spirits; even Abner Violette had been through with his equipment and given the place a clean bill of health, protoplasmically speaking. We often saw deer out our window, skunks, raccoons, eagles, and owls. Tom had numbered all the doors (the living room closet was number seven and my office was number five) and designated one of his bedroom doors a fire exit.

Cristina looked so gorgeous, a lozenge of turquoise at her throat, the wet luster of those full lips and lugubriously sensual eyes, that Detective Kevin Warren, as it had been the first time I had met Cristina, could only stare. Her English after much struggle had become serviceable and she was so gracious in company that few would ever dream that at the drop of a hat she would throw an avocado through your window or ask you to kill her. Tom took Rhonda out to the backyard to show her his "stick store," a little nook under the crabapple tree with a toilet (plastic wheelbarrow full of dirt), a refrigerator (Styrofoam cooler), a desk (bush), and a smoke alarm (old branding iron hanging from a branch).

Cristina cooked *chilaquiles* and we had some good Italian coffee we'd gotten in Rapid City and we sat under the skylight as Rhonda continued to cast about for book ideas. Like many adults, but not a single child ("I don't like *girls*," he said to me once, "but I like women"), she'd bonded quickly with Tom and took delight in his pronouncements and his two rubber skeletons, Thing and Baby Love, who sat quietly with us throughout the meal.

"What about a book on autism?" she proposed.

"I think it's already been done seven million times," I said. "Unless you want to do an autism cookbook."

"With ghosts," Kevin added.

Rhonda told about a friend whose son had been red-flagged for autism because he had delayed language, a high IQ, and would eat nothing but lentils, though nothing had come of it. I was often comforted by neighbors and friends with similarly alarming stories that seemed to be stimulated by the new clinical standards of educational conformity (No Child Left Behind), where every individual who does not comply is tagged with a "disorder." When you have a "special" child you will also be regularly treated to the story of Einstein (possibly autistic), who did not speak (depending on the story you hear) until he was seven. I liked the story of Truman Capote myself, probably not an autistic, who was deemed at a point in his childhood to be mentally retarded and who even as an adult could not say his ABCs.

I explained that no matter what I said, no matter how eloquently or logically I stated my case, I was unable to convince anyone familiar with autism that my child was not autistic. The only medical professional in my corner was Dr. Norden, the boy's GP, who had supervised Tom's prenatal care, delivered him into the world, watched him grow, and insisted that the boy's problems amounted to little more than being (like his father) a late bloomer. But Norden, a lowly GP, had no authority in the matter, and as the saying goes: "If 10 men tell you you're a horse, you'd better turn around and look for a tail."

I went on to say that Tom was definitely different, very observant (he'd walk into a room and instantly find the missing tiles or the burned-out light bulbs), that he was deft with numbers, and his memory was exceptional.

"Well, I wouldn't worry about *that*," said Rhonda.

Kevin, meanwhile, was intrigued by the fires that had swept through the panhandle only a few months before. He had seen the hundreds of miles of charred hills and incinerated trees from the window of the plane coming in. I recounted the Spotted Tail Fire, as it was called (it was also called the Strong Canyon Fire), one of five major summer fires that almost destroyed Chadron. The Spotted Tail Fire is studied to this day by firefighters for its extraordinary speed, intensity, and its freakish ability to move against the wind. Half the town was evacuated and several homes on the outskirts were reduced to concrete slabs. The most frightening feature of the Spotted Tail Fire, for those of us in its path, was the voracious crunching sound it made as it poured over the hills. We could hear it the way a damsel tied to a railroad track hears an oncoming locomotive. The night skies were an infernal blaze, sirens howling, hot ash and embers raining down. Folks were packing up their cars and some were headed out before all the roads were closed. The Chadron State campus was evacuated and then Chadron itself was evacuated from the south all the way to Sixth Street.

Cristina, Tom, and I lived on First, along the railroad tracks, on the very northern edge of town, where the deer and the antelope played. Our car was packed, too, and we were ready to fly. We were fairly sure the town would burn to the ground. But we waited, as one waits for a marriage to congeal, or a novel or an identity to blossom, against all hope. We had no insurance of any kind. There was only one escape route left: north. We all huddled around the radio straining at the crackle of news, and hoped for a miracle.

Six hundred firefighters, many of whom had not slept for days, saved the town.

"Let's go have a look at it," said Kevin.

Rhonda had no interest in blackened hillsides and incinerated prairie forests and said she would stay and chat with
Cristina inside where it was warm. She had these new sleeping
pills that absolutely knocked her silly and she felt well-rested
for the first time in a year, and if Cristina was up for it, she felt
like shopping.

Cristina brightened at the word and abruptly resigned her
misgivings about these strangers (jealous of Rhonda, I hate
to say) and went into the bedroom to change for the fourth time
that morning.

17.

The incinerated forest

KEVIN, TOM, AND I HEADED UP MAIN STREET. THE CLOSER you get to the small state college, the bigger the houses, the prettier the lawns. "Quaint little town," Kevin remarked, his breath a series of frozen clouds.

"Yes, you expect Rod Serling to come around the corner any minute and talk out of the side of his mouth."

"Submitted for your examination," Kevin quacked out the side of his mouth. "A town lost in time ... "

On the courthouse stairs we caught Shawn Conaghan, our county sheriff of more than 20 years, a well-liked and respected figure by just about everyone he hadn't cited or incarcerated or defeated in a repeated landslide election. A native of Deer Park, Long Island, the Irish-Italian Conaghan admits that growing up he could've been a "goodfella." Instead, the right people straightened him out before it was too late and he took the long hop west to enroll at Chadron State College as a High Plains criminal justice major. He tended bar for Jeanne's mother at the Olde Main in that ripsnortin' go-go-girl cave as a student before joining the Chadron police force. In time he found his calling in elected service as the county sheriff, which he will describe in various unflattering terms as "aggravating," "thankless," and "Maybe I won't run for re-election this term and become a greeter at Walmart." When he called in the SWAT team from Rapid City (96 miles north), for example, after the five Montana knuckle-heads who'd just stolen a car and committed three armed robber-

ies including the Stateline Casino in South Dakota and were headed into our already locked-down town, he had about 80 seconds
to make a decision, made the correct one, and drew criticism for
it. Later, he was commended officially for his foresight in the
apprehension of the five dangerous felons. The sheriff is not particularly moved by awards and was not in attendance at the 21st
Annual Nebraska Law Enforcement Coordinating Committee
Conference to accept his.

It was easy to like Conaghan. He looked you in the eye.
He told you without many trimmings what he thought. He told
senators and governors, without many trimmings, what he
thought. He confided to me once that the secret to looking busy
was never washing your car. "Drive it like you just came off the
rez," he said, "and everyone will think you're working overtime."
He called "good afternoon" to his coworkers when they arrived
late in the morning for work. He wore glasses with orange-tinted
lenses (reminiscent of Rod Steiger in *In the Heat of the Night*)
and was bald as the Dalai Lama. I'd heard him called "trigger-
happy" for the time he'd shot and killed a man from Angostura
who tried to gut him with a knife, though "self-defense" seems
more fair. He had the same sort of hard-bitten and self-effacing
sense of humor as Kevin, which along with the fact that I'd told
Kevin that Conaghan was "nobody's man," I think was the reason
Kevin liked him right off.

Shawn spoke with a faint but discernible New York accent.
"What brings you out this way, Detective?"

"We're hoping Poe can come up with a best-seller," Kevin
replied. "Otherwise my fiancée has to go back to printing comic
books in China. You don't happen to have any juicy crimes lying
around?"

"The big cities get most of those before we can have a crack
at them. We don't get a murder but every 10 years or so."
Conaghan cradled his chin. "Had a bank robbery last summer.
Hardee's arson was a good one, too," he said. This had been the
year before, when the assistant manager of the Chadron Hardee's,

Michael "Pepper" McFarland broke into his own restaurant late one night, stole $1,163 from the safe, then arsoned the place to cover his tracks. Pepper was doing a little time now, and despite early optimism, the Hardee's would never reopen.

I watched Tom tightrope the brick terraces that ran athwart the three flights of stairs leading to the courthouse entrance.

"Those wildfires we had last summer were something else, too," the sheriff continued, "and there was the mysterious death of Phoebe Krakatoa's fiancé. Autopsy ruled heart attack, if you trust the autopsy, which I don't. Our coroner is a pinhead."

"Case of the Pinheaded Coroner," Kevin said

"Except I'd have to interview Phoebe," I said.

"Now that would be interesting," the sheriff said. "I'd love to read anything this guy writes. His past is wilder than mine, and that's saying something. Well, if you'll excuse me I've got prisoners to feed."

"Good to meet you," said Kevin as the sheriff ambled up the steps and disappeared into the courthouse.

On King Street we came across Sam Killinoy, the tall, fit sports fan with perfect snow-white hair who liked to argue more than my wife, standing out in front of his mother's house, raking the front lawn. Born in Chamberlain, South Dakota, along the Missouri River, Killinoy had been the grounds director at Chadron State College for many years, then had left for Spokane in 1985, where he'd worked in retail and for the Department of Energy. The children from his numerous marriages ran the gamut from prison inmate to touring country-and-western artist.

Sam had returned to Chadron about the same time I had, though he'd had less luck finding work. A longtime Cave Dweller (his regular table was right behind the open well), he was now a fixture at Jeanne's Longbranch Saloon, sitting by himself with his bottle of Bud, a pile of change and a pack of generic smokes in front of him, his head scanning the crowd for someone to disagree with.

Sam was so eager for conflict that unless you were belligerent yourself you learned eventually to talk only about sports or simply agree with everything he said. One time before I'd learned this Benedictine Strategy he'd argued with me about chicken-fried steaks, our Wednesday special at the Olde Main, insisting that they couldn't really be from scratch since Larry over at the Grocery Kart cut them for us, though I would wager that if I'd cut and pounded the steaks with a meat mallet myself they still wouldn't qualify as scratch since I hadn't raised the cow.

Kevin and I stopped for a minute to chat as Sam raked his lawn. Dead leaves filled the gutters. His mother's home was immaculate, neat lawn and trees trimmed geometrically. A gallon of Ortho weed killer was parked in the grass nearby.

I introduced Sam to Kevin. Sam looked the detective over. "We could use a cop around here who knew what he was doing."

"Conaghan knows what he is doing," I said.

"We need a new police chief," Killinoy said. "Last one got fired. Got the dispatcher running the department, believe that?"

"I believe it," said Kevin.

"Where you two going?"

"To have a look at the fire damage."

Sam plucked one of the steel teeth on his rake and recollected the Spotted Tail Fire. He was one of many mandatorily evacuated. He'd been up on his roof, watering, the embers tumbling from the sky, when the police had told him he and his mother needed to go.

Behind us Tom had grabbed a juniper bush and was giving it a violent shaking, his eyes unblinking and feral, his expression fixed in trance, like a kid on an acid trip. If you let him, he'd shake a bush for an hour. "We gotta go, Sam. Come on, Tom."

"Testy chap," said Kevin as we moved away. "Reminds me of that Monty Python routine, the Argument Clinic. *You're not arguing with me, you're simply contradicting everything I'm saying.*"

"You should meet his sister," I said, and explained how his sister Phoebe was even more contentious. She was the woman who Conaghan had been talking about whose fiancé died under mysterious circumstances. Phoebe had once been brilliant, now she roamed the streets, crowds scattering in her path, pedestrians literally vanishing as she turned corners into sunlight, armored coiffure gleaming, that joyless grin plastered across her face. Phoebe haunted the public and college libraries and the three grocery stores, seeking to trap the unfortunate listener. Word was she had single-handedly disbanded the local bird club. Long ago, Sam had told me, she had published three papers in *The New England Journal of Medicine* and been on the vanguard of cancer research, but somewhere along the way she had "snapped an axel." Conaghan insisted she was undiagnosed bipolar. Sam blamed Janet Reno, the embattled attorney general under (but never directly under) Bill Clinton, though he'd never specified why.

"Warn me if you see her."

"I've never actually met her," I said. "Only noted her from afar."

"Lucky you."

We entered the Chadron State campus, its old red-brick buildings giving it the aspect of the college Rod Serling had attended in Yellow Springs, Ohio, in that Year of Enduring Twilight. Once a teacher's college, now a liberal arts school, CSC was one of the cheapest accredited four-year public colleges in America. The college was so old, five of the campus buildings were on the National Register of Historic Places, and dinosaurs and other antiquated beings in bifocals and hearing aids still roamed the hallways. The enrollment at Chadron State College was about 3,000, I told Kevin, and the campus was "dry."

"Right," he said.

CSC's southern border marks the end of town. Beyond that was scorched grassland and light, mostly burned pine forest to the horizon. Off to the east past Sandy Burd's May Queen Cattle Ranch was our pale-blue water tower written with the name of the town, its tipped "C" a crescent moon. To the west was the hamlet called Hidden Valley, where the only houses in the summer wildfires were lost. You could see exactly where the fire-fighters had turned back the flames and saved the town. My son always demanded that I read the marker erected in their honor:

> July 26–Aug 3 2006
> Wildfires caused by lightning burned 68,000 acres in Dawes and Sioux Counties. This marker is dedicated to the firefighters and volunteers from seven states and the people of the communities that fought the fires. Three homes were destroyed. No lives were lost. The Spotted Tail Fire burned to this point.

From there we climbed a blackened C-Hill, the most prominent landmark and the best view in town. Up there the air smells of wild roses, turnips, sometimes licorice and cinnamon toast, sometimes ocean and rusting trains. The wind seems always to be blowing. Tom claimed he could see California, where his grandparents lived.

18.

The so-called Christmas party

6:34 a.m. A caller at Third and Elm advised the Doritos truck had missed the corner and went into the ditch. Contacted someone about bringing the front-end loader out and pulling them out.

KEVIN AND RHONDA WERE LEAVING IN TWO DAYS AND I could see they were enjoying themselves at 3,400 feet on the snowy treeless plains with the ghosts of cowboys and Indians and the crenellated sunsets like tangled velveteen curtains on fire and all the nutty people who called this place home. The peace and vast distance and big skies of the prairies can get in your blood.

Before they left they joined Cristina, Tom, and me at Steve and Cheryl Welch's bonfire party, which came to be described later in the newspapers as "The Christmas Party." No one of course knew that two days later our gentle math professor, Steve Haataja, would vanish.

There were weekly parties at Steve and Cheryl's house, bon voyage parties, welcome-home parties, garden parties, let's-have-a-party parties, fire-blazing, picnic-table-full-of-potluck parties, which my wife and I often attended. The Welch house, only a block from us, was Wingding Ranch. Cristina, a self-admitted homebody, felt more comfortable here than most settings since both Steve and Cheryl spoke more than the usual *es-muy-bonito* Spanish and there was a big totem pole out front engraved with the word WELCOME. Cheryl, a Vermonter, taught high school Spanish in Hay Springs, 20 miles east. Steve, a jack-of-all-trades, possessed the ultra-logical scientific mind and resented irrational myths such as the Christian story of Christmas, so this wasn't by any means a "Christmas Party," and it was too early anyway, but primary storytellers (mythologists, journalists, and advertisers) can only sell what consumers will buy. Indeed factual stories are so cumbersome, ambiguous, unexciting, and difficult to understand most of the time that they are almost always instantly reconstructed and condensed for better emotional digestion into folktales with foreign villains and blue-eyed saviors. We'd rather have satisfaction and the maximum titillation than real information, and so history, I insist to my good friend Steve Welch, isn't a cold sequential list of facts, it's a prize anthology of the best fiction. Whether it's the ancient Israelites, Homer's *Iliad*, James Frey, or a Hearst newspaper, whoever spins the best yarn wins. And until science can come up with a story more compelling than protein globules congealing in some random electrochemical frenzy over four billion years to assemble somehow into Jesus in the manger, we're going to stick with the more colorful version of the mystery of how Christmas came to be.

Mostly musicians attended the "Christmas Party," Jack and John from The Bald Mountain Rounders, Shawn Marie Delinger, who is inhabited by a Gaelic faerie and teaches private music lessons for 10 bucks an hour, including a weekly Friday bongo session with a kid named Eli and my son. Community choir director Daisy Mavis was also there. Both Steve Welch (a tenor) and Steve Haataja (a bass) belonged to the choir. Violette, who never missed a drop of the Draft Called Life, was at the party too. Cristina attended under the provision that we wouldn't stay too long, while Tom came eagerly on the promise of an outdoor fire. It was a Saturday night so he could stay up late. He informed everyone there that his mother put soap in the toilet and that people were made of bones.

Since I had quit the Olde Main Street Inn I was utterly free these days due to a trickle of royalties and the sale of two or three magazine pieces a year as well as the occasional paid appearance, so long as I got up at three every morning and walked over to Safeway to sweep, scrub, and buff the floor. Once a week they locked me in at 10 p.m. and I stripped and waxed a section of floor and got out at three or four in the morning, whenever the stockers and the first bakery people came on or a truck pulled up to the back dock to deliver groceries.

My incorrigible spine went out that night from a sneezing fit of all things, and I walked around as if I'd been hit by a snow-plow. It got so bad that when I stood up from my chair I could not take my gaze from the floor. It was chilly and before long all of us moved inside, except for Tom, who wanted to watch the fire and play on the swings. He said if he went inside his blood would turn green.

Within 10 minutes of drinking a 90 Shilling beer I had an asthma attack. Kevin asked if I needed CPR or a ride to the hospital for anaphylactic shock. I said I'd be all right. The doctor in Mexico who'd agreed to prescribe me Valium had also provided three syringes and three vials of lumbar epidural steroids to get me through the next year and recommended back surgery within the next two years.

I limped home and *la doctora* Cristina gave me an epidural steroid shot, the last one in my arsenal, which almost immediately relieved my breathing. Within the hour the deep root-snag in my spine had begun to relax and I felt suddenly two inches taller and ready to contend for the major league baseball home-run crown. When I returned to the Welch house, Kevin was sitting on the couch talking to Dr. Haataja, who wore a white T-shirt, blue jeans, his trusty Birkenstocks, and was drinking a Corona, a smile on his face that I can only describe as a reserved and pensive sweetness. His usual companion, a laptop, was nowhere to be seen.

I watched Haataja that night and I couldn't help wondering, since I'd read so much about autism, if he wasn't at least on the edge of the spectrum. His intense intellectual interest, inter-personal awkwardness, compulsive neatness, solitary habits, pattern fascinations, aversion to touch, reluctance to meet your gaze, and perfect pitch all pointed in that direction, though like

Tom, he was warm (once you got to know him) and had a marvelous sense of humor. He was ruddy tonight, maybe from beer, though it seemed more to me like the familiar vitality that comes from a fresh start, bracing weather, and walking a few miles every day. His round wire-rimmed glasses rode high on his plump, prominently chinned face. He seemed to be in exceedingly good spirits.

Steve Welch, who knew Haataja better than any of us because they were in the choir together and because Haataja's car had broken down upon arrival and Steve often gave him a ride home from the college, told me that the professor had tried to kill himself the year before, wanted to hang, but "chickened out" and overdosed instead. Subsequently, he'd been diagnosed with MDD, or Major Depressive Disorder, and had been prescribed antidepressants, specifically Lexapro (a selective serotonin reuptake inhibitor [SSRI], which comes like many antidepressants with an FDA warning about suicide). Steve said that Haataja had weaned himself from the Lexapro because he didn't believe he needed it anymore. Steve thought that the pressure of the doctorate and all the time it had taken Haataja to recover from his broken hip had been the cause of his malaise, not some mysterious mental illness.

I told Steve that because I couldn't afford a psychiatrist, I'd never bothered to get a diagnosis in my 20 years of sighing heavily and wandering around the country like a corpse looking for its own funeral, though it was obvious by my suicidal tendencies and my custom of staring out the window entirely uninterested in my future that I would've been labeled with a depressive disorder, too. Eventually I obtained a bottle of Prozac, also an SSRI accompanied by an FDA warning, from an addict friend who was a psychiatric nurse. Prozac shrank my bone marrow, made my teeth itch, and made me feel as if I had an avocado pit embedded between my eyes. In my case, as in the majority of "depression disorder" cases, I suspected, symptoms were being treated, root causes were not being explored.

Some indeterminable aspect of my "brain chemistry" was thought to be "imbalanced." The cause of my "disorder" was not "brain chemistry" but being alone, poor, powerless, and not having any success at my primary pursuit, a set of circumstances that no drug in the world except maybe heroin could ever hope to address. Once I'd married and begun to publish regularly, I said, my depression went away. It seemed that something similar had happened to Haataja.

Overhearing my conversation with Steve that night, Violette in his baggy green Hawaiian blouse leaned over us suddenly. "Suicide is a mistake," he said, wagging a finger. "Trust me. I've talked to a few of them from the other side."

The conversation trapdoored from this into Violette's favorite avocation, and while he showed around some his mist photos from the Indian Creek Wreck of two years ago, I got up to see how Tom was doing and try my luck at another beer (a Heineken this time, God Bless the Dutch) and found Rhonda in the kitchen with Cheryl, who had an idea for a pioneer cookbook.

You look back on a night like this and try to recollect what might've been done or said, what significant or unusual details stood out, what hints might've been dropped: The event glows with preternatural meaning. Did Haataja's reference to the film *Man Without a Past* have significance? Why would he choose to explain to Steve Welch the graphing of polar coordinates to locate a star? Welch thought it uncharacteristic of Haataja that for the last hour before leaving the party he talked about his parents, who owned the Rim Rock Lodge in Spearfish, South Dakota, the sort of place that for its rugged vistas and breakneck precipices Alfred Hitchcock might have chosen for a scene in *North by Northwest*. Haataja said he hoped his parents were pleased with him. Steve Welch snapped a photo that night. It's the only photo I have of Professor Haataja, besides the two printed over and over in the newspaper. In the photograph he is smiling and holding his Corona in the air.

19.

Haataja disappears

AFTER EXHAUSTING ALL THE POTENTIAL GHOST, COOK-book, crime, autism, and cartoon possibilities of Chadron, Rhonda finally agreed the day before she and Kevin were scheduled to leave that I would write a novel, which I'd laid out already, about a Lakota Indian boy who accidentally kills his stepfather then flees the reservation to become a stand-up comedian in Las Vegas. Rhonda said she could see the movie already, though I could tell her heart was not altogether in the project. Nevertheless she wrote me an advance check for $2,000. She figured she could sell 5,000 copies, God willing, and that might help keep her company afloat for one more year.

Kevin and Rhonda were booked to fly out at seven the next morning, which meant I had to be at Safeway locked in by 10 so I could be out by 3:30 or 4 a.m. when the first stockers and the bakery people arrived. Tom and I went to the Olde Main to bid them a good evening in their General Miles Suite, said that we'd see them in the morning around six, and headed home from the hotel.

Wherever we went in those days, whatever the weather, Tom liked to push his old stroller. Once a passenger he was now the driver, and carried a number of his prized possessions, rubber lizards and skeletons, clothespins, ring boxes, a taped swizzle stick, a belt named "Poopy," a SpongeBob ball cap, a clipboard, and a weed he'd just pulled from the ground, all piled together in the seat.

Haataja lived only two blocks away from us on the corner of Second and Bordeaux in the same apartment where Dee, the one-time editor of *The Chadron Record*, had tried so hard to drink himself to death. Dee was evicted because Crawford, the land-lord, feared that with all the newspapers about, and Dee being a heavy smoker in an alcoholic stew half the time, he would burn the place down. Dee had to move to Pony Park, one of the seedier trailer parks in town, to finally get the job done. Those apartments on Second and Bordeaux were not exactly what you'd call lucky lodging for the single gentleman.

As Tom and I came down Second Street, we saw the com-motion at Haataja's apartment, two police units, cops filing in and out the front door. Several people were standing out front, including literature professor Kathy Bahr, who'd recently assigned one of my books to her class.

The police blotter for that day reads:

Dec 5 – RP [reporting party] advised he was informed of a missing instructor by Gary White who is the dean of Language and Literature at the college. Gary advised Steven Haataja hasn't been seen since yesterday at four thirty p.m.

Tom and I wandered over. "What's going on?" I asked Kathy.

Kathy, so cool she's almost blasé, is a gray-eyed redhead with a fondness for fellow Georgian Flannery O'Connor. She also likes true crime, Cormac McCarthy, Bret Easton Ellis, and Edna St. Vincent Millay, who penned the famous rhyming poems, "Renascence," "The Suicide," "Afternoon on a Hill," "Ashes of Life," and ended up at the bottom of her grand staircase, heart attack, broken neck, hard to say which came first.

Kathy wore a gray quilted down jacket and red earmuffs, and it was cold enough with the wind blowing in from the north that she had her hands stuffed into her pockets and her head turtled into her collar. "Steven missed a couple of classes," she said. "No one's seen him since yesterday."

"I saw him two nights ago," I said. "He looked fine."

"I saw him yesterday," she said. "The cops say that nothing

looks out of the ordinary, except his bike is gone. It's getting me a little peeved," she said. "If he's out on his bike they need to go look for him. It was five degrees below zero last night."

Kathy, a self-described "Army brat," has lived in almost as many places as I have and therefore has more empathy than the ordinary person for the new kid in town. Haataja had only arrived four months before. She'd also been the one to hire him (she'd been a dean that year to fill a vacancy), knew of his troubled background, his occasional "helplessness," his "gaps in employment," his numerous "illnesses." They'd gone out socially a few times, especially happy hour at the Sinister Grin, that loud cement-floored dive owned by County Defender Paul Wess.

Tom watched Kathy closely. If you got mad he'd often get mad too. He jerked his stroller in a restless circle and then scuffed the sidewalk with his shoe. To the west was an ominous cloud that looked like a forming tornado, though Chadron tornadoes are as rare in December as vanishing professors.

"We're going out to look for him," she said, pointing to the apartment. "The cops aren't going to do anything."

"Where are you going to look?"

"I just talked to Deane. He thinks if Steve was around town, someone would've seen him, so we're going to try the trails south of campus. Deane said he'd meet us up there. Do you want to come?"

"Do you want to go up to the college, Tom?"

"Oh, yes," he said. The college was the only place in town besides City Hall with "elvegators" and every building contained at least two of his cherished fire exits.

"We'll have to drive."

"Can we take the stroder?"

"No stroller. We're going up to C-Hill."

"We'll meet you at Math and Science," Kathy said. "We don't have much light left."

I made a call to the Olde Main to see if Rhonda or Kevin

wanted to go, but Jeanne said they were out. Back Tom and I went to the incinerated hills south of the campus, a one-mile trip from Haataja's apartment. I let Tom sit in the front seat and he played with the radio and the temperature controls, then announced suddenly: "I saw a drain!" I drove up Bordeaux Street on the outside chance I'd see Haataja walking in a daze, or peeking out from behind a curtain or a tree.

I parked in the empty lot at the Mathematics and Science Building. Deane Tucker, my occasional drinking companion, an old Floridian beach bum, film buff, and tenured professor of philosophy there, was waiting for us, as was Kathy and a pre-dental student named Paul Nelson, who Cristina and I often talked to because he knew the golden path to professional dentistry. Paul wore a goatee, had ski racks on his Honda, looked like a young man escaped from a Jon-Luc Godard film, and was always going off on vacation to places like Italy and Peru.

"Know what?" said Tom to Paul.

"What?"

"Red ants are going to come out of the ground and *eat* people."

That was the last laugh of the night. Light fading fast in the sky, we split up, Deane and Paul Nelson heading east, Kathy, Tom and I branching west. Tom said, "What are we looking for?"

"A teacher," I said.

"Why?"

"He is lost."

"Does he have a mother?"

"Yes, in South Dakota."

"Why is he lost?"

"We don't know yet, Tom."

Moving through a twilight landscape of blackened grass and dead licorice-stick trees, Tom announced that we were taking the "porky pine trail."

Among his many talents Tom was an amateur botanist, and he named all the trees for Kathy and me as we went, among them seaweed trees, nuffin trees, fancy trees, and stand-up trees, even if they were all ponderosas. They did look different, some twisted, stunted, some branchless, scorched, some scarred by lightning. As we made our way up the burned escarpment, scorched tubers of yucca lay about, unregenerated. The thin stands of flame-blasted ponderosa pine had not been able to regenerate either. The ponderosas in this part of the world are smaller and scrubbier than their counterparts north and west, where the temperatures are more modest, the rainfall more abundant. Botanists often facetiously refer to this hot dry zone between the Black Hills and the Platte River as "the banana belt." The lumber interests complain about these scrawny ponderosas, but what kind of commercial yield should you realistically expect from a short-grass prairie? The hills have been reseeded, though it will take a generation at least for this forest to recover, and it may never recover.

Now and then Tom would pause to grab a bush or a tree branch and wearing his fierce spasmodic trance face give it a mighty rattle.

Kathy, Tom, and I hiked to the signal tower, then back across the trail that followed the private land boundary of Sandy Burd's May Queen Cattle Ranch.

On a ridge to the west, we saw a herd of 13 mule deer, frozen in their tracks and staring at us as if we'd just called each by name. The taffy-pink sky swirled to purple. A few stars began to show. The terrain was too rugged to navigate in darkness, and that iceberg wind out of the north was freezing our knees.

"He can't possibly be up here," I said, "not at least on his bicycle."

We headed back, finding Deane and Paul waiting for us in the parking lot. Deane, who'd been out many times socially with Steve, including to his apartment, said that Haataja rode his bike everywhere, and that it was always parked behind the couch, so the police should not have missed it.

Sergeant Chuck later told me that Steve's apartment was

exceedingly neat, socks color coded, those plaid shirts that he favored on their wardrobe rack, even at the shoulders, all facing the same way. The little boxes of Sunkist raisins he liked along with the cans of Slim-Fast and packages of ramen were arranged fastidiously in the cupboard. Books in stacks were everywhere, but even the "clutter," as Sergeant Chuck put it, was neat. Sergeant Chuck described the room as "gloomy," with natural light only coming through two small windows above. The sergeant said to me that he would've been depressed in there too. There was a mattress on the floor, a statement after four months of residence that says to me: I don't plan on being here long.

"I hate to quit," said Kathy.

"He's OK," said Deane, flat-voiced, hands in pockets. "Probably rented a car. You know his father is dying."

Paul said he had seen Haataja in the library on Saturday, the day of the Christmas Party, checking out old genetics books. Paul wondered what the purpose of checking out a book on genetics from the 1970s was.

"It's too cold to ride a bike," said Deane.

"I feel sick," said Kathy, turning and heading for her car.

Tom had to ring the victory bell outside of Don Beebe stadium before we left to go visit Cristina, where she was a janitor in the Administration Building. He whanged on that clanger four times and then took a high-arced pee on the lawn. The air was so cold the toll of the bell was still echoing through the hills as we walked away.

20.

The Lakota comedian is set aside

SINCE I'D WORKED IN THE BAKERY AT SAFEWAY AND now cleaned floors there seven days a week, I knew all the Safeway employees and would learn before the police did that Steve Haataja had bought a bag of charcoal there just before the store closed at 10 p.m., Monday, December 4th the last night he was seen. Jennifer, a CSC student at the time, now in Wyoming working as an accountant, sold him the seven-pound bag of briquettes. She said there was nothing unusual about him that evening. He didn't seem drunk or despondent. No panic or alarm was evident in his eyes. He wasn't any more brooding, restive, or upset than any other shopper that night. He was alone, as everyone else who saw him that night reported.

The next morning, after two hours of sleep, I drove Rhonda and Kevin to the airport. "Maybe you've got your book now," said Rhonda quietly from the backseat.

"I'm sure he's all right," I said, not believing this in the least.

"A mystery anyway," she said.

"Not much of a cookbook," said Kevin.

"He'll turn up," I said. "What do you think happened to him?" I asked Kevin.

"All that stuff about MDD and antidepressants and suicide attempts?" he answered, shaking his head. "And five degrees below zero last night? We'd better hope that wherever he rode his bicycle it was indoors."

The plane was a few minutes late and had to be de-iced

twice before it could leave. Tom and I waved good-bye to Kevin and Rhonda, whom we could not see through the tinted passenger windows. Tom played with his OSU beaver mascot and sadly wondered when his good friends would return.

We drove back to Chadron and after I dropped Tom off at school, I puttered around town, thinking of Haataja and wondering where he might've gone. His story in many ways felt like my own, this gentle but awkward middle-aged man who lived alone with a mattress on the floor and kept having to start his life over. My instincts told me he had walked away. Whether or not he survived, if he was hanging in a motel room, or chattering along the side of the highway, or running off to join the Foreign Legion or heading out to start his life over in Reno as an Elvis impersonator, I was bound to the outcome.

21.
This wacky fandango

FOR FEAR OF APPEARING INFERIOR, CRISTINA WOULD resist speaking the English she'd learned, even if rule number one of learning a new language is that for a good two or three years you must be willing to go out and look like a complete fool, and long after that an outsider with a foreign accent. But Americans will understand, I assured her, they will help you. We are all of us from somewhere else. Only the *pendejos* will laugh. How many times did you laugh at me when I said something wrong? She thought it was hilarious when I put the wrong accent on *árbol*, the Spanish word for tree. Early in my career I'd asked a young woman how many *anos*, or anuses, she had, and remember the time I ordered *juego de araña* at the juice bar, not orange juice as I'd intended but "game of the spider"?

I told her that everyone's life was difficult, everyone was uncertain. I'd lived on the brink of desperation much of my life.

"You?" she said. "You're strong. You're an oak tree. You're in your own country. You know what everyone is saying."

Every two weeks at the minimum we had "the talk." Do you love me? But do you really love me? I have this pain in my chest. *Is it her heart*, I wondered? Her grandmother had died in her 40s of a heart attack, but then the pain, refusing to be treated or traced, would migrate to her neck or knee.

I wanted this, us, to work out. I was done with jumping ship. I'd stayed the course with writing and it was beginning to pay off. Now it was time to commit to flesh and blood. I wanted to give her confidence, to find and eradicate those sources of chronic insecurity and pain. I believed that once she could command the language, once she was comfortable with the culture, once she held a respectable job, once she learned how to drive, once she gained some independence from me, and so on, everything would change.

Still we fought, always over trifles that would build and lead to threats and curses that never achieved anything except to frighten our child and create these eerie islands of sterile domestic silence. There had to be a way to stop this, I kept thinking, to recognize the trigger, to avoid the bait, but we were both too stubborn to give in. We each knew the other was selfish and wrong and needed to change. What we needed, what I needed at least, was more time to figure out this wacky fandango of irreconcilable wills and desires called marriage. To wit, when you get married no one tells you the rules of the Can't Win Game, though it's very simple to play (rather like being a pinball caught between two bumpers), and it always begins with a question that you must recognize as a statement. Let's say we're planning a trip from Chadron to Colorado Springs, about a six-hour drive. Cristina does not want to take the interstate because it makes her nervous. She would rather take the back highways, so she "asks" me which route I think we should take, and since I'm driving it's "my call." If I make the mistake of saying we should take the interstate because we can save an hour, and then concede quickly to take the back highways after her obvious disapproval (and it really makes no difference to me) she will insist indignantly that we take the interstate, thereby assuring a snit (and an argument) no matter which way we go. The Can't Win Game is about anticipation, the illusion of a discussion, and capitulation without it being recognized as such. It took me five years to understand (i.e. avoid) this game, which is simply doing what Cristina wants. Which way would I like to go to Colorado Springs? Why, the back highways, of course.

Tom got upset when we shouted and demeaned each other.

He blamed me for these outbursts. I was supposed to be the strong one. After one of our daily skirmishes I'd lie on the floor with my sock feet up on the couch and marvel at my labor of futility.

And then along would come a laughing Tom to jump on my chest. "Easy, buddy. Hey, can you sit up a little higher?"

"Why?"

"It makes my back feel better. That's it, right there."

"Make a spider!" he commanded. "Make two spiders!"

These finger spiders I made, Spidey and Whitey, were his only non-adult friends. Spidey and Whitey loved him, kissed him, crawled up his shirt and made him giggle. In turn he cared for them, made sandwiches for them, put them to bed, housed them in his tents, and made sure they got through the dark woods safely where they attended spider school and sometimes spider church. They were also the bridge when he withdrew emotionally.

I'd make two spiders and then everything would be all right.

22.

Chuck in charge

ON DECEMBER 7, 2006, NATIONAL PEARL HARBOR REMEM-brance Day, Sergeant Charles Chaffwick of the Chadron Police Department was assigned the lead in the investigation of the disappearance of Steven Haataja. Chuck had seen a total of one murder in his 26 years as a Chadron police officer, missing persons cases were about as rare, but in his 12 years at Wisconsin 5-0 he'd investigated a number of complicated cases, including murders and missing persons (and you don't have to be missing for 48 hours to officially be designated a missing person, he informed me), so he was very probably the best officer for the job, and better prepared than most were willing to concede. Chuck's recent successful battle with prostate cancer and his imminent retirement, however, probably didn't sharpen his appetite for more police work, especially anything as complicated, extended, mystifying, and disturbing as the Haataja case would turn out to be.

Neither was it the best timing for the Chadron Police Department. The chief, Jerry Crews, had recently been fired, and the dispatcher, Margaret Keiper, had taken his place. Both Sheriff Conaghan and Sergeant Chuck informed me that Margaret was much better suited for the job than Jerry. Chuck insisted that Margaret's leadership style had a coherent and soothing effect, and would've had the force back in good shape given time. In fact, if the professor hadn't done his disappearing act, both men agreed, no one would have likely ever noticed, the department would've coalesced, and she'd still be running police headquarters today.

Whatever your opinion about the dispatcher running the department, her appointment did little to assuage the aura of tumult, resentment, and public distrust that had been hovering around the force ever since one of the officers, Charlie Puchner, had shot a dog. The story passed around had a number of variations, including her (yes, Charlie is a she) emptying her handgun into the dog because she was afraid of dogs, but the fact was she'd never shot the dog. Her father, a deputy sheriff from the next county over, riding with her, had shot the dog. The dog, which would not let the officer out of her car, had provoked several calls.

The townspeople preferred their own dog-killing-inept-policewoman (whose deputy sheriff father got her the job in the first place) story and liked to include various fabricated embellishments, including the passage of bullets intended for the dog into the house behind the now dead dog. We are a community like most small communities, probably all human communities, that prefers excitement and a good show over order – the truth is so demanding and hard to keep straight! – or as the saying goes, "Never let the facts get in the way of a good story."

Not long after the dog shooting, two police units responding to the same call had met in a fabulous smashup in front of the newspaper office. My friend George Ledbetter, the editor of *The Chadron Record*, a native of Pierre, South Dakota, an ex-beekeeper and a devout, guru-trained Hindu, always appreciates when news is brought directly to his office. The cruisers were responding to a domestic disturbance call, the third or fourth call that day from the same household, a life-threatening situation, and in their haste the two drivers approaching from opposite directions met in a spectacular collision, one car leaping the curb. George got snapshots from his office window as wheel covers wobbled away and various dangling and swinging parts came to rest. The officers jumped down, ran around, scratched their heads, briefly assumed silent movie poses, and bent to examine the damage. The radio chattered. The senior officer leaped into the only drivable car and sped away to answer the call. Both refurbished autos were recently sold at auction at an excellent discount.

Not much later came the coup de grace, a wrongful-death suit filed against the city in what many considered to be the mishandling of the Craig Chizek suicide case. Craig, a railroad employee in his 30s, had armed and secured himself in a garage, while officers stood outside preventing family members from entering. Craig died before anyone could reach him. Many thought that his family could've talked him out of it. This last episode, along with Police Chief Jerry Crews's general decline in performance and attitude, finally got him the axe. Sheriff Shawn Conaghan described the FBI-trained Crews as an excellent policeman, a good drug investigator, but a poor administrator. Sergeant Chuck said that Jerry had trouble being honest with the citizens he had sworn to protect, which only worked against him. Chuck said, "Tell the people the truth about how the dog got shot and they won't have to make up stories."

Sheriff Conaghan said about Crews: "Toward the end there he just crumbled. It was the Peter Principle in action: a man rising to the level of his incompetence."

Crews's administration was also marked by what Sheriff Conaghan describes as the "Super-secret-James-Bond-if-I tellya-I-gotta-killya attitude." This atmosphere of lax management and Cold War secrecy prompted many of the more seasoned and competent officers to move on, leaving green cops to train more green cops, a Green Cop Cycle, if you like, and this culture still pervaded the force.

A quick note on jurisdiction: while police authority is confined to Chadron proper, the sheriff's department handles all calls and complaints within Chadron and Dawes County, which includes the city of Crawford, the village of Whitney, the virtual-ghost-town of Marsland, and all points, ranch and rural, in between. Chadron police and the sheriff's department often cooperate and respond to the same dispatches within city limits. The county sheriff is elected by the people, answers to the people, and hires his own deputies. The chief of police, as much a politician as a policeman, is appointed by the city council, answers to city council, and relies on state commission statutes to hire his or her own officers. Conaghan had absolute power in the county, even over the FBI, though with only two deputies, his workload was stretched, so he let the better-staffed and funded police force handle the majority of violations and calls.

Conaghan told me that one of the reasons the police force had so much trouble "was that they were poorly trained and poorly disciplined." He said there was a real lack of public trust. At that time the sheriff's office was getting four calls a week from people who did not want the police department to handle their case. "Margaret Keiper did the best with what she had," Conaghan told me, "but they didn't give her enough authority, enough tools. The police department was in chaos."

> 11:30 A.M. Caller from Chadron advised that he wanted to speak to someone about the burglary in his home on Sunday. Caller was advised that the Dawes County sheriff's office was handling that case and he needed to speak with them. Caller stated that he had seen people in town selling his items and he expected that someone would be out arresting them before they sold it all. Caller also stated that the sheriff's office had told him that the Chadron Police Department was holding up the investigation. Caller was further advised that the sheriff's office is handling the case.

23.
Speeding tickets and cats in trees

FROM THE BEGINNING OF STEVE'S DISAPPEARANCE THE Chadron Police Department did not seem especially motivated or concerned. Small town constabulary is not ambitious by nature. If they wanted exciting, high-profile law enforcement challenges they'd be in Denver or Cheyenne. Sheriff Conaghan defended their initial inaction. "Because of the college, this is an itinerant town," he told me. "People are always coming and going, students, professors. You're ready to serve papers on a guy and you find he's already been gone for six months. Steve could've been anywhere, on a vacation or a flat tire up in Rapid. So it took us a while before we recognized this as a missing person's case. It isn't an excuse for no response, but it was a reason."

Nor do I insist that being a small-town cop in any way is easy. Matthew Red Shirt, for example, gets drunk and lies out in the middle of the road until he has to be physically removed. Like several of the homeless Indians in town, Matthew is sometimes on very cold nights allowed to sleep in the lobby of police headquarters. Matthew is so mean-spirited and vile many insist he will never die. He swears blue fire and threatens to kill your family and burn down your house. One night, staying in the police HQ lobby, he took his cane to an arriving dispatcher. Matthew claims boastfully to be a descendant of the war chief Red Shirt, who participated in the successful plot to kill the Great Lakota Hero, Crazy Horse. The police wear masks and plastic gloves and slide him onto a stretcher. Matthew is crippled, has tuberculosis and hepatitis, so they can't put him in jail. There is nowhere really to put him, so Joni Behrends, the Hot Cop, smokes a cigarette with him or drives him around for a while in the back of her police car. She likes Matthew and is not afraid of his cane, his tongue, or his tuberculosis, and she loves it when he speaks Lakota. In a few days he will be lying in the middle of the road again, drunk as Caligula, metal crutches scattered, laughing and demonically cursing his rescuers.

And there are, of course, the normal challenges presented by the residents of a small college town: drunken football players, all-night parties, bar fights, domestic disputes, assaults, suicides, car wrecks, child abusers, house fires. It isn't all cats in trees and speeding tickets. I have heard more than one complaint from Chadron police officers that *The Chadron Record*'s Police Beat trivializes their work.

> 5:51 A.M. Caller from East Second St. advised he was on his way to work and found a gun at the above location. He requested an officer remove it from his lunchbox.

> 2:17 P.M. Caller from the 800 block of Pine St. advised that she had just left someone's home and she forgot her jacket, and requested an officer to get her coat.

> 10:20 P.M. Caller from the 300 block of Lake St. requested an officer at the above location to unplug the light in his garage as he is not feeling well and is unable to get it turned off.

24.

The war god descends

ONE DAY MY ATTRACTIVE YOUNG IMMIGRANT HISPANIC wife came home all atwitter about a man named Loren Zimmerman, who'd been hired the year before as an assistant criminology professor at the college. I recalled the buzz among the professors when Loren Zimmerman was hired. Landing an instructor who had more than 20 years of hands-on homicide experience seemed a lucky strike for the criminal justice department. An ex-Marine who'd once been poised to invade Cuba after the Bay of Pigs fiasco in 1961, Zimmerman had six children from several marriages and was a Vietnam veteran. Robin Smith, instructional design coordinator at CSC, who'd also served in Vietnam, told me that Zimmerman had been a "tunnel rat" there and enjoyed reminiscing about those times. Robin said that Zimmerman laughed when he told the story of how he had killed a Vietnamese soldier on a reconnaissance mission, shot him in the back, done his sworn duty. You don't often meet the Nam vet with fond memories of the war.

The intensely blue-eyed and modestly balding John Shafer, who left a good job in Oregon television to return to Chadron about eight years before to take over his grandfather's farm southeast of town (and would die of a heart attack before I could finish this book); who played double bass and sang lead in the bluegrass band called The Bald Mountain Rounders, and who had also attended the "Christmas Party" at Wingding Ranch, worked as a telecommunication technician at the college setting up video conferences and helping the professors with audio/visual problems. John helped Mr. Zimmerman set up a slide show one time for his Forensics II class. The slides, according to Zimmerman, were of canoes, but instead they turned out to be autopsy photos of L.A. gang members, one of Zimmerman's many areas of expertise. John didn't know that "canoe" is police lingo for a corpse after it has been autopsied ("canoe maker" is cop slang for coroner) so it took him by surprise, these Crips, Bloods, Sureños, and 18th Streets, all laid out on steel tables with tags on their toes and bullet holes in their young blue chests, and all Zimmerman could do was chuckle and remark upon the tattoos. War and crime were Zimmerman's elements, canoes apparently entertained him too.

Loren Zimmerman had been a cop in L.A. for 20 years, but since then he'd been on the move: Texas, New York, Maryland, back to California (San Diego), and now Chadron. Five jobs and five states in six years. He was too old to be itinerant so he had to be running from something. *Running from himself most likely,* I thought, *and don't I know all about that?* The presiding opinion was that Zimmerman would not last. When I heard he'd been married not once but twice to a woman from Argentina, that he was keen to the cause of the immigrant Hispanic (especially, I was guessing, the attractive young female immigrant Hispanic), that he spoke Spanish and liked his *chicas del sur,* I began to feel a little ill.

And even though Cristina and I had been fighting at least once a day, sometimes three or four times a day, spitting and swatting at each other like cats over issues unrelated and long separated from the actual issues themselves, both of us knew the real issues. Cristina was honest with me about almost everything, honest enough even to tell me that she didn't trust me. She smoldered about the women from my past, was vigilant about the women in my future. Once when Laurel, an artist from New York City, came to visit us for two days, Cristina chased her out of the house, and Laurel had to spend the rest of her stay at Deane Tucker's place.

I still had faith we'd one day find that path to connubial harmony. A marriage worth having is work. I understood it was the cultural transition, her struggle with the language and her fear of losing her identity, of being swallowed whole by America, that was putting the strain on her and making her more possessive than she'd otherwise normally be. It takes most people a while to understand my sense of humor, too, some never get it, and Cristina didn't get it either. It perplexed me for a long time that whenever I sold a magazine piece or got an advance on a book, I'd give her a chunk of it, and invariably she'd concoct an argument within the hour, blindsiding me in the self-congratulation of my generosity. What was most difficult to accept was her attitude toward my writing. Literature was a waste of time, and though I made a few thousand a year at it, she thought I should get a full-time job with the Department of Transportation.

"Why do you write that crap?" she asked me the first time she got out her electronic translation dictionary and read one of my pieces, intensely jealous over the woman in the story who had preceded her by 20 years. "You tell everyone everything."

"Not everything."

"Aren't you embarrassed?"

"To the contrary. I feel liberated."

"Why can't you write something nice, like children's books? Or something that makes money."

"Like what, mysteries, romances, murder books? A story about a Bavarian shoemaker who finds a genie in his toaster?"

"Why not?"

"I don't care about them for one thing. I don't read them. Why would I write them?"

And so on, *que gacho*, until we hit the flashpoint and went up in flames.

I was not used to being berated on a daily basis, of being the object of exasperation and scorn, of living under a cloud of distrust and disapproval, of not being allowed out of the house without a pass, though I realized this was the matrimonial package I'd signed up for. Nevertheless, I continued to believe that once she'd acclimated to the culture, had mastered English, had learned how to drive, had found herself a better-paying job, could appreciate my oddball sense of humor, and realize that I had only her best interests at heart, that I really really did love her and was not going to run off with some jade the second she turned her back, everything would change, balance and complement would be restored, and she'd burst through the door with a baguette and a cold bottle of gin, immediately roast a beef round with orange zest and 27 cloves of garlic, throw on some jazz records, and exclaim the while, "I feel just great."

Because she made no attempt to hide her pleasure in or the regularity of exchanges she had with Crime Professor Loren Zimmerman, and because she was open, familial, and religiously scrupulous, I was able to quell my misgivings. If you can't trust your partner, then why are you together? When he invited her out to a barbeque or to his house to watch the Nebraska Cornhuskers opener, she made these invitations known to me (I was never invited) and she politely declined. I wasn't sure how a janitor and a professor could have such frequent routine contact (I almost used the word "intercourse!"), outside of the fact that – why didn't I just admit it to myself then? – he wanted to slide through the reeds, prop open his jaws, and gobble her knickers off on the dusky, sun-dappled shore.

Though I'd made an ingenuous promise when I brought Cristina from Mexico to America that we'd find her a good-paying job, or at least something related to her field, I hadn't been able to come through. I'd been a *maestro* in Mexico, teaching English for two dollars an hour, but in America I was a *peón*. I had worked pipe dreams and bottom-rung jobs all of my life and I was now 51 years old. It had taken Cristina, 33, a while to realize I was truly poor and had little influence in this wealthy society of big dreams and opportunity that I supposedly represented.

There were four dentists in town, and we'd gone around to each one twice with an introduction and her résumé and a lot of grinning and bowing without anything coming of it.

"I'd like to present to you my wife, an excellent dentist, I know this firsthand. She can do root canals, crowns, extractions, administer nitrous, take X-rays, the complete professional package. She worked for two years in a two-chair clinic before we came here, and her English is good (even if I am doing all the talking, I always do the talking, but she'll be gaining confidence soon, filling out her own applications and writing her own résumés and everything). She'll be getting her naturalization papers before long. Oh, yes, she's perfectly legal to work. Impeccable work habits. You won't regret it."

The looks we got, the paper rustling, throat clearing, brow cocking, the quizzical simpers and constipated stares, were almost identical at each office.

So she was a maid among ghosts before she worked with me in the Olde Main kitchen, then she was a food server at a camp in the woods for troubled and disadvantaged youths (Job Corps), then she worked in the bakery at Safeway for a few weeks. After Safeway she got a job with the state as a janitor at the local college with her best friend and *compatriota* Suzie Maria Greenwheat, a wild child from San Benito, a *pueblito* two hours east of Monterrey, Mexico. Suzie lived in a modest house across the street from a pair of pet geese that never shut up. You could hear their raucous gasping squawks for blocks causing even committed vegetarians to consider an early Christmas dinner.

Suzie, about four feet nine and 37 years old, had come to America as a photo bride 14 years before. She had hustled and scraped all her life. A nice-looking woman, she was actively dating after her recent divorce from Denny Greenwheat (brother of the prolific letter-writer and diatribist Jonas Greenwheat), so I wondered what the holdup was in introducing her to Hispanicophile Loren Zimmerman. I called Suzie Greenwheat "Telenovela," the word for "soap opera" in Spanish, for the madcap misadventures that seemed to follow her wherever she went. She was in the habit of calling Cristina at least once, sometimes four times a day, to gibber giddily in Spanish and report the latest episode from her action-packed life: She was tearing suicidally down the highway at 90 per; she'd just caught her ex-husband with an Indian girl in a South Dakota motel room; she'd met this doctor in Denver, who wanted to fly her out for one night of fun, etc.

Cristina worked nine-hour shifts. She seemed to be gone all day and well into the night. *Zacatecanos* are renowned for their work ethic. Hire a *zacatecano* and forget about the Chinese. My wife, besides being sweet, honest, pious, and polite, was an exemplary employee. Not only was she trustworthy, loyal, helpful, friendly, courteous, kind, obedient, thrifty, brave, clean, and reverent, her floors shined, her toilets twinkled, and she never called in sick. The custodial position was regular and secure, with good benefits, but it only paid eight something an hour, and she longed to return to the challenge, familiarity, and prestige of her field. So when Zimmerman stated his intentions to get her a better job, she began to speak of him as if he were a war god descended upon mortals, or upon peons, as the case may have been.

Cristina worked nights. I worked milkman hours and was done every morning just before Safeway opened at seven. This was the best arrangement for watching our son on his autism carousel. Because of this schedule, I was able to spend most of my day with Tom. We built tents, played trains, rode elevators, listened to music, and wrestled on the floor. We talked for hours about yellow dogs and blizzards and old age, about fire exits and hailstorms and that candy dish of silver in the sky called the moon. He confessed to me once that a hundred years ago he had been a dancer. For a time he was worried about that hot place under the earth his Catholic mother often warned him about where the bad people went and wondered if he might just spend a night there to see what it was like. I read to him from his mother's Bible the first line of Genesis: "'In the beginning God created the heavens and the earth.' It says nothing about hell, Tom. That came later with the membership drive."

I often drove to the college to visit my wife in the evenings. Tom particularly enjoyed these trips because he got to ride the "elvegator" in the Administration Building, where she worked. It was on one of these occasions that I saw Loren Zimmerman for the first time, talking to her in the first-floor hall. Cristina stood behind her custodial cart with its vertical mops and brooms, its cleaning chemicals and vacuum cleaner, and verily basked in his spell. As I moved toward them down the hall Zimmerman glanced up at me with a sort of amused disdain, and slithered away without benefit of an introduction.

My wife, unlike Zimmerman, was pleased to see us this evening. It encouraged me that she showed no signs of disgrace, remorse, annoyance, or chagrin. (Again, her frank admiration for him and open discussion about him, while it deepened my disquiet, also exonerated her because I assumed she was being fully forthcoming.) She only regretted that I'd just missed Mr. Zimmerman, who she was very excited about because he'd had a word with his acquaintance the dentist, who happened to need an assistant. He had no doubt she would get the job.

At last one evening at Safeway I was allowed to meet Crime Professor Loren Zimmerman formally as we came upon him leaned over his shopping cart in the meat section. Cristina presented him to me. Mr. Zimmerman was thick in the chest and upper arms, gray-headed, loose-skinned and yellow-toothed as an old crocodile. I estimated his age to be approximately that of Satan. This is Mr. Zimmerman, she said. This is my husband. She never used my name in introductions. This was either cultural, reflective of her discomfort in American social situations, or a result of being knocked unconscious by a drunken driver a few years back in Mexico. She used the title "Mister" in addressing all of her male elders, including her ESL teacher, whom she called Mr. Don.

"How do you do?" I said, offering my hand.

Little effort was expended on his part as he raised to me a listless claw, grinning with those yellow teeth the while, the same sort of amused contempt I'd caught in his demeanor the first time. Something was definitely tickling his funny bone. I decided after a while that my attempt at friendliness was only being interpreted by him as weakness.

A few weeks later, thanks to Mr. Zimmerman, my wife landed that beaucoup job with the local dentist. We'd been to this dentist, Terry Owen, a Seventh Day Adventist, twice over the years with résumés, and we'd talked to the receptionist, Brenda, a.k.a. Mrs. Terry Owen, a very kind, helpful person who said there were no openings but why didn't Cristina think of teaching at the University of Nebraska in Lincoln, since no actual license was required to teach, or perhaps she could pass her boards in Omaha after only one or two years of additional study?

An argument could've been made (and I was getting good at that) that Cristina's English hadn't been up to par the first and second times we'd been there to see about a job, and neither had she been a citizen (her naturalization hearing was not far away and no one except Cristina doubted that she'd pass), though she was legal to work, and doubtless there were a number of other obstacles to consider. Nevertheless, with one nod from the Old Crocodile, my wife was in.

She couldn't thank him enough, was dizzy with his influence and thoughtfulness, wanted to bring him gifts, to erect a statue of him in our front yard, thought to rename our son Zimmerman Junior. The position, however, was only four days a week, with several unpaid vacations a year. After a year she'd be eligible for paid vacations, and her hourly wage would be high enough to absorb whatever time off the dentist and his wife took for their annual trips to Hawaii and charity trips to India and the like. In the meantime, she looked for another job, without much luck, but when she asked Mr. Zimmerman if he knew of anything, lo and behold, she had a job cleaning his house once a week, Friday mornings, $10 an hour.

25.
Exit the rainmaker

9:45 A.M. Subject at PD stated that she thought she saw our missing professor at Hammond and Canal St. number 32, in Hot Springs near the boot sign. Caller requested an officer to go check if he's there.

SERGEANT CHARLES CHAFFWICK WAS A CLOSE FRIEND of Jeanne Goetzinger of the Olde Main Street Inn, and shared with her a fond reverence for the Large American Motorcycle. He belonged to a local group of enthusiasts, a "social riding club" called Brudenschaft, which I was told meant "Brotherhood," though "brotherhood" is *bruderschaft*, with an r, not an n. *Brudenschaft*, as far as I can gather, means literally either "Nazi underground," or it's a German/Polish drinking toast. Strictly speaking, "brüden" (with the umlaut over the u) means "exhaust vapor" and "schaft" means "barrel" or "shank." Whatever the meaning they were a recreational, often charitable group of hearty fellows, not the Mongols by any means, even if they dressed like brigands in black leather, chains, bandanas, and knives, all of which made Chuck and his crew even more endearing to Jeanne. One time I was at the bar and there were 30 Brudenschaft members roaming about, including Sergeant Chaffwick, who was being shown a knife made from a motorcycle chain. At the bar were mostly Indians who'd just bought Girl Scout cookies from Jeanne's granddaughter, and the boxes were stacked before them.

Fifty years ago these Indians would have not been sitting at any bar in town, especially with Girl Scout cookies in front of them, and these black-clad rogues (whose prototypes in the good old days often controlled large networks of drug traffic) would've thundered into town on their Large American Motorcycles, moistening the nether regions of the local citizenry, and in the movie version been met with a rifle-toting officer of the law, someone like Sergeant Chuck in other words, and his shivering posse comitatus. Bikers have since come to represent a more mainstream image of an *Easy Rider* way of life and rebellion against authority, even if you are an accountant or a police sergeant not far from retirement. Over the years bikers have also become a reliable source of revenue for Chadron as they rumble through for two weeks every August on their way to the Sturgis, South Dakota, motorcycle rally, seven days of contained wildlife, outlaw masquerade, marquee rock music, and brisk T-shirt sales.

Because of his prostate cancer and those apocalyptic summer fires that had nearly wiped our town off the map, Chuck had missed the rally this year, a virtual pilgrimage for the motor-cycle club enthusiast. I ran into him in Rapid City that summer, where he was getting treatment, and we gabbed for a time and he seemed down at the mouth. I liked Chuck. By all accounts he was a good cop with a pretty solid record, a better record than I would've amassed (surely I would've shot someone, probably myself), but the cancer ordeal and the years of working the small-town beat in a hapless John le Carré environment had drained his vigor. "Chuck," Sheriff Conaghan told me, "was burned out."

And no one blamed Sergeant Chaffwick for not doing much about Steve Haataja's disappearance. Those who did not know Dr. Haataja well, including me, thought he'd walked away either to start his life over somewhere in the west as a window washer, a gas station attendant, or a carnival barker, or to end his days in the most private and nameless way so as to cause the least pain to the ones who loved him, as I'd so often fantasized in my own days of wanderlust. *Exit the Rainmaker*. It was tragic but perfectly understandable. There was not much use in wasting time looking for him. He had our utmost sympathies.

The possibility that Haataja might've met some sort of dia-bolical fate was also discussed, but mostly discarded. Murdered in our small town? Abducted? There was no evidence to support such a proposition. He had no enemies. Most of his friends and family declared that he was happy in his new surroundings. Most vehement in this was his best friend and colleague of two years in Sioux Falls, Tim Sorenson, who said that Haataja's emails and phone conversations were "upbeat," that he was "excited" about his new position and home, that he seemed to be getting more upbeat as the days went along. And this was a town where not only did most not lock their doors, some even left their car keys in the ignition. Ignore the Sherlock Holmes remark about the evil that lurks in your average country home. It simply couldn't be.

Fair or not, the general impression persisted that the police were not heavily invested in the missing professor, that the Haataja investigation had concluded in essence with the first-day walk-through of his apartment on Second and Bordeaux, when Sergeant Chuck had not seen the bicycle because it was behind the door. Sergeant Chuck told me that the police department *did* conduct searches, and that they were concerned by and sympathetic to Haataja's circumstances.

In the meantime, a few searches by citizens were organized, including one on horseback.

26.

The dead in strange houses

TOM'S NIGHTMARES BEGAN IN EARNEST AROUND THIS time. Perhaps it had something to do with all the hollering his parents did at each other. Maybe it was all the tense talk about the man who existed one minute and did not the next. Children are more sensitive to their environments than we usually give them credit for. Both the recent fires and devastating hailstorms had put their frightful stamp on him, too.

Tom was growing at an astounding rate, his mind especially, and he'd reached that stage of independence also known as being contrary:

"Today's Tuesday, Tom."

"No, it isn't."

"Those are cows over there."

"No, they're not."

One night he was having a particularly vivid nightmare, calling out, "No no, please, I can't."

I got up to console him. "It's going to be all right," I said.

"No it isn't," he said, still asleep.

Cristina's nightmares also seemed to be worsening. She described them as "dark, dark dreams, soulless dreams." Their sameness year after year was disturbing. We'd be sitting at the breakfast table and she'd say, "I had a horrible nightmare last night."

"About dead people," I'd say, because they were always about dead people.

"Right." And she'd look at me closely as if I might've been in the nightmare with her, though I was never in any of her dreams.

"In a strange house in Mexico," I added, because they were always in a strange house in Mexico.

"Yes."

The dreams were always about dead people in a strange house in Mexico, but they did have variations. Sometimes her sister was there, her father, an old friend. Sometimes the corpses were eating each other. Sometimes they were chasing her, trying to kill her. Sometimes the dead would be indistinguishable from the living, as one often encounters in certain suburbs in California. Whatever the case, they were always wrenching, moving, chilling dreams that soaked into her waking hours.

And I couldn't avoid reading the symbolism: the dreams meant change, I told her, fear of change, refusal to change, refusal to leave behind the past (if you don't leave it behind it will consume you), though she wasn't persuaded by my pseudo-psychoanalytic interpretations or perhaps felt helpless or satisfied in some untoward way, as if the dreams were a judgment upon or a recompense for her (very modest compared to my) sins in this world.

My own nightmares these days were negligible. My "philosophy," work-hard-be-honest-don't-sell-out-give-more-than-you-take, though it made me a chump in America, kept the devil and the dead at bay. At the center of every molecule is a moral mechanism, or in other words: If all matter is transient, then only the deed remains. And I'd learned a trick over the years, perhaps from having to get up at such odd times, whether it was from work obligations or noisy neighbors, rats, or cockroaches. When I dreamt I usually knew I was dreaming. A good dream you let run, perhaps only adjusting the tint or volume. A bad dream, well you can fly in them, fly above it all. You can control your dreams, Cristina, you really can.

She thought this was funny, funnier than breathing to

control pain when she was giving birth (can I have the anesthesia now, please?).

How could such a pious Catholic girl, with saints and Bibles and crucifixes everywhere she turned, who believed so thoroughly in everything Catholic – grace, forgiveness, the next life – be so possessed of these wretched dreams?

I often asked her, "Why don't you trust God?"

"I do trust God," she'd reply.

But she didn't trust God any more than she trusted me or her own father. Her faith was closer to magic (she'd stopped going to church two years before) and she knew that whatever it was we were talking about, it wasn't going to work out, the pineapple was bad, there were no jobs to be found, we were going to be late and miss the appointment, the team she was rooting for would lose, the garden would fail. By predicting failure, she could at least own the satisfaction of being right. By denying joy she could never be deprived of it. She had no control over her life – this was her one true law and only unbending creed, that black ace that by its absolute negation trumped all possible disappointment – and it took me a long time to accept that this was simply the way it was going to be.

Along with the nightmares, Tom was often sick that year. A cold would go straight into his chest and he'd cough all night. Once he got started there was no rest for any of us. We tried every medication available, Mucinex, Triaminicin, Claritin, Singulair, albuterol, VapoRub (one person recommended that we slather the soles of his feet with it, which worked one night but not the next), ibuprofen, and many others. We closed and opened his bedroom door. He slept in other parts of the house, on the couch, in blankets in front of the heater. A humidifier brought no relief. His only chance for a good night's sleep was prescription cough syrup with codeine, which he protested so strongly he'd sometimes vomit.

So I'd mix the cough syrup with Baileys Irish Cream to make it more palatable, he'd down it without complaint, and then he'd be out like a catcher trying to steal third base. Peace would reign over the household. I realize the combination of alcohol and codeine is synergistic, potentially lethal, and I know Dr. Norden, his GP, would have beaten me vigorously with his stethoscope if he knew what I was doing, but remember, we're dealing with preponderantly inert sugar matrices in the half-tablespoon range.

When the codeine cough syrup was gone and the appointment with the doctor for a refill was still two days away, we hoped that we'd get lucky, that our son would simply sleep for a change. Not a chance. The cough was worse than ever. He coughed and coughed and then howled in anguish. Cristina had already given him a useless allergy pill and gone to bed. I stayed up, distressed and unable to sleep. I had the choice of either going to work now, since a reset crew would be at Safeway all night, or going in later, at 3:30 when the bakers and first stockers came in. I poured another drink and listened to my boy hack and scrape and howl for another half an hour. Finally I loaded up a tablespoon of Baileys in an oral syringe, hoping the alcohol would give him some peace. Cristina came in as I was administering.

"What are you giving him?"

"Baileys."

"No you're not."

We argued in elementary yes-no playground fashion while the boy continued to cough.

"Why don't we just *try* it?" I said. "Nothing else works."

"You will not give my boy alcohol."

"It's just a *tablespoon*, dear. Seventeen percent alcohol. There's more alcohol in a chocolate-covered cherry…"

She stood fast. Tom sputtered and gagged. Exasperated, I blasted her pajamas with the Baileys. Shocked, she began to shriek at me. Our son continued to gurgle and choke. I loaded up another syringe of Baileys and gave it to him while Cristina yelled at me. The Baileys didn't help at all. Cristina and I shouted at each other as I drew a syringe full of bubble-gum-flavored ibuprofen. The ibuprofen helped this time, perhaps in combination with the Baileys, and he fell asleep at last.

Cristina was furious and would not accept my apology. I stayed up a while and stared at the wall. I knew I was wrong and that I'd been a prick, but I did not feel guilty. I threw her pajamas into the washing machine and went to work that night at Safeway. The reset people were there and Barb, who was supervising, let me in. I stripped and waxed the soup and juice aisles and returned home about three that morning. I slept on the couch, of course. In the morning Cristina would not speak to me. I apologized again. Our son, with about six hours of straight sleep for a change, was better rested than usual, and eager for school.

27.

Speculation & hooey

7:14 P.M. Caller from Regency Trailer Court advised of a dead bird that caller stated died for no apparent reason.

AS A MARRIED MAN I DIDN'T GO OUT MUCH ANYMORE. I didn't go out at all, not by myself anyway. Cristina did not like to be "alone," and there was Tom to look after, but on Friday nights I'd drag the boy and the wife to the Olde Main Street Inn and try to sit in for an hour or two of lively conversation at the President's Table in the corner of the Longbranch Saloon over by one of Jeanne's five pianos, where the Artists and the Bohemians convened. Sometimes there'd be 10 people packed around the President's Table, the snowflakes tumbling sidelong across the windows. Kathy Bahr was usually there, as was Vince Hazen, an art professor who did fantastic science/art studies like jars full of giant pickled wolf spiders and strung bluebirds in formaldehyde. The convention was usually presided over by the merry-eyed, coarse-haired Professor Deane Tucker, surrealist surf-bum poet, proponent of French Modernist Philosophy, and challenger of your shitty taste in music.

I call Deane "the Minister of Debauchery" after his talent for late-night revelry and his complaint that there are no decent clubs in town, not even a strip joint. Like me, Deane grew up along the ocean. After graduating with a film-philosophy degree from Florida State University, he went to Hollywood to work in movie production. He hated it. Every bad thing they say about Hollywood is true, he claims, multiply that by 10. For the two years he was in California he surfed up and down the coast, Lower Trestles (San Onofre), Solana Beach, Santa Barbara, all these places I know well myself (I lived in Solana Beach for a while). Eventually he returned to the gulf of Florida to his surf-nut roots. He waited tables and surfed for two years –

"Wait a minute, Deane. The surfing is no good along the gulf."

"That's what everyone says. The surfing is *great* along the gulf."

Youth and a future in restaurant service dissolved into a PhD. He lived in New York for two years. He lived in France for a while. He lived and surfed all over the East Coast. He surfed in New Jersey –

"Wait a minute, Deane. The surfing in New Jersey is no good."

"That's what everyone says. The surfing in New Jersey is *great.*"

A lot better than the surfing in Nebraska, I suppose.

In spite of all his grousing about the provincialism of Chadron, Deane calls this part of the world "mystical and beautiful," and feels "penned in" whenever he travels back east.

I've never lived in a place where it was common to see an ad in the local newspaper for an English or a Spanish professor. For many with ambition Chadron is a stopover, the bush leagues, a quick notch on the résumé. There isn't much here for the homesick cosmopolitan or the delicate urbanite, and professional salaries though lavish in respect to the cost of living, are comparatively low across the board. The Big City, Denver, is a good five hours away. You have to be a special type of person to be content here, to subsist solely on friendliness, flannel sheets, books, pink-cauldron sunsets, cool summer nights, high, star-smashed skies, a cupboard full of homemade jams and salsa that your neighbors have made, deer in your backyard, Friday night at the President's Table, and Police Beat entries.

8:22 A.M. Caller from the 900 block of Morehead St. reported that someone had taken three garden gnomes from her location sometime during the night. She described them as plastic, "with chubby cheeks and red hats."

9:03 P.M. Caller from the 100 block of Main St. requested an officer at the above location. Caller advised there was a man who seemed to speak only Spanish and was making some girls uncomfortable, and no one could get him to stop.

9:06 P.M. Caller from Ann St. stated her husband was stuck in the tub and unable to get out.

ON THAT FRIDAY at the President's Table after Steve Haataja went missing, December 9, 2006, there was only one thing on our minds. Bald Mountain Rounder John Shafer was in attendance, as was choir director and music professor Daisy Mavis, pre-dental student and Excellent Vacationer Paul Nelson, literature professor Kathy Bahr, and Minister of Debauchery Deane Tucker. My wife was also present as was her acquaintance, JW, the Spanish professor (Cristina would always get to know the Spanish professors). JW, a tall, youthful, slender WASP fluent in Spanish and married to a man from Mexico City, had only been at CSC one semester but was on her way out, she said, because she had a better position in Denver.

She was also receiving creepy 15-page letters from Jonas Greenwheat, Suzie Greenwheat's devoutly Christian ex-brother-in-law, who along with his wife was attending both of JW's beginning Spanish classes. Jonas was a man of unusually numerous contradictions: fanatical with a sharp business acumen, a plumber who opposed indoor plumbing, a voluntary outcast who actively sought society, a fundamental Christian who warred with his neighbors, a proud, self-educated man who thought of himself as a world-class intellect but who rented privies and pumped out septic systems for a living, a man who prided himself as progressive but who virulently opposed what he perceived as "the homosexual agenda." He lived in town but had a wind generator, solar panels, his own well and septic system, and was presently at a standoff with the state over what he deemed the unnecessary requirement of a septic-pumping license.

When Jonas was upset with someone, he sent them a letter. A good half of the CSC faculty, including deans and the chancellor, had received letters from Jonas. Spanish wasn't going as well as he'd planned, and he intended to straighten JW out on a few matters. Greenwheat's voluminous screeds were laced with prophecies, veiled threats, queer criticisms, recommendations, sesquipedalia (long words), and bizarre pleasantries. His favorite subject was his opposition to the college's "homosexual agenda." He also noted how nice the women smelled and how nice the men should smell. He plainly liked JW, hand delivering his spooky missives to her home, and tried to soften his diatribes by saying he thought that women were better teachers, cleaner, that they could set an example for the men. He described JW as an "inexperienced teacher," and urged her to abandon her immersion system (having been a language teacher myself, and having finally learned Spanish by living in Mexico for two years, I will also cast my vote for immersion as the best method of language acquisition). JW was unnerved. They were disturbing letters even when they managed to make sense, and their grammar, she noted, was poor.

That Friday we tried to figure out what had happened to Steve Haataja. Missing for four days, we wondered if he'd left town. But where would he have gone? He'd left his Birkenstocks under his desk. His beloved laptop was also found in his office. His bicycle had been found in his apartment. We discussed what he might be working on. Steve's best friend of many years, Tim Sorenson, head of the math department at Augustana College in Sioux Falls, South Dakota, where Steve had once taught, had suggested that since Steve was "an introverted math wizard," if one of "his doctoral arguments had crumbled," it may have been enough to bring about an emotional collapse. He did not believe, however, that depression, the so-named depressive disorder, was a factor.

Violette the Ghost Hunter joined us at the President's Table with his pitcher of beer. He was off to La Junta, Colorado, in the morning to raise an antenna for his new radio station, 107.3 KRKV. "Any theories on where the professor might be?" I asked him.

"Afraid I'm not up to speed on the thing," he said.

"Not much information so far." I painted the highlights, told him about the bicycle and the laptop.

"Suicide note?"

"None found so far," I replied.

Violette wondered if there might be a clue, a puzzle, a note in code, on the laptop that used Linux as an operating system and that Haataja carried with him everywhere.

"The police have the laptop," said John Shafer.

"Well, that's the end of that," said Deane.

Choir Director Daisy Mavis rolled her eyes.

"What kind of mathematician is he?" Violette asked.

"Theoretical," Deane said. "Though he taught algebra and trigonometry."

Kathy Bahr stated flatly that she thought Haataja had killed himself.

"Balls," said Deane Tucker. "I saw him the day before he disappeared. He was in fine fettle. He was joyful."

"There was a lot of pressure on him," said Kathy. When Monty Fickle, the department chair, was diagnosed with cancer, she explained, all the other professors in the math department, including Steve, had to pick up his classes, and Steve was barely keeping up as it was.

Daisy Mavis agreed with Deane. "Additional classes" were not an impetus for suicide. She'd received an email from him the day before he disappeared. He was very much looking forward to the upcoming choir season. Already familiar with the schedule, he'd made a joke about having to perform on April 15, the day income tax statements would be due. "I hope we won't be performing for the IRS," he said. Not the words of one who is intending within the next few hours to walk away permanently from everything he knows.

Daisy was upset not only at the disappearance of Haataja and the inertia of Sergeant Chaffwick and his Green Cycle Underlings, but because Loren Zimmerman was sending her flowers. She'd asked him to stop, but the flowers kept coming. She thought he was a creep, but she was afraid of him, and Tim Hardy, her boyfriend, was out of town. Daisy had also become the first victim of rumor. Tim, a professor in the math department at CSC, had transferred to Wayne State just before the arrival of Haataja. Haataja appeared to have replaced Tim, and because Daisy and Haataja were seen together, in the choir and at other related functions and on one or two occasions at happy hour at the Sinister Grin, some misguided suspicion had fallen on Tim Hardy. The "jealous lover" angle.

"All right," I said. "If he didn't leave, and if he didn't kill himself, what's left?"

"Foul play," said John Shafer, who believed more strongly than anyone that Haataja was gay, that this was central in the deed. Living in Portland, Oregon, for many years John had seen hundreds of gay men arrive from other places, especially small towns, far enough away from their parents and geography teachers and den mothers to pursue unashamed lives, but there were also a lot of guys who hated themselves for it. Steve seemed like that kind of person to him. "Maybe he killed himself," John suggested. "Or maybe he got mixed up with the wrong people."

"He had no enemies," said Deane "Look, I knew the guy pretty well." He glanced at his watch. "You guys want another drink?"

"Everyone has an adversary," I said.

"Everyone liked him," Deane countered, waving to Jeanne for another round.

"Maybe a student," said Paul, who remembered seeing the words "Die Fag" written on the chalkboard with what looked like a caricature of Steve in Memorial Hall.

"Or Jonas Greenwheat," said JW.

"Jonas never took a class from Haataja," said Kathy.

"Yeah, but he hates homosexuals."

"Do you think Haataja is gay?" I asked.

"No, I don't," said Deane.

"No," echoed Daisy Mavis, brooding, preoccupied, her blue eyes on the window, as if Steve Haataja might lumber past at any minute, pull open the door, and join us for a drink.

"He was married for 10 years," said Paul Nelson.

"That doesn't mean anything," I said. "Oscar Wilde was married."

"So was Rock Hudson," Violette added.

"I think he was probably gay," said Kathy. "Maybe he didn't know it. I don't think he was as happy as everyone said he was."

John Shafer, who spent his days organizing video conferences and audio-visual programs and therefore knew all the teachers on campus, agreed. "The man was not comfortable in his body. When he was around me I got the vibes, the way his eyes moved on me."

"What difference does it make if he was gay or not?" blurted JW.

"If he was living a secret life…" Kathy said.

"Do you think he was a virgin?" I asked.

Deane laughed.

"Let me put it this way," I said. "Can you picture him with a woman?"

"When he was going to college maybe," said Paul Nelson.

"What are you driving at?" said Deane.

"The possibility that Haataja might be autistic," I said. "Gifted mathematicians are twice as likely to be autistic. Newton, Tesla, Turing, Dirac were all probably autistics. Ted Kaczynski, the Unabomber, a brilliant mathematician, is probably autistic. Autistics have higher rates of depression and suicide. Turing committed suicide."

"It's true," said Violette. "I worked with a bunch of them at NASA. They have higher divorce rates, too."

Handsome Sam Killinoy, the Inherent Conflict in All Things, had been sitting at the corner of the bar, nursing his Bud and listening in. "You want to know what I think?" he boomed. "He's playing a trick on you. The man's smarter than all of you put together. Dead or alive if he wanted to be found, he would've been found. He's dead in my book, and he'll never be found."

Jeanne arrived with the drinks. "No way he killed himself," she said.

Kathy said, "Can we please talk about something else?"

28.

A sad-eyed lady

5:23 A.M. Caller from the 400 block of West Third St. advised that he was at the above location at noon when a man came in who looked a lot like the missing professor. Caller stated the man was wearing a black leather jacket.

WHENEVER MY SON AND I WENT TO CASPER TO VISIT Dr. Weld, the autism expert (or the "college-ist" as Tom described him), it was tradition to go to McDonald's afterward for a small order of fries and a small chocolate shake (no variations on this) and then, TV clown hypnosis abated, on the way home we'd stop in Crawford, that crumbling old railroad, uranium, and winery town of 1,000. My boy liked the city park there, a regal expanse with rusting swing sets and obsolete tractors and giant trees and a turned-off fountain and an icy spring that snaked its way under two bridges through the grounds. Panels of walkway are inscribed with the names of Crawford citizens and businesses alike, and though dedicated to the living, most of the dedicatees have since passed on, the businesses have closed, so the effect under the broad shade trees is more funereal than intended.

On the way home that cold December day, not long after Steve Haataja had vanished, we drove down Second Street and I saw the door to Haataja's apartment open. Someone was inside. I thought for a moment Haataja had returned. A sad-eyed lady with shoulder-length, coal black hair came out and hung a rug over the porch rail.

I thought there might be a new tenant already. Later that day, Steve Welch told me it was Steve's sister, Sheila Speaker, who he'd met at Maverick Junction only a few days before when his car had broken down there. She was putting up posters of her brother. He said she was optimistic that her brother would soon return. It made Steve tear up to think how much she obviously loved and missed him and the possibility that he would not be coming back.

Since Sheila lived in Rapid City, she came often to help in whatever way she could. Later I would talk to her several times on the phone, but she never trusted me, so everything I learned about her came from the journalists, police officers, and others, like Steve Welch and Daisy Mavis, whom she did trust. What is important to extract from her testimony is that everything in that punctiliously neat apartment suggested that he planned on coming back. He'd just bought groceries and had taken nothing of value with him, nothing he might need for a long trip. He had also paid his rent the very morning he vanished, as I confirmed with his landlord, Sheryl Phillips. Sheila thought he'd worked too hard for that doctorate to walk away from it. And their father, who would pass away in less than three months, was terminally ill, so it was hard to grasp why Steve might have left voluntarily. She added that she couldn't fathom why anyone would want to hurt him.

I drove slowly past the apartment that day, and when I got home I put some fish sticks in a pan for Tom, poured him a glass of milk, and thought of my sister and my son and what it would be like to have them disappear, to lose them without a trace. I opened a beer and sat down and wondered if my father were on his deathbed and I was depressed if there was even a remote chance I'd abandon him or take my life.

Two days later Sheila's birthday came and went without a word from her brother. Steve had been gone 13 days.

29.

On the road again

CRISTINA STUDIED FOR HER NATURALIZATION TEST AN
hour and a half every night, stared into her study guides and
sample exams, floating in and out of Cristinaland. Every few minutes she raised her head. "I forget what the difference between
omit and commit is." And I would explain this, and once again the
cause of the Civil War and the reasons people left in droves
from Europe to embrace the fabulous ideals of the New World.
Cristina wanted to know what had become of America, why it was
so bloodthirsty, why everyone drove a big muddy pickup truck,
why so many Americans were robots and pigs. She wanted to know
why America did not come as advertised. I explained that most
people flocked to America for "opportunity," a code word for
"wealth," and that many of the good traits, habits, and values im-
ported along with a hope for "opportunity" were quickly
exchanged for the aggressiveness, selfishness, and cheating
required to compete successfully with all the others who have
come to America for opportunity.

I wasn't crazy about America either, I told her, but I'd
stopped holding it to an impossible standard. America was not
a picture book, it was just people from other places under pressure intensely competing, the results of which were infinite
variegation and brilliance in form, just as Nature played it in her
own park, but as in Nature there were many dropped in their
tracks and savaged by jackals on the open savannah and also

nervous breakdowns, migraines, suicides, depression disorders, and homeless people asking you for change.

But it still beat the pants off of living in Albania. America with all its admitted problems was also compassionate, energetic, tolerant, generous, and capable of laughing at itself. Few Americans were standing in line to emigrate to its rich uncle, China. The border patrol was not yet amassed at the frontier of Texas preventing undocumented Americans from entering Mexico, not yet anyway.

Having a passive outsider's personality, I'd never see an argument coming. We'd be conversing in a perfectly civilized way and then she'd make a remark about how "we" (meaning I) needed to make more money, or how "we" needed a bigger house or a bigger TV. The word "need" was usually anchored in there somewhere, though I don't think she was baiting me. Acquisition was more an expression of her general dissatisfaction with her new status-minded country and the attendant belief that more and bigger somehow made you better. More money, lifestyle, and our future (for which you need lots of money) were always our points of contention. I wanted the simplest possible life and she wanted three cars.

When a morning job cleaning the Pizza Hut opened she thought I should take it. I explained that mornings were when I worked, I should've said "wrote," because "work" to her meant at least minimum wage, not the three dollars an hour I averaged as a writer. When she'd first come to America with me, she was convinced I was rich, as were all Americans in her mind, and it was still hard for her to stomach that I wasn't rich and would probably never be rich, worse yet that I wasn't even trying to be rich. Since I could meet all my financial responsibilities and we already had two cars and I already "worked" 60 hours a week, another job for me, I explained, was not "more money," but "less time." "More money," I continued, was the same as "never enough." The inevitable squabble began, we both knew how to get under each other's skin.

Tom was listening to Canned Heat's "On the Road Again," over and over, it was that underlying, oscillating psychedelic jangle I think that drew him, and it drove Cristina crazy, these songs over and over again, Tom singing or humming the parts that attracted him, and using his fingers to express note construction, a ritual that looked like gang signs or American Sign Language. Normally he'd try to ignore us when we fought, then run to his room if a doozy started, but this time, before it got out of hand, he turned off the stereo and said: "You wanna go somewhere?"

"Where you wanna go?" I said.

"To the park, where I work."

He meant the park by his school. I was trying to instill in him early the notion that life is mostly work, so when I dropped him off mornings at East Ward Elementary I would say, "Have a good day at work." He liked this and the notion of working like his parents.

"OK," I said, "go get your shoes on."

"We can throw the ball for Lightnin'," he declared. That was his favorite game, even though I always threw the ball for Jackson, aka Lightnin', our golden retriever, so named for his lack of speed, while Tom pushed his stroller or rode around on his three-wheeled scooter.

Cristina accompanied us to the park, trailed along dourly with the dog, scolding him most of the way.

Tom said: "Momma got the dog so she could be mean to it."

"No, Momma loves the dog, just like she loves you and me, she just doesn't know how to show it very well."

It was 50 degrees, a warm day for December, with light rain falling that would turn to snow by nightfall. We had a small, bent blue umbrella that we'd use as a canopy in the construction of our fort. Tom pushed his stroller filled with the usual items; this batch included a calculator, a tequila brochure (his "map"), an egg timer, and a play camera he used "to take pictures of photographs."

It is a mile walk or so to Tom's school. The elementary, middle, and high school are all in the same complex right across from the state college. Tom and I set up camp, played on the slides and the swings. We threw the ball for Lightnin'. Every few minutes I glanced south, expecting some sign of Steven Haataja, a flash of his plaid shirt, a wave from a window, the sound of his laughter, his figure in the distance in the light forest above Math and Science. The pressure had gotten to him, I decided. He'd fled, hitchhiked out of town, and was hiding out in a mountain cabin or living in a residential motel with a lonely divorcée. Eventually, because of his family and all the work he'd put into that doctorate, he would return.

The rain finally stopped.

"Are you ready to go?" Cristina said.

"You don't bring a child to the playground for 20 minutes, dear," I replied, trying to keep the edge out of my voice.

She nodded, took the dog for another walk around the park, and left for home without saying good-bye.

30.
True crime

BY LATE DECEMBER I'D AMASSED SO MANY NOTES, NEWS-
paper pieces, blogs, and Police Beats on the Haataja story that I
had to begin organizing them in files, dividing them out of habit
into three preliminary sections: The beginning I labeled *Disappearance*, the middle indicated *A Good Deal of Headscratching*, and
the ending, I reluctantly and finally allowed, would *Not Be a
Happy One*. A "true crime" book was possibly taking shape, the
last thing I would've expected or asked for, for most "true crime"
is an exploitation of another's misery, a callous milking of
human misfortune, a picnic round a corpse with plastic forks and
all the photographs, the bloody mattress and the poor mangled
hookers and the lonely killer with the funny eye, and as long as it's
happening to someone else and there aren't too many psychological "explanations," I suppose it's great sport.

I haven't read much true crime, though I do admire when
luridly charged material is used for more aesthetic and less
graphic or ghoulish effect, such as *In Cold Blood* or *Midnight in
the Garden of Good and Evil*. There is also the more substantial
category of "true crime" composed by someone in the middle of
one, someone who knows all the players, someone who is not
simply boarding an airplane with a tape recorder and staying at
a nearby hotel to catalogue and "exploit for profit" (I'm in my
fifth year of working on this book and have made $1,000 so far)
the sorrow and horror of perfect strangers. Ann Rule's *The
Stranger Beside Me* is one of these, the account of the infamous

maniacal vampire and mass murderer Ted Bundy, Ann's good friend and partner on the suicide hotline at the Crisis Clinic in Seattle, Washington. Ann Rule actually dined and drank white wine and had many heart-to-hearts with dashing young Ted, a psychology major at the time, and every other week or so he'd slither off and kill another girl.

Ann Rule had been a police officer, a student of criminology, and was a detective and a crime writer during the time she knew Ted, but I had no experience in any of these areas, and so I wrote for advice to Detective Warren in Portland, Oregon:

> Dear Kevin:
> I've begun to organize the math professor book around numbered scenarios, possible explanations of what might've happened to Steven Haataja as the evidence comes in, but I'm wondering what term a detective would use in his official reports. Theories? Hypotheses? Let's Go Grab Another Donut and Raid the Topless Place Again? Your role in this will be essential, hope you don't mind, but I'll never reveal your secret affection for toenail polish and young freshly shampooed poodles.

> Dear Poe:
> I'm always happy to let you in on official police vernacular. First of all, scratch "hypothesis." Too hard to spell and it makes you sound like you talk with a lisp. Here's a list of acceptable words or phrases to describe working premises of criminal investigations, listed in descending order based upon the likelihood of solving the case and the investigator's personal concern, which we affectionately refer to as our *Give a Shit Level*.
>
> 1. Theory: Everybody knows this word and most are smart enough to understand what it means.
> 2. Possible Scenario(s): When you've used the word *theory* too many times. Although rare, some investigators are sympathetic to redundancies.
> 3. Wild Ass Guess (WAG is official abbr): This really gets your reader's attention. Especially when that reader is an attorney.
> 4. Fuck It: Similar to Let's Go Grab Another Donut and Raid the Topless Place Again, only less wordy. Let's face it, if you're at level 4 you really don't want to take the time to type all that out. But you could substitute Beer for Donut and still be within acceptable limits.

31.

Zimmerman hijacks the Haataja case

FOR WEEKS FOLLOWING STEVEN HAATAJA'S DISAPPEAR-ance the police were tragic burlesque figures shrugging with upturned palms. They were often quoted in the paper, "We're baffled. We're puzzled. We're confused. We've turned up no clues. We have no information. He's vanished. Our shoulders are tired from shrugging. Our scalps are sore from scratching."

From *The Chadron Record*:

> Sgt. Charles Chaffwick of the Chadron Police Department said there is nothing new in the case.
>
> "Right now, we're still hoping something turns out," Chaffwick said. "We sure haven't quit trying."
>
> "We have absolutely no idea where he went, or why, or how," said Charles Chaffwick. "There are no hints. No clues. It's as if he went out to check his mail and never came back."
>
> "We're at a loss here,' Chaffwick said. "We're grasping at straws here."

Despite the fact that he had no authority whatsoever, it almost made sense when Crime Professor Loren Zimmerman stepped in before the year was out and effectively took over the Haataja investigation. He wasted no time. He was a savvy, hard-boiled veteran of many such campaigns. Contacting relatives, alerting neighbors, interviewing subjects, and conducting searches were all second nature to him. Zimmerman professed a personal interest in this "exceedingly mysterious case" and pronounced his willingness to work nonstop, since so much valuable time had already been lost.

Zimmerman traced the possible routes, organized two formal searches, one of 20 students, another of 25, searches that looked remarkably like those mock searches for staged and invisible corpses he'd conducted in his Forensics II class. He contacted and interviewed friends and family members. He urged Haataja's colleagues to look in every closet and other out-of-the-way locations.

Zimmerman iterated the difficulty Steve would've had navigating long distances or rough terrain due to the five hours of surgery after breaking his hip in an ice skating accident in 2005 (at a rink in Lincoln called the Ice Box), though this is simply another popular fallacy about Steve that got in the way of determining his actual whereabouts. Steve walked at least two miles a day, sometimes 10. He walked regularly to and from Walmart, a four-mile round trip with plenty of uneven terrain and long stretches without sidewalk, a bag of groceries or two in each hand. And he liked to hike in the hills south of campus, the reason two of his colleagues, Kathy Bahr and Deane Tucker, had first gone to look for him there.

Zimmerman admitted the possibility of suicide but stated that people who take their own lives rarely do it in a place where they will never be found. His evaluation of Haataja's situation supported that of Haataja's sister Sheila: unlikely that a man would buy groceries or pay rent before planning to leave town, and if he had left town, he'd taken nothing that he valued or would've needed with him. Zimmerman restated police-established facts: no bank or credit card activity, no Internet contact, no phone calls, no contact with family, no public transportation records (Chadron is a hard town to get out of on foot without anyone noticing), no recent car rentals, etc. For the record, Zimmerman remained optimistic. Privately he laid it all out in plain English for Sergeant Chaffwick: *the man has not left town, which means he is very likely dead.*

From Zimmerman's first day of involvement, he dominated every news piece about Haataja's disappearance. He was able to provide what the police appeared to be short on: action, zeal, method, sympathy. His broad background and advanced degree in forensics qualified him as an expert. He won the confidence of relatives and friends. His ability to orchestrate communication with the press (he even swung a TV appearance!), to give updates through the campus email system, and to alert farmers and ranchers, made the police department look even more lackluster than it might've been. He explained that the locks on Steve's apartment had been changed so he couldn't be hiding someplace and returning to the apartment at inconspicuous times. Though he was for the most part echoing the same blank anthem as the cops, he would remain the expert in the case until the end.

Zimmerman, as quoted in *The Chadron Record*:

> "He's just not around, but we don't know how he could have left town."
> "He might be right under our noses someplace, but we can't figure out where that would be."
> "There's nothing to indicate anything."

Sergeant Chaffwick was understandably miffed about having the show stolen out from under him. He moped about, grumbled and shrugged, glared dimly at interlocutors, dumped a little more ketchup on his buffalo burger, and when he got his chance at a quote in the paper, he tried not to sound petulant. "If somebody wants to search places that haven't been searched, we say go for it and let us know what they find." Or: "We haven't given up, but we really don't know where else to search. We have no direction where else to look [sic]."

Zimmerman countered: "If you sit back and wait, nothing's going to get done. You've got to search somewhere. It's better than not doing anything, and even if you don't find anything, you've eliminated something. We needed to look, especially in the areas south of town, because if it snows and hard winter sets in, that area's going to be off limits until spring. We needed to do something now rather than later."

Sheriff Shawn Conaghan, who describes Zimmerman as

"an asshole," and "a bucket of shit," was convinced that Zimmerman tried to take over the investigation to make an impression on the town so he could become its next police chief. "He was in it for his own personal gain. He didn't care about Haataja," he told me. "And nobody could challenge him because of the hands-off policy toward the college. There was never any rape, alcohol abuse, or football players assaulting anyone up there," he said facetiously. "As far as this town is concerned, the college is all rainbows, lollipops, and unicorns."

Others weren't convinced that Zimmerman was the New Messiah. Sergeant Chuck welcomed Zimmerman's help at first but soon felt denigrated and dismissed. Later, he confided to me, he began to believe that much of Zimmerman's impressive résumé was invented.

Randy Rhine, vice president for student services, told me the college was upset that Zimmerman was using his students to conduct searches, which included, in his words, "digging through trash." He did not think these students should be digging through trash, and what if one of them came across a corpse?

It was nice to have a few as irritated with Zimmerman as I was. I was also grateful that Mr. Zimmerman had found a project other than my wife to occupy his time.

Loren Zimmerman's vault into the limelight and the relish and aplomb with which he handled his role as de facto lead investigator in this case may have cheesed off those officially in charge, but it did little to repel any who were interested in actual results. Journalists, local and national, gravitated toward his ability to use the right phrases and the self-assurance he emanated along with the way he could express sympathy with the flickering muscles in his reptilian forehead. It was widely believed that the local police force, whose officers, many recruited directly from the criminal justice program at the college and installed in the Green Cop Cycle to start at a wage of $11 an hour, were simply not equipped for such a formidable task.

Zimmerman had seen so much blood, mayhem, and

wretched sorrow in his day, and had liberated so many Hispanic ladies from their underwear, that it was clear to many that he was the only man for the job.

32.

Zimmerman tries to hijack Cristina

IT WAS HARD TO SEE HOW CRISTINA, ALREADY WEAK TO Zimmerman's enchantments and enlisted as his personal housekeeper, could not be completely swept off her feet by his exhilarating new celebrity status. He had a job with benefits and he'd been on TV. He could woo my woman at will and if I didn't like it, he could shoot me in the leg, and the only people who could help me were the police, and no one was taking them seriously anymore.

Indeed, Cristina at this exciting, distressing, and confusing time began going out on her evenings off, leaving my son and me home to entertain ourselves. Though I was sure she was seeing Mr. Zimmerman on the sly, she insisted this was not the case. My gloom surrounding the subject of Mr. Zimmerman nonetheless mounted, even if bias, suspicion, instinct, alarm bells, and faltering matrimony were my only foundation. Outside of her exuberance for Zimmerman she'd never given me a reason to doubt or mistrust her. She was so jealous and possessive it was impossible to believe she'd think of cheating on me. She was only taking what she could find, I reminded myself, using her limited connections, resources, and feminine appeal. She was grateful that someone had helped her achieve her goal. What could possibly happen in a few hours on the town or a Friday morning of dusting and mopping?

Up to this time she'd objected to my going out without her, because we were a family, because, as I said, she was not comfortable "alone," because she was still trying to make the arduous cultural transition, etc. Up to this time, we'd spent most evenings in, as she preferred, watching movies, listening to music, drinking wine, filling out Immigration and Naturalization Service forms, squabbling with one another, and watching our son grow. Though she was not social, she tolerated the occasional party, always making an excellent impression. Her fellow workers and her neighbors liked her for her genial nature, Old World manners, and irreproachable work ethic.

On her evenings out she barhopped with Suzie Greenwheat. When Cristina left the house to go out with Suzie, she'd invariably say: "I'll be back in an hour." And each time it was three or four hours. We'd fight when she returned. I had to get up at three in the morning for one thing, and it seemed much as I loved my little lad that I was getting the brunt of the caregiving. She'd apologize, promise never to go out again. After a week or two, she'd go out again. I would have been more encouraged to see my diffident and cautious wife blossoming socially had it not been initiated by the attentions of Ye Olde Tunnel Rat, Mr. Zimmerman.

Still, I had no grounds for complaint. Compared to my degenerate upbringing, she was the picture of virtue. I recall coming home one night not long after I'd shown her how to use a computer and finding her sitting dejected on the couch. "I've done something bad," she confessed to me in Spanish.

"What is it?" I said.

"I don't know how to say it. I don't know how to tell you."

I thought someone had intruded, that she'd been robbed or raped. "Tell me. Tell me."

"I was using your computer."

"You broke the computer?"

"No."

"Tell me then."

"I can't."

"You must tell me. What happened?"

Her hands fell from her knees. "I looked at some dirty pictures. Oh, I feel so terrible. I feel so bad."

"Is that *all*?" I said with a laugh.

She was crying and pleading with me not to think badly of her. "Please erase them," she kept saying. "I have never done anything like this in my life."

We turned on the computer and erased all the dirty pictures that had come up when she typed the word "sex" into the search box, the same thing I'd done when I got my first crack at the Internet. "Oh please don't think badly of me," she said every five minutes until we finally went to bed.

But then one evening she had to meet Mr. Zimmerman about some housekeeping details, and they met of course where most housekeeping details are ironed out: at a bar. "I'll be back in an hour," she said from the door, all dolled up and smelling good. Two hours later she returned. We fought once more. She made the usual sniffling teenage recants and promises, and though I suggested it was time to part ways with him professionally, that $20 or $30 a week was a nominal sum in the face of a disintegrating marriage, she kept the job cleaning Zimmerman's house.

33.
Sniffing horses

4:37 P.M. Caller from the 600 block of West Second St. advised that her 11-year-old son was misbehaving, had not gone where he was supposed to after school and was now being very disruptive. Caller advised he had thrown spaghetti outside.

IN LATE JANUARY I CALLED DETECTIVE WARREN TO ASK for some help on the development of my "Theories" which were closer to "Wild Ass Guesses," and after I mentioned that no record could be produced of Haataja leaving town, no sightings, car rentals, contacts, banking records, etc. (though it is possible that he hitchhiked out without being seen, if he got a ride quickly enough, or that someone he should not have trusted offered him a lift), Kevin said that unless someone had kidnapped him or he was hiding in the organ loft of the opera house, Haataja was dead. In a city like Portland, someone missing under such circumstances might turn up alive years later just about anywhere, or the body might never be recovered, but in a town as small and tightly networked as Chadron, with people having seen him numerous times on the night he went missing, it was a good bet he wouldn't be coming back. The remaining "mysteries," Kevin said, were where the body would be found and what the medical examiner would determine as cause. And since Haataja was probably still in Chadron somewhere, Kevin wanted to know if the Chadron PD had used dogs, helicopters, or surveillance planes to search for the body.

I admitted I didn't know. I told him I hadn't read or heard discussions about anything like that.

"You might want to drop a clue on them," he said.

"My understanding," Sheriff Conaghan told me, "is that State Patrol offered the two dogs at their disposal, as well as a surveillance plane, but Chaffwick turned them down. He insists they have everything under control. The police presume, like a lot of people, that Haataja has left town."

Sergeant Chuck told me that he did not recall such a proposal, though a rancher in Crawford had offered "sniffing horses," which Chuck claimed were as good as dogs for search and rescue. Unfortunately, their olfactory talents (like the dogs) were negated, Chuck said, because so much of the surrounding area was burned.

I told the sheriff: "My homicide detective friend from Portland says that he's probably dead."

"This isn't my case," he said. "And it isn't State Patrol's either. If the PD wants either of our help, all they have to do is ask, but they haven't asked. For the record, I agree with Detective Warren."

I thanked him, hung up the phone, and wondered how you found a body when it hadn't left town.

34.

The girl mosquitoes are *grass*hoppers

ABNER VIOLETTE AND I WERE STROLLING DOWN MAIN Street, my son in wool cap, gloves, and winter jacket, trailing us with his stroller as he tracked his reflection in the shop windows. On this frosty, calm evening, in addition to the usual items, the belt named "Poopy," the rubber lizards, and so forth, Tom had heaped in the seat a Styrofoam biplane, a slide whistle, and three colored plastic eggs, each containing a rock.

Violette had all his toys with him too, the belt around his waist arrayed with a gaussmeter, an EMF meter, an infrared pyrometer (used to measure temperatures), a voice recorder, a motion detector, and a compass. Hanging from his neck were two cameras, one digital, the other a standard Olympus set for slow shutter exposure and filled with 400 film, so if he caught something, he would have the negatives for a record. He was committed to helping me find evidence of Haataja's electromagnetic afterlife, if it could be determined. This was his first detective ghost project, and he was so excited and in firm belief of our imminent success I thought he might float away on me like Mary Poppins.

It was dusk, the time of day, Violette insists, when the dearly departed are most accessible to their breathing brethren. We all have the ability to interact with paranormal phenomena Violette says, though most of us (like me) would prefer not to. When you enter a place spectrally inhabited at dusk, Violette says, this is why your skin crawls, your hair stands up, your body turns when there is no sound. This is what makes you leave a room eerily perplexed when you have no real justification for leaving a room eerily perplexed.

I told Violette, "I remember a certain office in the Ames, Iowa, City Hall that I used to clean in the evenings that literally terrified me. I'd be in there and the light would be draining from the window and the trees outside would be stirring and waving and I'd feel unnerved in a way I can't explain and I'd stumble through doing the very minimum and get the hell out as soon as I could."

"You never learned the history of City Hall?"

"It was an old building. I never really cared to know. I mean what difference would it make if I knew someone had died in there?"

"It would make a big difference if you knew who it was. You could talk to them. Most ghosts are agreeable to interaction."

"I've known friendly ghosts before," I said, "like when I lived in a small apartment in Colorado Springs. I had poltergeists, I know it. They'd hide my clothes. I lost a contact lens down the drain one time and found it the next morning on top of the back of the toilet. I've also known confused ghosts, like Metal Head Ted. That was when I lived in that trailer in the Black Forest at 8,000 feet out in the middle of the woods all alone with my dog. Metal Head Ted died there in the back bedroom (where I refused to sleep because it was so cold and because something was wrong in there, I could feel it) and every week or so around midnight he'd come clomping up the deck stairs and just stand at the door and my dog's hackles would rise and she'd growl. It took me about three months to get the nerve to open that door – when I did there was no one there. I think Metal Head Ted was one of these who didn't know or refused to believe he was dead."

"Why was he called Metal Head Ted?"

"That's what I called him. His wife, who was too old to take care of the place anymore, said he had a metal plate in his head, that's all, and his name was Ted. He wasn't that scary once I figured out who he was and what he wanted, which was just to come home from his walk in the woods and have a cup of hot cocoa or whatever. But this office ghost, I believe was malevolent."

"I'll check it out online," he said. "I can almost guarantee you of an unnatural death in that room, maybe a suicide. The suicides are the meanest."

"You told me that."

Violette crouched and took a snapshot down Second Street. "I've captured a lot of mist on Second and Third Street," he said. "Don't know why that is."

"There was a pedestrian killed by a speeding motorist last year on Third," I said. "Probably never knew what hit him, the driver was alcohol-powered. Haataja was also seen a number of times walking up and down Second and Third the night he disappeared."

"May or may not mean anything." He adjusted the strap around his neck. "You want to go and try to talk with him? We'll go to his apartment first, then the Math and Science building."

At Haataja's apartment on Bordeaux there was no one who might let us in and nothing of note appeared in the viewfinder of Violette's digital camera. We wandered around the outside of the building with the voice recorder on and asked a few questions. "Are you here, Steve? Is there anything we can do to help? Can you tell us where you might be found?" Tom listened to us with big eyes, head perched to the side, and carefully avoided the bushes all around the house where the Daddy mosquitoes lived ("And the girl mosquitoes," he will tell you, "are *grass*hoppers.").

At the Math and Science building, Violette found some cold spots in the hallway around Haataja's second-floor office, which could easily mean that this part of the building was simply not as warm as the rest. Beth Wentworth, the mathematics professor in 214, the office next to Steve's, stuck her head out. "Oh," she said sadly, "I thought I heard Steve."

In one of the glass cases in the hallway was a diagram of

Turing's bombe, a cryptanalytic machine, with its central cryptic logical theorem in caps at the bottom: "FROM A CONTRADIC-TION YOU CAN DEDUCE EVERYTHING."

"Do you know what this is?" said Tom, indicating the figures on the diagram. "It's a thunderstorm connected with *dots*. And those are *old* numbers there."

Suzie Greenwheat, a.k.a. Telenovela, my wife's best friend, who worked as a janitor in this building and had seen Haataja almost every day since his arrival, came along pushing a dust mop and wanted to know what we were up to. Violette told her and she reacted with a mild nod as if our work was as routine as hers. Telenovela said she had seen Haataja the morning of the day he disappeared. He was talking to a handicapped student, one whom she often saw him with, though he was always talking to students and there was nothing suspicious about the conversation. She also said that one morning when she was waxing, he'd come along and walked right through her third coat of freshly laid wax, spoiling the job, without apologizing or saying a thing.

Tom was off to find the fire exits, which he'd stand before in adulation and sometimes even kiss in a vulnerable moment. The Math and Science building also had a spiral staircase and a giant gravitational pendulum suspended from the ceiling that pleased him to no end.

For the services of the NASA engineer's paranormal exper-tise, all Violette asked in return was a pesto pizza. Jeanne didn't make pesto pizzas, nor did any of the other pizza joints in town, neither did the two pizzerias in Huntsville that used to have them on their menus. Pesto pizzas had gone out of fashion. Violette liked them with "white" cheese, chicken and mushrooms, a few tomatoes, and my scratch dough version had chopped raw onions too. He talked about pesto pizzas as some people talk about first love. I had dough rising at home, grated mozzarella, and the pesto sauce.

Violette reeled off a few dozen pictures with his digital camera, then finished two rolls of standard film. It was dark as we left the building. To the south there was no light except for the stars and the water tower with its tipped-up *C* glowing a dim silver-green. For a moment out the corner of my eye I saw something flicker up the trail into the incinerated forest, deer probably, then it was gone.

35.

A birthday party 100 years ago

LIKE CERTAIN SONGS, TOM WATCHES "MOVIES OF MYSELF" over and over, home videos of the blizzard in April, the hailstorm in July, our new puppy, Lightnin', riding scooters out front, taking a walk along the paved apron of C-Hill, Christmas morning, a family New Year's Eve party. He is five years old and already longing for the "old days" when he was "young." His favorite episodes are those of himself at his fifth birthday party at his grandparents' house in Mexico. His uncles, aunts, cousins, and mother are all in attendance. There is a lot of jubilant racket in the open patio where the party is held, Cristina's mother's wild birds chattering in their cages, Tom and his cousins squealing and shouting and blowing party horns, laughter echoing off the ceramic walls. I am on a book tour in the Pacific Northwest, so I can't be with them this time, but Tom at his mother's bidding suspends the festivities long enough to look into the camera and give me a message: "I love you Daddy." Tom's birthday party in Mexico is like a birthday party 100 years ago: a gentle jubilee of indolent bliss and no hurry to stuff it all into garbage bags and get the kids off to soccer practice. My wife's family sings in that open courtyard full of potted geraniums and trilling tropical birds. Everyone chants the song *dale dale dale, no pierdas el tino* (hit it, hit it, hit it, don't lose your aim) as Tom blindfolded and grinning tries to whack open his piñata. Everyone is speaking Spanish and he has no idea what they're saying, but it doesn't matter.

As Tom begins to open his gifts, Cristina instructs her son

on what to say. She won't teach him Spanish, perhaps owing to the stigma she perceives of being Mexican, another of our many areas of contention. "Say *gracias a tu Tia Liz, Thomas,*" she exhorts. "*Gracias a tu Tia Liz,*" he repeats, as his little cousins gambol all about, angling for the cake and playing with Tom's new toys.

Cristina, too, is content. Her velvet dark eyes are placid in a non-Cristinaland way. She jokes and laughs and claps her hands and sings. This is the modest, peaceful, breezy, composed, and often funny woman I married. I recall our old-fashioned courtship, sitting in the parlor of her parents' home with her toy poodle, Zeus, taking long evening strolls under the lilac trees, watching Almodóvar movies with subtitles in the theater down-town, moving through the clubs and little cafés and internet satellite cafes and staying out too late kissing on the couch of whatever home I might've been watching at the time. There was never much talk then, no need for it. She was *mi favorita,* I declared, *mi super favorita del mundo, mi super dooper flooper favorita,* eventually shortened to Flooper, a pet name that made her dizzy and laugh.

I don't often get to see my Super Dooper Flooper in the States – she's too worried about finances, can't understand what's being said, is under some sort of imagined or real pressure (they end up being the same), in a dither about our old house or our young son and the possibility of me having smoked a ciga-rette. I do my best to cook the native dishes she likes (though I use too much cilantro. "I've never had more cilantro in all my life," she quipped once) and the MP3 player is loaded with her favorite artists, La Ley, Hombres G, Enanitos Verdes, Mana, Ricky Martin, Vicente Fernandez. I also try to do more than my share of work around the house, all the cooking, most of the dishwashing, the principal care and entertainment of Tom, but I'm rarely able to induce the kind of mood I see now on the patio in the house where she was raised.

36.

Snow and mystery deepen

HEAVY JANUARY SNOWS SUSPENDED THE SEARCHES FOR Steven Haataja. If he was out there alive, wandering or holed up in a cave, there wasn't much any of us could do for him. The number of news articles waned (George Ledbetter, *Chadron Record* editor, was commendable in his refusal to bow to the temptation of increased sales by printing anything that wasn't strictly factual) and those that appeared were largely iteration. The babbling declarations – we're baffled, he's vanished, we have no idea – began to subside. Steve was dead (or had transformed himself into a new person if you insisted on being optimistic), it was as simple as that. Steve's sister from Rapid City, Sheila Speaker, was using the word "closure" and had begun packing her brother's things.

Most of us, however, would've preferred the mystery solved, the uneasiness put to rest, the possibility of evil lurking allayed. There was also the chance that he was disabled somewhere, hurt or sequestered or stricken by madness or fugue, or lost in a forest or trapped in a tunnel or a collapsed mine. All the cops running around in clandestine circles seemed only an aggravation of his potentially imperiled circumstances. Made-up stories about him continued to circulate. He'd been sighted. He had called. Sheila Speaker had received an email from him. Another resident who'd moved to Phoenix had seen him on TV there. It was suggested that because he was a lover of puzzles that this was all somehow a game. He was looking down on us from somewhere, amused at our bungling, our inability to extract a single clue about his whereabouts.

37.

DNA hero

UNDER PRESSURE FROM BOTH THE COLLEGE AND THE Chadron Police Department, namely Sergeant Chuck, who threatened to throw him in jail, Loren Zimmerman reluctantly stepped down from his podium and out of the spotlight, the flatfoots in the back still scowling and grumbling. With all the fun dried up and more time on his hands now he began to regularly call my wife on her cell phone. Right in front of me she'd chat with him cheerfully about nothing in particular for 10 or 20 minutes, then hang up, look over at me and say, "What?"

Mr. Zimmerman, like most opportunists, was capable of making a good first impression, but the something-wrong alarm usually went off soon after. He wasn't in his fifth state in six years, simultaneously courting two women both spoken for, and about to lose his job because life was unfair. It was funny how Cristina could not trust God, me, or her father, yet this flimflammer had won her complete confidence. I chalked it up to her newness to the country. She was also undoubtedly mesmerized, like any tender prey, by the twinkling rotation of his carnivorous yellow eyes.

I suppose there is a Loren Zimmerman in every town, cap tilted jauntily, tapping the sidewalk with his rosewood cane as he goes, nostrils twitching from the scent of dark equatorial flesh, striding chest first into the saloon to challenge all the cuckolds glancing sidelong at him with timorous eyes. If he hasn't arrived yet, he is on the way. The full spectrum, the laws of natural selection, the moral mechanism of the molecule, demand it. The laws of reality, dynamic energy, and spiritual process demand it. I've played the part myself, with gusto, oh I was a young scoundrel and a rake, although I stopped trying to sleep with other men's wives in my 20s.

Perhaps if I'd torn a page from the Book of Zimmerman, I wouldn't have had all those years of lament and deprivation. I'd venture to say that Mr. Zimmerman was rarely melancholy or suicidal, and never corralled or herded by a finicky society or shunned to the edges of the Pepsi Generation. A good American goes for it, just does it, slakes it, eats it, kills it, the more the better, damn the torpedoes! The real winner knows that the rules are meant to be broken. All my modesty and compunction had ever gotten me was a noble self-disgust.

I looked Zimmerman up on the Internet one night. Since he sought the spotlight, information on him abounded. He'd served as a Marine in the Vietnam War, where speaking of his time as a platoon sergeant there, he said, "I led 26 Marines in the rigors of laying and breaching minefields, disarming booby traps, and just blowing stuff up." As quoted a hundred times in various reports, he'd been a policeman and a homicide detective in L.A. for 20 years. Intimate with the prominent L.A. cases of the last two decades, Rodney King, O.J. Simpson, and the Rampart scandal, he also knew many of the players, including Defense Attorney Johnnie Cochran and Detective Mark Fuhrman, finder of the bloody glove and the only person in the O.J. Simpson criminal trial to be convicted of charges. Detective Zimmerman had spent many years working in some of the toughest neighborhoods in L.A.: Compton, Watts, Griffith Park, and *enjoyed* it. I read in some detail about a cold case he'd investigated in Los Angeles in 1988, before DNA testing, but seeing DNA testing on the horizon he'd frozen some blood samples. Time had passed, but there is no statute of limitations on murder, and the killer by Zimmerman's foresight was brought to justice.

"I got out of the Marine Corps," he said in one interview,

"and joined the Des Moines Police Department, where I became somewhat of a legend in my own time. Even today young officers in Des Moines tell me they heard of me and my shenanigans. But I was a good cop. I had seven Officer Involved Shootings [OIS] in Des Moines. But Des Moines was too quiet, so I moved to L.A. I got in my first OIS on Thanksgiving Day in 1978. Hey, he had a gun and shot first. The South L.A. gangsters, and my fellow homicide friends, didn't call me 'Z-Dog' for nothing. I was a bloodhound, an attack dog, a pit bull that didn't let go."

In that same interview he said, "I think like a killer. Homicide cops do that. Robbery cops think like robbers. That's called 'The Thin Blue Line.'"

Oh good, I thought: *He shoots people, thrives in the jungle and the ghetto, and thinks like a killer.* In one piece about the marital problems of police officers he confessed that his second wife, the Argentinean, had regularly cheated on him, they'd divorced, he'd remarried her, and then she'd wronged him again, leading to divorce number two and a more cynical view of matrimony. I discovered that his favorite singers were Marty Robbins, Johnny Horton, and Hank Williams (not Jr.), that his favorite ice cream flavor was banana, that he liked "hot little Mexican and Italian women," and that he enjoyed "living life on the edge." The character he despised the most was "the backstabber."

Zimmerman held a master's degree from National University in San Diego, was a proud gun owner and defender of the Second Amendment, and had published several apparently jocular papers on sexual harassment and morale, one of them called "The Theory of Pure Version." He was a leader of seminars and appeared often as a public speaker. Except for his LAPD service, he'd jumped around considerably, had literally and admittedly "been around the world." It seemed that, like me, traveling and new places had always been his modus. But he was moving faster now, pulling up stakes and starting over when the vast majority of people his age, even an escaped-electron like myself, were slowing down. The motive for this pattern wasn't difficult for me to discern. Wherever he went his appetites got the better of him and before long he'd have to blow town.

One evening he announced over the phone to Cristina (as I sat there across the room watching her) that he was going to California and taking his 10-year-old son, the one from the Argentine marriage, with him. Could she check his email, feed his cat, go over every day and make sure everything was all right while he was gone?

When she hung up the phone I stared at her. She arched her eyebrows, expressing a lack of sympathy. I said, "Don't you think this is inappropriate?" She told me instead she intended to manage his estate.

"How much is he paying you?" I said.

"He's not paying me."

38.

Love letters in my hand

ONE DAY IN OUR MAILBOX, ALONG WITH THE ELECTRIC bill and a catalog from Lands' End, there was a letter addressed to Cristina. The envelope had a local postmark and appeared to be written in a masculine hand. Instead of her married name the sender had used the words *"La Flaca,"* which means "The Skinny One." I turned the letter over and over, held it to the light. I saw a little rose inside and my heart flipped. I sniffed the envelope, which had a crocodilian fragrance. Cristina was at work and with that Elvis song "Suspicious Minds" lurching up in the old juke-box in my head ("We can't go *onnn* together...") I opened the letter and read with a tumbling heart about Zimmerman's love and dedication and his intention to be with her soon in Mexico.

I was shocked, of course, betrayed, appalled, befogged and benumbed, but I said nothing. I kept the letter, hoping that it was somehow a mistake. Two days later another letter arrived with the same confessions, promises, little red roses, and gaudy talk of wine and Venus and shining stars.

That night I took Cristina into my office, closed the door, sat her down, and read aloud one of the letters. She blushed and groaned. I began a tirade, coarse and lowdown. In all the times we'd fought she'd never heard me talk like this before. I had never used the word divorce, either, a dirty word, especially when you have a five-year-old child. "How long has this been going on?" I wanted to know.

"Nothing happened," she said, holding her head in both hands, her eyes bulging.

"If you really love him go on and live with him. He doesn't love you. He just wants a piece of ass. You want to go with him, go with him, but you won't take the boy."

I thought she might faint. "Oh, no."

It felt good to have my suspicions justified, to be able to rightfully vent my anger: "What kind of hypocrite are you?" I went on, "trapping me in this house with all your jealous compulsions and your meaningless *topicos* about trust and communication and the family being the most important thing?"

For once there were no shrieks of exasperation, no empty threats of leaving me, no snarling or theatrical sobbing or throwing of vegetables. She explained calmly that nothing had happened. "Ask him," she said. "Meet with him. He will tell you. Nothing happened." Her head dropped.

I gnawed on this awhile. I knew by her gaze, her record of discretion, her sturdy values, and the way she'd settled without hesitation into the admission that she was telling the truth. She was young and someone had helped her and made her feel good, that was the size of it. I realized also that she had no idea who he was, that she was unaware he was making overtures to other women, that she saw in him no potential danger, no open long-toothed maw, only flattery and the manly efficiency of the polished scoundrel. I explained how dangerous he was, unstable, moving about the country undoubtedly repeating the same behaviors, a man well over 60 years old still bird-dogging other men's wives.

"Do you realize what you've gotten yourself into, what you've gotten me into? I don't have a gun, don't even know how to use one. He's a cop, baby, a homicide detective, and he could off me, or you, so easily in this hick town that no one would ever figure it out."

"No," she said.

I reminded her of the bumper sticker on his pickup: *Guns Don't Kill People. I Kill People.*

She grew more and more distressed. "Forgive me," she said.

"Give me a few days to think about it," I said.

As she came around to the realization of what she'd done (actually she hadn't done that much except swoon under his amphibious spell), she became ashen and repentant, groaning out loud occasionally as she undoubtedly ran some scene through her mind. She asked me over and over to forgive her, and after about the third day I did.

From that point on she broke off all relations with Zimmerman. She gave his house key to Suzie Greenwheat to return to him. I suggested once again that since Zimmerman liked hot little Mexican numbers whose citizenship had already been paid for, then the divorced Telenovela might be the ideal companion for him, though I wondered since she was divorced and officially single if she would meet his criterion for "living on the edge."

I would've liked to confront Old Zimmerman. My mind swarmed with plots. But there were several problems, including my longevity, and no need to make it publicly known that Cristina had made a mistake, one I had made of my own volition more times than I care to enumerate (oh, a little karma there, eh babe?). I also hoped to interview him about his role in the Haataja case for my book so there was no need to antagonize a potentially valuable testimony. I knew also that Zimmerman didn't really care. His was an ancient habit that I wasn't going to change in any profound way, except perhaps to help him lose his job, which he was already well on the way to doing all by himself.

39.

The headlock of wedlock

1:36 A.M. Caller from the 900 block of Main St. requested an officer at the above location. Caller advised he could smell marijuana in his bathroom and thought it was coming from the apartment below him. Caller advised he is allergic to marijuana and is getting sick.

I'M AT HEART, AGAINST MY WILL, AN IDEOLOGUE, A romantic if you insist, the sort of person who talks and reveals too much, who believes that everything has a reason, who believes that everyone is basically good, who believes that beauty is truth and in turn truth is salvation, who overvalues the opinions of others, and who needs to be liked and understood. A born fool, in other words, but why put up the sign? Why wear the cap?

My best memories are of being alone, in a room with books, sleep, cigarettes, snow without footprints, no obligations, no one to answer or apologize to, no one reprimanding me or stepping on my daydreams, the peaceful nights, the long projects, Death sitting next to me in his bumblebee pajamas, legs crossed, nibbling from a carton of real-butter popcorn – "He who loves nothing is invulnerable," Master Zhuang tells us – and when it is time to go: the one-way bus ticket out of town.

I began to yearn for those days, that safe distance from intimacy and linear simplicity of moving on whenever the notion struck. You're going to die anyway, your life summarized in one trite and forgettable paragraph, preferably no photo, so who needs all the complications in between?

Five years of doing the matrimonial shuffle had only shown me that Cristina and I were not compatible. I was a crusty, profane old wanderer, set in my ways. She was a sheltered, middle-class child accustomed to an unencumbered life managed by a mother who cooked and cleaned for her, and a macho father who flawlessly provided and never showed weakness or emotion.

All I'd managed with my ideal of helping Cristina fulfill her dreams and trying to "make her happy" was to undertake the upbringing of two children.

I'd always known why I would never marry. And now here it was, loss of freedom and the implacable mate. The headlock of wedlock. Why had I demanded the proof? What sort of arrogance was it to suppose that my marriage would be any different than all the others I had ever observed?

Leibniz, co-inventor of infinitesimal calculus, never married. He considered matrimony at the age of 50, but the woman he had in mind asked for time to reflect. This gave Leibniz time to reflect, too, and so he was saved.

Oft-quoted journalist H.L. Mencken ("No one ever lost money underestimating the intelligence of the American people."), who called marriage "the end of hope," finally married at age 50 to a Southern woman 18 years his junior, just as I had. He changed his mind about marriage, changed his mind as well about the South. When she died five years later, he was desolate.

Every day or two I contemplated taking Tom and leaving Cristina.

Mencken or Leibniz, Mencken or Leibniz.

If Cristina and I had only been a couple of bumpkins from different countries who idealized each other because of a language problem, then married out of hormonal momentum and lamentable judgment, it would've made sense to split.

But Tom changed everything. Recite what you like about what's good for the children. I know firsthand the importance and superior survival rates of intact families. No, somehow, Cristina and I were both going to have to unhinge our pasts and swivel our hips around to the fact that an innocent life required our utmost attention. For the good of the child and everyone else, somehow we were both going to have to grow up.

In the meantime, the boy and I traveled together. We

tramped about town, visited our friends, shopped for good-look-ing tomatoes. We walked along the railroad tracks. He'd often wear his "singing shoes," Mexican black dress shoes that could not have been comfortable but held important meaning for him because he'd been in a school performance with them and loved to sing. He'd gotten in the habit of saying, "Let's dine out," and then in a tone as if withering from starvation: "I need some junk food." Everywhere he pushed his stroller full of rubber lizards and other prized possessions.

"Hey, Tom, you've put your pants on backwards."

"I can live with that."

"Tom, don't you think it would be better if I walked in front for a while?"

"You can when it's your birthday."

"What do you want for lunch today?"

"French toast. And remember (lifting a forefinger), don't give me any healthy stuff because that makes me t'row up."

40.

How's that Subaru?

HAZEL DEVINE WAS THE ONLY PERSON I'VE EVER KNOWN who could drive by and wave with one muscle. He navigated his burnt-orange 1976 convertible Impala top-down with the toes of his bare left foot gripping the top of the steering wheel, his other foot wedged firmly against the accelerator pedal. I usually saw him on Tuesday, his day off from the lot. He pulled along next to us.

"How's that Subaru running?"

"I think the fuel pump is going out."

"Why?"

"Every time I start it up it leaks gas."

"Probably just a fuel line." He shut off the engine and began to bob his head up and down, an indication that I should help him to ignite his cigarette. "How's the mileage?"

I got one started for him. He smoked it fast. My son watched in awe. "I don't know. I quit driving it. I never wanted a car anyway. My wife has her own now."

"Why don't you bring it in?"

"All right."

"Any news on that math professor?"

"Nothing I've heard of. What do you think happened to him?"

He shook his head, pressed foot to face and took a thoughtful drag. "The cops won't ever find him. They couldn't find their ass with both hands." He grinned out of his pockmarked head red as a Costa Rican mango, finger spinning like a windmill.

I took his cigarette end and crushed it on the ground. "Someone will find him eventually, I suppose," I said.

"Won't probably make much difference."

"No," I agreed. My son was squatted down now, extracting a thorn from one of the wheels of his stroller.

"Gonna go to the Fave," he said, referring to The Favorite, a bar right next door to the Sinister Grin. "Drink a few more."

"Have one for me," I said.

"We should get together some time."

"Just like the old days." The grin on his face was wistful, at best. "You've got a beautiful boy," he said. "Sure he's yours?"

41.
Grasping for straws

11:57 A.M. Caller from Regency Trailer Court advised they had captured the "elusive" husky and would like someone to come and get it.

ONE COLD MORNING IN LATE FEBRUARY, I SAW THE POLICE searching Millie Heiser's old house, which had been abandoned since I came here the first time in '94. Though it had once been grand, it was now tumbled-down and hail-shattered beyond repair, the place where you'd shoot the remake of *The Ghost and Mr. Chicken* (one of Tom's favorite movies). Millie, who'd owned the bowling alley for many years, had recently died and for the last 30 years had only used her mansionette for storage. A hunched but spry old lady, she'd spent her last few years working at Wal-mart. Millie's house was just a block east of Haataja's apartment.

When next I saw Sergeant Chuck, I asked him what was going on over at Millie's place. I hadn't seen anyone on those grounds except the phantoms in the curtains for years. "Yeah, well," he said, hitching up his trousers. "Some psychic from Iowa called and said she thought Haataja got run over on a one-way street by a disgruntled student. Supposedly, he took the body and stowed it in a basement." Chuck shrugged and looked offended. "We checked every abandoned basement all the way west to the RV park."

"Find anything?"

He clapped the back of his neck and looked askance. "Mice."

Chuck was getting calls from all over the country about Steve, one where empty boxes of raisins, the kind that Haataja liked, had been found behind a dumpster in Sioux Falls, another where a man who exactly matched the description of Haataja had jumped from the Golden Gate Bridge, except he turned out to be black.

I understood that Chaffwick was not dicking off as much as everyone believed, that circumstances more than style had led him to this pantomime, but having little else to go on, and having seen lots of psychics on television solving prominent cases (there is no credible record of a psychic ever solving or preventing a crime, finding a kidnap victim or a corpse), he'd been induced to follow the lead. Bordeaux, the street on which Haataja lived, was coincidentally a one-way street.

"Who was the psychic?" I asked.

"Wouldn't give her name." He stuck his tongue into his cheek and hung his thumbs on his belt. "She called from a pay phone in Dysart, Iowa."

I knew Dysart, which was near Waterloo, where I'd gone a few years back to live, and though I hadn't stayed there I had settled in Decorah, not far north, for around 10 months. John Wunder, a history professor and bawdy storyteller from the University of Nebraska who comes to the Mari Sandoz conference every year and stays with Jeanne at the Olde Main, and is a native of Dysart, told a story at the bar one night about a strange young man there who sucked off a certain part of himself with a vacuum cleaner. He also told the story about the woman who'd died falling from a building when he was living in Cleveland. Apparently she could only achieve climax hanging out a window while her lover made a crucial exploration with his toes. No one believed the story until the paperboy, who'd witnessed the event, confirmed the details.

42.

Town of the unknown psychic

SINCE I'D BEEN INVITED TO READ AT THE UNIVERSITY of Iowa (where they'd been studying some of my essays!) the following weekend, I thought I might take a jaunt up to Dysart to see if we could locate the anonymous pay phone mystic. I'd never met a real psychic before and did not think it would be hard locating one in a city of a thousand. I figured John Wunder probably knew her.

Iowa City, home of the University of Iowa and its storied writing program (Flannery O'Connor, Thomas "Tennessee" Williams, and John Irving among its luminous alumni), is about a 13-hour (back highways) drive from Chadron. Cristina did not travel well and would not drive. It had been five years since we'd almost been killed by a one-armed farmer pulling a trailer who turned in front of us as I was passing him on Highway 20 on our way to Immigration and Naturalization in Omaha in the rain (I managed to land us unharmed in a ditch, but what a lot of screaming that was!), so along with getting flattened by a drunk in Zacatecas, Cristina's frayed highway nerves were understandable.

What wasn't understandable was her lack of empathy. She was never deliberately cold or mean, she simply didn't have the patience or ability to appreciate someone else's perspective. We were squabbling more than ever, Tom between us half the time. Marriage was an equation without a solution, the vortex of an intangent divided by the square root of a misconception. No wonder the divorce rate among mathematicians was so high.

When I asked my mother how she'd made it 50-plus years with her husband-who-was-too-much-like-me, her reply was no more than a convoluted smile, as if to say, good gravy, man, don't ask me. I suppose it takes nine years for the typical married couple to learn how to live together, that's the average point of an American marital breakup at least, the point at which two people believe they've given enough of themselves and worn out every bird-witted cliché and all their handed-down pop-cult expectations of romantic love as if it were supposed to be some sort of electrical current piped in from the Hershey's chocolate factory through a KC and the Sunshine Band song.

Neither were the tricks and conundrums of a successful marriage going to be revealed to me on my Yahoo! home page or by a bald psychologist escaped from the Oprah Winfrey Show. Marriage was more like falling down a rabbit hole at the bottom of which an archaic Romanian dialect was spoken and all the rules of physics had been changed. Here in this accidental country of half-finished rainbows and sniggering hedgehogs and games you could never win, you had to sit in the crooked chairs and endure the tambora buzz and the wandering cuckoo bees, learn the customs and the lingo and accept whatever passed for root beer and whole wheat noodles and be a jughead for a long time. Eventually, somehow, it would all make sense, and years, perhaps decades, later you'd be returned home reformed and barely recognizable but fluent in bastardized Romanian, a wanly convoluted smile on your lips, and when anyone asked you about marriage and its rabbit-hole riddles you'd only be able to respond with all candor: good gravy, man, don't ask me.

This was the sort of flapjack batter that ran constantly through my mind as I cast about for answers, though I knew that like all warring parties interested in each other's music, literature, soft drinks, black pepper, and gold, there were three steps to rapprochement. First, détente; second, mutual understanding; third, a night out arm in arm with a cold bottle of gin under the stars. You needed that first step though, the cease-fire, the chance at least to contemplate and discuss peace before any progress was going to be made, and it didn't seem like that would ever happen. Fortunately we were both stubborn enough to hold on.

We were put up by the University at the downtown Sheraton, where I spent most of that evening and the rest of the next morning running the halls with Tom, going up and down the "elvegators," filling buckets from the ice machines, investigating the swimming pool area, fiddling with the controls on the "ang-sang-dang-dang-a-der" (air conditioner), or picking him up so he could stand on the window ledges and look down over the city. The french fries of Iowa City were better than Nebraska french fries, he declared, and he still hasn't forgotten to this day which room we stayed in: 512.

My reading was at the Mill: a bar and restaurant only a few blocks from the Sheraton. Cristina always makes sure I have new clothes and shoes for my readings, so that I look like I'm in fifth grade and my mother has dressed me, but I indulge her and avoid another quarrel. Here comes the drifter, why does he look like a preppie? About 36 people attended. I read a condensed version of "Methamphetamine for Dummies," which I don't think went particularly well, and it rained violently the whole time as if the gods disapproved, then I shook hands, chatted with a few patrons, picked up my cash, declined the after-reading party, and said thanks for putting up with my nonsense.

We were off the next morning to The Town of the Unknown Psychic, a short jaunt up 380 that would put us back on 20, an easy route back home. Cristina agreed with the psychic that Haataja had probably been killed by a disgruntled student. Her Catholicism, consistent with the authority of many fundamental creeds, was derived from the Notion of the Angry but Somehow Just and Loving God. Acts of random violence or tragedy were always explicable through conduct: if you did something wrong you were punished for it, and if something awful happened to you, you probably deserved it.

In Dysart, population dwindling, I pulled into a bar on Main Street and asked the bartender where I might find the local clairvoyant. He smiled and said, "You must mean Kat the Swami Queen," marking her title in the air with two-finger quote marks. He didn't know the address but described her small green house (with ruffled asbestos siding, white aluminum awnings, and a big green elm out front) two blocks south. "She's a flake, though," he said.

I found the house and parked. There were no fortune-teller signs out front, no "Palms Read, $20," just an ornamental well trimmed with trellis and a birdbath gone dry. Cristina stayed in the car with a headache that she thought might kill her. She had no desire to meet the Swami Queen. Tom accompanied me. Though he disliked most children, he was always eager to meet and talk with adults. "Do you feel any vibrations?" I asked him as we came up the walk.

"Is this an automatic house?" he wanted to know.

"Automatic as any other, I suppose."

"Does it have 'lectricity?"

I told him it probably did, unless there was a power outage like from a tornado. Tom did not like tornadoes, he said, thinking I meant the main ingredient in spaghetti sauce. I explained it was not that kind of tornado but the kind where high wind spun into a black funnel and ripped your house up into the sky. He said he did not like that kind of tornado either.

I knocked on the door. Three black kittens staggered toward us. Tom said "oh," and knelt to pet them. He had a special relationship with cats, possessed some rare feline magnetism. They often ran to him as we walked around town and then they would follow him for blocks.

A lady, much older than I expected, with a thin, drawn face, cold pale eyes, and long middle-parted white hair in the fashion of a folk singer from the 1970s, opened the door. A laptop was open on the kitchen table and the place smelled strongly of cigarette smoke. "Hello?" she said.

I introduced myself and my son, who was still kneeling with the kitties. "Tom loves cats," I said.

This made her smile.

"We are from Chadron, Nebraska," I said, "the town where the math professor disappeared?"

"How did you find me?" she wanted to know.

"Well, we just asked. Do you remember John Wunder?"

"My goodness. John Wunder hasn't lived here for years. He was our paperboy."

Behind her I saw that her house was filled with more cats and plants. The cats were principally black, the plants were principally fronds and ferns. The windows had green tinting on them, giving the place the atmosphere of a private cat jungle, with cigarette smoke. "Come shake hands with the lady, Tom," I said. "She is a psychic. That means she can see things that other people can't."

Tom shook hands. He was often very much in attitude like a grown-up, the way he carried himself, the enthusiasm with which he listened to Mozart's "Mass in C Minor" or Vivaldi's *Gloria*, the way he sat at a piano or in a chair with his legs crossed pretending to read a newspaper, or the way he shook hands with a psychic. "When I grow up I am going to smoke," he said.

"He is also going to drink wine for breakfast," I added. "He got that idea from his Uncle Mario, who works as a room service waiter at the Aladdin in Las Vegas and drinks wine with his breakfast. He's not a wino," I said.

Kat giggled this time and flicked back her hair. "Would you like a cup of coffee?"

"My wife is in the car," I said. "She has a whale of a headache and we'll probably get running here pretty soon."

Kat the Swami Queen nodded. I was glad Tom the Icebreaker had come along.

"They checked all the basements and could not find him," I said. "I don't know if the police missed him or what, but nobody has any idea where he could be."

She licked her dry lips and looked down at the ground for a spell. "I get these pictures. I don't always see them clearly." She smiled as if she had gas pain. "I still see him low." She pushed her hand down against the air. "It's possible he froze to death."

"Where?"

"I don't know. I'm sorry I can't be of more help. I wish I didn't see these things. I don't sleep."

"I appreciate your trouble. I know it can't be easy. What do I owe you?"

"Nothing," she said, waving me off. "Tell John Wunder I said hello."

I gave her 20 anyway, not a bad rate for fiction, and now I figured I was up to speed on the case, or at least I knew as much as anyone else.

43.

Steve's first martini

5:37 P.M. Caller from the 400 block of Ann St. advised that his sister had come into his home and was pretending to be his wife.

ONE SUNNY AFTERNOON A WEEK OR SO AFTER OUR MEET-ing with the Iowa clairvoyant, I was having a beer with Deane Tucker in his backyard. Rana, Deane's young wife, an ex-student of his, was off counting a newly introduced herd of bighorn sheep in the wilderness somewhere to the west. That was actually her job, counting sheep (Do you find yourself having to drink a lot of coffee at work, Rana?). Rana was 16 years younger than Deane. Cristina was 18 years my junior. Deane and I, the cradle robbers, were commiserating over the problems of marrying women young enough to be our daughters.

Marrying a woman young enough to be your daughter was often like having a daughter, a double-bonus if you took the right view, but so long as you hadn't cornered her when she was 15 and kept her hidden in the backyard in a tent, there was always time to catch up and grow together and become contemporaries and even surpass your expectations and treat each other kindly in the memoirs. I admitted that our marriage wasn't progressing as well as I liked, despite all her recent material victories such as the job in dentistry, the 401(k), a car of her own with automatic transmission, an eBay account, a bigger TV, and contact lenses. We were fighting as much as ever. But we had advanced in that one crucial area, agreeing not to discuss things we'd never agree on, such as our financial security and the ownership of more than one car. I was also going to continue to write whether I made a hundred dollars a year or hit the mother lode. And she'd get her three-story Second Empire with the mansard roof, dormer windows, picket fence, three-car garage, spiral staircase, and a property tax bill higher than our current annual mortgage the very *moment* I hit that mother lode. Poco a poco, we were working it out.

Deane's dog, Jasper, half German shepherd, half Nigerian wildebeest, was running around in frantic circles, hoping someone would throw him the ball. My son was off exploring the upper floors of the house and he'd occasionally appear and wave from a window, like one of the phantoms in Millie Heiser's abandoned mansionette.

"You got any idea what Steve was working on before he disappeared?" I asked.

Deane sipped from his bottle and smiled, like Sartre's Absurd Man. "No one, not even his colleagues, understood what he was talking about when it came to his own work," he replied. "We did have a few conversations about logic. He mentioned once or twice a project that near as I can make out was some application of the unity of opposites."

"You mean like a unified field theory?"

"Maybe not quite that ambitious." He crossed his legs. "Far as I can tell he was just interested in quantifying natural antagonism, the Marx-Engels idea that everything in existence is composed of equally contradictory forces. I can see why Steve might've been attracted to this because it's basically algebraic: a puzzle about balance."

I wiggled my bottle. "Like an ancient Eastern parable."

"I have no idea how he codified it, or how far he got. It wasn't an idea that should've gotten him into any trouble, since all numbers lead back to zero." He drained his bottle of beer. "Maybe that would've done it. That's what always trips the mathematicians up, the idea that the universe is perfect. God would never make a perfect universe because it would be dull."

"I didn't know you believed in God."

"I don't. It's just an argument."

Deane and I often differed on the utility of philosophy. Deane didn't believe that philosophy could actually provide anything of use for the layman. Philosophy as we knew it was dissolved long ago by the Cynics, who taught us that everything in the end can be disproved. What we've been left with is an esoteric method of skepticism guarded by the professional intellectual for the purposes of insuring his tenure. My position was that philosophy should be an organization of thought for the benefit of all humanity, like psychology tries to be: "love of knowledge," had to mean something other than winning an argument or making a test difficult.

"Did I ever tell you about Steve's first martini?" he said.

"You did not."

"It's one of my favorite stories."

"Tell it."

"Do you want another beer?"

"Maybe one more. I have to work tonight."

"Too bad," said Deane, who was on sabbatical that year.

He retrieved a pair of chilled bottles, threw the ball for Jasper, seated himself, crossed his legs, and began the story of Steven Haataja's first martini.

Several professors and students had been out one night for happy hour at Public Defender Paul Wess's bar, the Sinister Grin. Afterward they all trooped over to the house of JW, the Spanish professor.

"Let's have a martini," Deane proposed.

Steve had never tried a martini, 46 years old, imagine that. JW mixed martinis on the rocks. Deane Tucker said no no, thanks all the same, but these are not real martinis. The *bon vivant* had to give a demonstration: you fill the glass with ice, you swirl and then discard the vermouth, the gin should be as cold as Dick Cheney's soul. I'm not asking for Spanish olives stuffed with almonds.

The reconstructed martinis were served.

Haataja said, "How do you drink one of these?"

"Well, you just toss it back," said Deane, the Minister of Debauchery. "And then you eat the olive."

JW was drinking more than usual these days, nervous about the letters that kept arriving from Jonas Greenwheat, who was also in the habit of regularly jogging past her window in his ridiculously short shorts. Why couldn't she just teach? Why was she a magnet for crazy people? She was looking forward to Denver, more lunatics, yes, but you could hide from them more easily in a big city and the police would beat them discreetly behind dumpsters with sticks. She leaned in toward Haataja, eyes closed, licking her lips. "Oh it's the best thing you'll ever try. What a sensation it will be on your tongue. It will be like dying and going to heaven."

"It will change your life," Deane said.

Steve liked the martini. He laughed in that wonderful way of his and thought it remarkable how vermouth could not only change your life, but the properties of oven cleaner as well.

"But never drink them on the rocks," said Deane. "That's not a martini, that's a travesty. If you order a martini like that in Britain they'll revoke your passport."

Steven Haataja was a modest drinker. Most evenings he spent in, reading, grading papers, working out chess problems, tinkering with a theory, singing, listening to a ball game on the radio. But when he wanted to he could also put it away. He was Finnish, a big man. He had four martinis that night, felt tingly, laughed. He admired JW and her slender youth. Deane walked him home that night and thought the math professor was the happiest he'd ever been in his life.

Deane shook his head. "I really miss him. He was good company, a great sense of humor. I really mean it when I said he was happy. He and I traded DVDs. He liked Russian and Hungarian movies. Have you seen Béla Tarr's *Werckmeister Harmonies*?"

"Never heard of it."

"The opening solar system scene." He kissed the tips of his fingers. "Beautiful. I still have the last DVD he gave me, a

Finnish film, *The Man Without a Past*. It's a good movie, too. I'll lend it to you."

"Is there a freezing-to-death scene?"

"Funny you would ask."

44.

Rowboating with hobos

I HAVE THREE GIFTS: I CAN MAKE AN EXCELLENT CREAM soup, I'm a good speller, and most people who don't think I'm a smartass or from Venus think I'm funny. Even my computer programmer ex-brother-in-law who never laughs and is probably to some extent autistic admits that I have a "sophisticated sense of humor." Cristina, however, didn't think I was funny. She took all my remarks literally. I'd say to her, "Why don't we walk to the store on our hands today?" and Cristina would frown and say, "No, we can't do that." Then I would say, "We'll hitchhike to Rapid City then, catch a freight train back before dark," and Cristina would shake her head somberly and frown. She couldn't fathom why I might want to hitchhike to Rapid and return by freight train or walk on my hands or steal a helicopter or go rowboating with hobos or contact my home planet or pull my pants down in front of the Queen.

When you read as much as I have about autism, everyone after a while begins to look autistic, everyone fits somewhere along "the spectrum," just as it was a few years ago when it was discovered that we are all gay, that we all fit somewhere along that spectrum (I suppose, consistent with this argument, we all fit along the heterosexual spectrum as well, but anyway…). It was interesting to see how many traits Cristina shared with her son, traits that in his case were numbered as symptoms under the broad canopy of Autism Spectrum Disorder (ASD): literal-mindedness, awkward personal interaction, dearth of social interest (except with family members), hypersensitivity to stimuli, wandering attention (Cristinaland), lack of empathy, rages when rituals were disrupted. Some of these traits, e.g. Cristinaland, could've been chalked up to the drunk driver who struck her senseless in Zacatecas, but she admitted that she'd always been spacey, not too social, that her personality hadn't changed markedly since it was formed.

That made me reflect on what Violette had told me after my remark about the preponderance of mathematicians bunched along the autism spectrum. He'd known a number of high-functioning autistics at NASA, one in particular an eccentric experimental physicist named Bunthram, who insisted that he wasn't autistic but Bunthram. Bunthram didn't believe in autism. What most people considered autism, Bunthram considered part and parcel of the genetic bundle of the logical mind. Furthermore, Bunthram didn't want to be social or touched or to go play volleyball, square dance, or sit around a bonfire singing "Kookaburra Sits on the Old Gum Tree." He wanted to work and be left alone. He liked his one-dimensional life and his job and his apartment, his cats and the TV shows *Battlestar Galactica*, *Airwolf*, and *Charmed*. He thought most people were oversocialized, but that was their business. His hero was Nikola Tesla, one of the landmark intellects of all time, who wouldn't have achieved that height without his ASD tendencies toward isolation, celibacy, pattern obsession, ritualism, and the rest of that prototypical geek package.

I am always relieved to turn to optimistic views on autism. I have long suspected that autism is a natural intellectual function correlating to our increasing need for specialized, nonlinear, incoherent, and advanced "thinking styles" and not a disease or a developmental "disorder." The work of Simon Baron-Cohen, not the comedian but the psychopathologist (do they call you a "psychopath" for short, Simon?) at Cambridge University, illustrates this view. Baron-Cohen has been doing genetic research on autism for years and has theorized that most autistics have a drive to systemize. Mathematicians, physicists, engineers, logicians, number theorists, software programmers, and quantum cryptographers are all good examples of systemizers, and in each of these pursuits, you'll find higher rates of autism.

Systemizers are much more likely to be male as well as autistic. About 80% of all autistics are male. Baron-Cohen proposes that autism is therefore an extreme male-brained profile. But this doesn't make it inherently psychopathological. In fact, autistics by their asocial predispositions, narrow preoccupations, tendencies toward ritual and repetition, sensory filtering, and so on are able to work long periods without distractions on deep projects that might bore other people to death. Think space travel and the overall management of a cyber-connected universe. At the end of any spectrum is dysfunction, chaos, madness, disease, and snack machines getting pushed over. On the political continuum both the left and the right lead unimpeded to totalitarianism. And I wouldn't want to rely too heavily on psychology or go all New Age on you and declare that autism is a gift. It does however seem possible that with its considerable claim on the population, its numerous talented representatives, its frequent association with rapid brain growth, and its continued ability through exhaustive research to evade cause or cure that what we're calling autism (and the heavy psychological inference of abnormality or "disorder") might well instead be cerebral evolution.

Cristina was a systemizer too. She'd gravitated to a profession that demanded close attention to detail and the need for emotional distance from pain and patients she was literally inside of. Often on Saturdays when we were courting in Mexico she couldn't go out because she had to "organize" her room. Everything in our house had a place, no one got to put anything where they liked, even the end table with my books, which I'd find in a neat stack each time I sat down to read. Whenever she worked with me, in the Olde Main kitchen or on a side job I'd pick up, we would end up arguing before we did it her way. I was constantly startling her as I came around a corner or out of a room, even though she knew I was in the house. Faithfully, like a prisoner in solitary, she'd put an X through each day on the calendar with a black ink pen. Staring at me as I explained something to her, she'd say when I was through, "You need to trim your eyebrows." She'd check the dishes after I washed them, remake the bed the way she liked it, refold the clothes after I'd done laundry, tell me what shoes to wear, much of this leading to an argument, since it seemed to me more like nagging and controlling than her drive to systemize. Her job was extremely important to her, the one place where she could totally devote herself, and she put so much into her work (she's the best worker I've ever known) that she barely had the energy to quarrel when she got home in the evenings or call the dog *pinche huevón* or *callejero cabrón cochino*.

Most noteworthy in all of this is that at the other end of Baron-Cohen's systemization spectrum, as we part from masculine science and sine-cosine-tangents, we find the feminine empathizers, those who have the ability to identify with others, read facial expressions, imagine how others feel, make a crawfish étouffée with steamed asparagus and jasmine rice, give change to panhandlers, and not intentionally say hurtful or antagonistic things. As a rule, systemizing and empathizing are opposed. If you're strong on systemizing, you don't want some goober to come along and mess it all up. If you're long on empathizing, it isn't likely that you'd stare willingly into an electron microscope for 12 hours or obsess about how the pillows are arranged on the couch. Systemizers are rule-based, less flexible, and more inclined to stick to patterns and positions. Empathizers are more emotionally oriented, freeform in approach, care less about rules than getting along, and usually give in when the argument starts because, really, what difference does it make what shoes I wear if I'm driving you all the way to Omaha?

Whether you believe that autism is a blessing or a curse, the result of an sv40 monkey-virus mutation (if you're interested in this angle, read Edward Haslam's *Dr. Mary's Monkey*) or the mercury-destruction of mitochondria, having a sense of humor is your pass out of ASD. Autistics are rarely funny, the reason both Einstein and Steven Haataja should be excluded from the list. Cristina was funny, too; she thought Randy Moss looked like Rudy from *The Cosby Show*, and she'd say that she looked like a fish or that I looked like a "homeless guy." Still, my droll, ironic style evaded her and she fielded every line I delivered literally. Most of this had to do with language, humor being one of the last things you learn in your new country.

But one day after Cristina had described a tyrannical patient from Virginia, a traveling temporary nurse who'd been working on the Indian reservation who was eventually told to leave the office after the volume of abuse she heaped on everyone, Cristina taking the brunt, I said, "Why didn't you just keep tipping back the chair until she slid out?" As usual Cristina only stared at me, trying to ferret out whatever nasty thing I might've been implying, and then the outlandish justice of what I'd suggested suddenly hit her, her face relaxed and opened, her eyes fluttered, she broke into a grin and laughed. And the way she stared at me for the next 30 minutes was like six years of reassessment, as if she were recalling all the other jests and joshes and jocularities solely delivered as God has provided to relieve tension and make life a little more pleasant and bearable. It was a revolutionary moment, a watershed moment, like nuns in a peanut field singing old Negro songs or rods of dusty sunshine poking through holes in penitentiary walls.

Once she understood that I wasn't criticizing or incriminating her or making preposterous suggestions to confuse her or tarnishing her public image or intimating that I didn't love her anymore, we had our first cease-fire. It also helped that Mr. Zimmerman was finally having relations with Suzie Greenwheat, a fortunate and practical alliance as far as I was concerned – one I'd proposed myself many times – except for the awkward fact that Suzie Greenwheat was my wife's closest friend.

45.
Pig roast under the pine boughs

4:41 A.M. A caller one and a half miles west of Chadron on Highway 20 requesting an officer run out to the location to see if there is a black cow on the highway.

EVERY WEEK OR SO TOM AND I WENT TO THE COLLEGE to check out the fire exits in the library and ride the "elvegators," especially in the 11-story student housing complex that would attract the five knuckleheads from Montana in the middle of their interstate crime spree because they thought it was a hotel. Sergeant Chaffwick was also moonlighting as a campus security cop at this time, and we'd run into him now and again. He was plainly vexed. The corners of his eyes and even his mustache drooped. Having lost much of the elasticity in his shrugging muscles, his shoulders had sunk as well. I must've seemed to him like a friend in contrast to the criticism he lived with daily over his failure to solve the Haataja case (especially that AP writer from Kansas who excoriated the Chadron Police Department for its purported inaction in stories picked up nationally) and also he'd finally grown accustomed to my face and no longer squinted at me as if I'd just climbed out of a special craft from outer space. My son also helped to cheer the weary, the embittered, the battered, and the besieged.

The sergeant and I might gab about UFOs, the authenticity of Bigfoot, whether or not Abraham Lincoln was gay, the upcoming Sturgis rally (I see him here dismounting his Harley in his black leathers and bandana, swaggering cinematically through the hot sun, then leaning down to a cupped match to light up a smoke in the manner of one who has seen *The Wild One* more than three times), or that pig roast next Sunday under the pine boughs. I'd told him about the Iowa psychic's claim that Haataja

had frozen to death, but he'd waved at me as if I had declared
Frank Sinatra wore nipple rings. Mostly I tried to steer clear of
the Haataja case. Chuck had suffered enough. He'd been changed
by this event, caught like a bather in a riptide and dragged
under. If I could've thrown him a line I would've. He was so close
to the palm trees and rum drinks and sleeping-in-late-every-
morning of retirement he could taste it, that was at least until the
biggest case in the history of Chadron had fallen in his lap, and
three months later: not a whisper of *corpus delecti.*

I should've thanked him. Every fascinating true crime case
from Bobby Fuller (who sang the hit song "I Fought the Law"
and died at the age of 23 under highly suspicious circumstances) to O. J. Simpson to the West Memphis Three is a study in
perceived police ineffectiveness. But all of humanity falls short.
The rarity is the job well done. How many times have I burned
the rolls or spoiled the soup or cut myself in the middle of a rush?
Which of us executes his daily tasks without flaw? The errors
of the policeman were no greater or careless or more egregious
than mine. It's just that my mistakes had comparatively little
consequence. My mistakes were forgotten.

Mark this as well, Sergeant: Everything in human experience is told and understood as a story. The news, history, religion,
evolution, Creation, dreams, every life is a book. Language and
time are the culprits. We are all subordinate. God is a playwright.
If there is no story one will have to be produced from the meager
facts available, from Yahweh to Y2K, from inorganic molecules
as the origin of life to planet earth as a wasteland brought to you
by ExxonMobil, the truth be damned. And the cop has the most
prominent theatrical role in contemporary society. There is no
more enduring and appealing formula than the police story.

So every officer should know his part. In essence, he has
only two choices: Good cop. Bad cop.

"When are you going to put me in one of your books?" he
liked to say.

Well, here you are, Sergeant, at last.

46.
Bluffers and raconteurs

FROM SUZIE GREENWHEAT, CRISTINA AND I LEARNED officially that Zimmerman's contract would not be renewed at the college after being an assistant professor for less than two years, purportedly for taking over the Haataja case and making unauthorized statements about Haataja and the investigation, although I was told by one administrator that he probably wouldn't have been rehired anyway. Among the long list of detractions, he was "bad-tempered," and "had a habit of doing things before asking." It was a heated confrontation with a dean, the administrator told me, that had sealed Zimmerman's fate.

It was difficult to persuade Cristina of certain obvious facts, but she realized finally that Zimmerman had never loved her, that he wasn't as he represented himself (you can't keep telling everyone you're a peach tree when you have onions and persimmons growing from your branches), that his continued troubles in keeping employment and cordial relations were a reflection of his character rather than his luck.

I don't think it was a coincidence that around this time, our cease-fire graduated to an attitude of mutual respect. Cristina and I were unusually mismatched, culture, age, background, personalities, placement on the system-empathy scale, and we were unfortunately alike in too many of the wrong areas. But we both came from solid families, we both believed that marriage was more than a "piece of paper" or an amusement park ride where you were supposed to gasp with joy at every turn, we were both truthful with each other, and neither of us intended to quit on the other. With no fights for a month, and a policy of mutual respect in place, it looked for the first time that we might have a chance.

Now able to engage in colloquial conversation and field half the cracks that came her way, Cristina was the first one dressed for our Friday evening trip to the Olde Main, one or two drinks, five games of dollar keno, Spanish speakers, the beatnik contingent at the President's Table, and whatever other bluffers and raconteurs had assembled in the Longbranch Saloon.

Of all the Olde Main regulars I'd known in the last three months, my vote for the most improved went to Sam Killinoy. Ever since he'd gotten a job with Community Action, helping poor folks work out heating problems and the like, he'd become downright likeable, showing the ability to joke and accept someone else's point of view. He could spend money now. He could afford a girlfriend. He'd bought himself a truck. One of his daughters was blossoming into a country-and-western star. Sam worked with the poor, and he was their daily advocate. He was like many men I've known, myself included, simply grateful to find somewhere he belonged.

No longer did Sam have to hang his head in his own hometown and neither did he sit by himself waiting around for someone to drift by so he could argue with them. Most of the time he had a friend to the left and a friend to the right, and the debates raged on about who was going to win the Super Bowl this year, or if the Broncos had the defense to compete in the west, or if the Huskers were going to make a Bowl bid this season with their new coach. I couldn't pass him without getting caught up in the debates myself. You're crazy if you think the Penguins can sweep the Avalanche. Sometimes we'd talk for an hour and he'd insist on buying me a beer. He'd begun to endear himself to listeners with confessions of weakness such as his propensity for attracting psychopathic women and his chronic insomnia that he remedied with a bowl of Kellogg's Frosted Flakes and two pieces of toast. Occasionally, just for the heck of it, he didn't just concede to your position but actually agreed with you. The story of the bitter man turned sweet is as good as any. He expressed admiration for Tom, always engaged my son in adult-style conversation, and had recently brought him a musical-zoological keyboard that Tom still plays.

One Friday night Mr. Mad Dog, the mortuary science student who'd taken my spot in the kitchen at the Olde Main, caught me down at the end of the bar. Mr. Mad Dog's real name is Mike, but there were so many Mikes around at the time, I gave him his nickname, in honor of his easygoing nature. Mr. Mad Dog told me that Sam Killinoy had been in the night before and had stated that he knew who had killed Dr. Steven Haataja.

Haataja was still officially a missing person without a crumb of evidence to suggest otherwise. I asked Mr. Mad Dog who'd killed Dr. Haataja.

"He wouldn't say. All he said was that it was not a stranger. It was someone we all knew."

Not only did Sam have a truck and a girlfriend and a sweetened Kellogg's cure for insomnia, he was the sole possessor of an intoxicating secret.

"Did he give you a clue?" I asked.

"He said that anyone who wanted to murder the professor would have had to know him very well, and would have had to observe him for a long period."

Cristina had joined us and kept shooting me imploring looks. Her English was improving by leaps and bounds, but fast colloquial speech still often left her in the weeds. Usually I translated on the fly, but sometimes, as in this case, she'd have to wait for the recap later.

"He said he'd already told the sheriff," Mr. Mad Dog continued. "Something about not wanting to be an accessory. Then he started talking about people with mental deficiencies and how they often bonded. People with mental deficiencies who are lonely. Then he said 'she,' and that's when someone said, 'You're talking about your sister (Phoebe),' and after that he clammed up."

"He thinks his sister did it?"

Two customers in black dusters and black cowboy hats entered the bar and were waiting to be served. I could hear pool balls cracking in the back, my son playing his version of cueless billiards.

Mr. Mad Dog took a peck from his smoke and said: "I'm thinking he did it – how else would he know so much – so I asked him sort of politely, 'Are any of the rest of us, you know, in danger of becoming a target?' He just smiled and said, 'No.'"

It was not like Sam Killinoy to speak frivolously on such somber subjects, no matter how many Buds he might've tossed back. He was an upright, proud, and civic-minded citizen who kept his mother's house shipshape and held strong and sometimes unbreakable opinions on various matters, but of all the many times I had sat with him in my cook's apron to blather about the Nuggets or the Rockies he'd never bounded off into the boondocks like this. I hadn't yet had the pleasure of meeting his sister, Phoebe, though I'd seen her from a distance as the crowds scattered in terror before her, and I'd come across her once asleep on a couch in the college library. She was a slight woman of about 50 years, and though she'd single-handedly disbanded the bird club and her fiancé had died under mysterious circumstances (the autopsy had revealed a heart attack), I doubted her culpability for many reasons.

And even though Sam had told the same story not only to Sheriff Conaghan, but to Hot Cop, Joni Behrends, whose mother lived across the street from Sam, I chalked this all up as more conjecture, rumor, and fanciful yarn. Yet Sam Killinoy's chilling tableau, independent of the means by which it had been proposed, suddenly made more sense than anything submitted so far. If the body couldn't be found, it almost had to be hidden. All of those who knew him, students, colleagues, and friends, insisted that even in the very unlikely event he couldn't face his responsibilities and had fled, he would've made contact. He wouldn't have missed his sister's birthday. He would've made an appearance at Christmas. He wouldn't have left his students hanging. He wouldn't have neglected his dying father. He would've never left this city or this earth voluntarily without a single word.

47.

A flicker of chaos

LESS THAN TWO WEEKS LATER, THURSDAY, MARCH 9, 2006, three days before Steve Haataja's comatose father would pass away, ranch hand Calvin "Slim" Buttes (who worked for Sandy Burd), a cranky old cowpoke with a bald white dome and a big twiggy black mustache, was down in a wash looking for a stray steer on May Queen Ranch, about three-quarters of a mile southeast of the Chadron State College campus. Buttes had parked his ATV and was now afoot.

The terrain in this area is a maze of rising hillocks and eroded ravines, punctuated by the occasional stand of elm, bur oak, cottonwood, and ponderosa. Snow filled the crags and clung in patches along the shady southern flanks of the hills. The crumbly, flinty earth was piled here and there with dormant anthills and the burrows of rodents. Rippled clouds like the expanding trails of moon rockets hazed the bright, faintly turquoise sky. The light of impending spring, sparkled with dust, has a certain clear and melancholy hardness about it.

Up ahead he saw carrion birds luffing aloft in ragged formation. He knew by their numbers that they were not attracted by a rabbit or a raccoon, more likely a deer or the calf he sought. Winter was fading. The days had just begun to warm and the process of decomposition had accelerated. Whatever these buzzards detected, he considered, might have only recently thawed.

He hiked down into the brushy hollow below. His eye caught a flicker of chaos. Streams of sunlight strained weakly through the branches. He was not aware of the outrageous proclamation of Sam Killinoy. All he knew was that the decadent heap sprawled below in the weeds looked more like a charcoal Gumby or a tackling dummy than any bovine form. It was also obvious to Buttes that whatever this was, it had been there a long time. Reluctantly, he drew closer. Like those who would come after him, it took a full minute to understand what he was seeing.

48.

Grapevine substation #1

JEANNE GOETZINGER CALLED ME ABOUT TWO HOURS later. I live three blocks east of her hotel, along the railroad tracks. I was looking out the window when she called. A train carrying scraggly ponderosas was creaking slowly east. Jeanne told me in a thrilled hush that she'd just received word that Professor Haataja had been found bound and dead in a ditch. That was all the information she had but she'd call me back when there was more.

Two hours later she called again. The body was burned and bound, not recognizable as a man or woman, she amended, and they were doing some tests to determine its identity.

"Who else could it be?" I asked.

49.

Twilight Zone shit

SHERIFF SHAWN CONAGHAN GOT THE CALL THAT THURS-day on his way back from a meeting 60 miles south in Alliance, a railroad city I call, for the entertainment of my son, "Alliance and Tigers and Bears, Oh My": 1065, dead body, about half a mile southeast of campus on the May Queen Ranch, Sandy Burd's place. He thought of course of the professor, who'd been missing now for more than three months, even if that area had supposedly been thoroughly searched. His thoughts were the same as mine: Who else could it be?

From the five boroughs of New York to the Howling Plains of Nowhere, Sheriff Conaghan has seen a lot in his day, hundreds of bodies and their misarranged parts, the muddle of minds and methods gone mad, the misery of passion overflowed, the love of excitement that runs roughshod over all reason, the lies that never stop being told. Having run the jail for over two decades, he'd witnessed the gamut of humanity, heard every story, prosecuted just about every crime. But he'd never seen a case like this one, nothing close.

1065s are not common dispatches in an agricultural county with a population of little more than 9,000. There are further code suffixes, J1, J2, and J3, to describe the circumstances, but none were given. There was a reason for this. Neither the identity of the body, nor the means by which it had ceased to function, could be ascertained.

It was a mild spring day, wind out of the southwest, those

furry, rocket-trail clouds crisscrossing the sky. Sheriff Conaghan drove south up Ridgeview Road, at the eastern edge of town, till it changed to dirt, followed the first 90 degree turn onto private property, the May Queen Ranch, and bounced up in the hills, the ridge ahead lined with burned ponderosas, lifeless as the shadows they cast, a black forest of the most literal kind.

Once you leave the unpaved ranch roads, and discounting the sidewalk that runs along the apron of the campus and the football practice and archery field, there is no thoroughfare to carry traffic into that area, only trails, washes, cuts, ravines. This area is negotiated by foot, horse, motorcycle, or ATV. Students occasionally roam up here for Mother Nature and beer. Their names and scholarly reflections are carved into the rocks: Lydia Jesus FUCK.

Conaghan slowed his white Ford F-150 pickup when he saw two emergency units, along with Burd's Yamaha Rhino, parked at the base of the ridge ahead. His deputy, Jarvis Wallage, was already there with Lieutenant Hickstein from the Chadron PD. Slim Buttes and Sandy Burd were also present, pale under their hats and blinking in the frosty slants of sunlight. Deputy Jarvis had been the first to respond to the call.

"Where's the body?" said Conaghan, making his way through the trees, looking around, seeing nothing, thinking it might've been a mistake or that the body was buried or had been moved.

Jarvis pointed.

Conaghan still didn't see it. He moved closer. "Holy shit," were his first words, followed by a more reflective, "Holy shit."

On first glance he thought the body looked more like a charred log tied to a tree. You might've walked right by it, he told me, if you hadn't been paying close attention.

Sheriff Conaghan couldn't tell at first if the black, ransacked mass straining against the slackness of its ligatures was badly decomposed or badly burned. As he drew closer it became clear that the body was severely burned. In his words, "99.9% burned."

Burned to bone and black as the end of time. What little uncon-
sumed flesh remained, such as the right calf and the back of
the right arm, had "leathered" and was marbled with red and
purulent streaks of yellow. The corpse was facedown, ankles
crossed, arms bowed as if embracing a lover or protecting a com-
rade from a grenade explosion. The round, wire-rimmed glasses
had been knocked askew but were still hanging from one ear,
lenses intact. Except for the smoked and ripped hiking boots,
socks, and a patch of blue jean, all clothing was gone. He was
more burned front side than back so after they unbound the body
from the tree and placed it on the pink rubber tarp it looked
more like a black mummy exhumed from the depths of an Egypt-
ian sarcophagus. Conaghan thought the cadaver looked like
something from a war photo, a napalm victim. A grotesque sculp-
ture of perpetual anguish. The left hand was so thoroughly
burned that it was free of flesh and cartilage and some of the bone
had gone to ash.

"You couldn't tell if it was a man or a woman," Conaghan
recalled. "Though we were pretty sure who it was. I was leaning
down there getting a closer look when a mouse blew out of the
chest. I said: 'Oh shit.'"

State Patrol was notified. The area was taped off. SHERIFF
LINE DO NOT CROSS. Deputy Sheriff Jarvis Wallage took a few
dozen photographs. The Mobile Forensics team was called from
Scottsbluff, two hours away. The officers started looking from
different angles, trying to figure out what might have happened.
Fresh talent kept arriving, Drinkwalter and Fitzgerald from
State Patrol, County Attorney/Coroner Vance Haug, and Officer
Joni Behrends, who would not sleep that night for the image of
the mouse infestation in the cadaver's chest.

"We all thought at first that it was a suicide," the sheriff told
me, "but the ankles were bound." Although the body was bound
by its midsection to a tree, the hands and arms were free. His
body at some point had apparently fallen forward into his campfire. There was an empty bottle of peppermint schnapps on the

ground, an unopened bottle of water, a scattering of charcoal briquettes, and a few other indeterminable items, melted or incinerated. There were a number of highly unusual features.

"You read about things like this, of course," Sheriff Conaghan said. "You're trained for it. But I had no experience. The upper body burned to bone and the tree that he was tied to not burned? The area all around him barely burned? How does that happen? It was *Twilight Zone* shit. And I didn't have the staff or time to deal with it. I got prisoners, paperwork. I was up to my ass in alligators. So I turned the case over on the spot to State Patrol. Matt Fitzgerald became the lead investigator."

Mobile Forensics arrived.

The body was ID'd from the serial number on the orthopedic implant.

No surprise.

50.
Circus time

NO ONE WAS PREPARED FOR THE NEWS OF THE DISCOVery of Steve Haataja or the way it would flood and capsize our quiet little town. Within hours of the announcement, an ABC news team appeared, followed quickly by 20 other out-of-town teams. Law enforcement of every star and stripe converged. The streets and bars filled. The courthouse overflowed. A legion of blathering, blundering international TV-trained Internet sleuths joined the fray. Fevered citizens in damp drawers flocked to the hills to see if they could locate the site where the professor had been found. Because there was so little information released, bloggers and other tattlers and fishwives, many samurai in the art of gossip, felt duty bound to manufacture their own facts. The hum and throng from these discussions rose to frenzy. The explosion of misinformation, consternation, shock, bewildered exhilaration, and whimsical conjecture ran panting circles around any circus or rodeo that might've rolled unannounced into town. The value of an innocent life was temporarily lost in the feast upon its misfortune. For the first time since Cristina and I had moved here six years before, we began to lock our doors.

From *The Chadron Record*:

> "It's just like somebody dropped a corpse out of the clear, blue sky," said Dawes County public defender Paul Wess. "Everybody imagined that when they found him it would clearly be a suicide or an accident." Wess said that violent assaults are rare in Chadron. "The worst case of violence we get around here is if somebody gets hit by a poolstick."

Denise Fleming, who lives in Chadron, said that some are rattled by the discovery and that during a church meeting recently some worried a serial killer might be on the loose.

Sheila Speaker of Rapid City, S.D., Steven's sister, said the family knows "practically nothing (about Haataja's death) and it's frustrating for the family." The family doesn't know how Haataja got from his home in Chadron to the place where his body was found. "I was hoping to hear something today but I didn't," Speaker said Monday. "I know now that he's not missing but... there's still a lot of questions that haven't been answered yet."

51.

The bubble-gum barber

8:46 A.M. Caller on the 900 block of Parry Drive advised a squirrel has climbed down her chimney and is now in the fireplace looking at her through the glass door, chirping at her.

SATURDAY MORNING, NINE DAYS AFTER HAATAJA WAS found, March 18, while Cristina slept, Tom and I went to Daylight Donuts, out on the highway (Third Street through town), for two bear claws and a "Daylight glazed" for Tom. Everywhere you went, the talk was of Haataja. The Daylight was a hive of buzzing customers. A popular shop, this Daylight franchise, even without a human sacrifice, was often completely out of donuts by nine. Today all that was left at 8:30 a.m. were the maple bars with cream filling, some lemon-filled, and two plain cakes. Tom would eat no other donut but glazed. And the glazed they fried over at Safeway he called "fakeful." Do you know what *fakeful* means? It means "yucky." They were heavy donuts over at Safeway, sinkers in the true sense of the word, even if they fried them "healthy" in pure canola oil.

"Well, buddy, no glazed," I said. "How about a cupcake at the bakery?"

Tom agreed to a cupcake at Cakes and Etc., the bakery over by Safeway. He wouldn't eat my cupcakes and didn't like Safeway's cupcakes either, even if they were made in a factory and frozen carefully and delivered by truck twice a week.

After his cupcake Tom decided he wanted to get his hair cut.

"Isn't it a little early to get your hair cut, Tom? I mean your follicles aren't even awake yet."

He grinned at me, slung his arm around my waist, and we wandered over to the shop on Main Street, the Bubble-Gum

Barber, as Tom has christened the place. One time we went up the street to the Ship Shape Shop, and Herb, the barber-proprietor there, had no candy, which was unforgivable in Tom's eyes. Herb seemed chagrined and promised to have candy the next time. As far as Tom was concerned there would be no next time. Roger, the Bubble-Gum Barber, is always tickled to hear this story and you'll never see his fishbowls of treats for the kiddies running low.

Roger's shop is that one from your youth with the combs in alcohol and weird Persian neck powders and occult astringents and the wooden church pew to wait on and the big bubble-gum machine that sends your gumball down a spiral chute to clank against the metal door. When we entered there was an Indian kid sitting in the chair, head down as Roger trimmed his bangs, and two big fellows sitting on the bench, one who wore suspenders, the other with blue jowls and a sharp pale nose. The pew was strewn with newspapers and magazines. There are no naked girl magazines here. If you want titty mags you have to go north to the place next to the pawnshop.

"If it isn't Simon and Simon," Roger greeted us. There was a television close to the ceiling playing the Weather Channel. It looked like it might be cool for the next week or two. Soon there would be Cubs games on that television. Roger was a big Cubs fan and tried to get to Wrigley at least twice a year to catch a game. "What's kickin' chicken?" he said to me.

"Well, the donut shop is out of glazed," I replied.

"Yeah," said Tom indignantly.

"All they have left is maple bars," I said.

Roger shook his head. "Holy Cats," he said.

Tom perched himself between the two men on the pew, picked up a newspaper and feigned to read it.

"What is your name, young man?" enquired the large man in the suspenders, who also wore tan Dickies on his lower half and crusty rubber boots and had ears hairier than a troll.

Tom looked up. "They call me Tommy because I'm a beautiful boy and sometimes I wear hats."

Everyone laughed.

"You solved the case yet?" Roger asked me.

"Where were you the night of December 4, 2006?" I said.

"Why, I don't recall."

The man in the suspenders said, "It sure looks like a homicide."

"How can you tell?" said Roger, who squinted as he snipped, wearing that bemused expression of concentration that you want for your barber when he is in possession of moving scissor blades. Like any good barber, Roger was strong on opinion, or at least whatever kept the conversation going. I often suspected him of changing positions just to stir the pot. "They didn't release any details from the autopsy report."

"They have to do that in case someone comes forward to confess," Blue Jowls explained. I didn't know either of the two men, but I guessed that Suspenders (by his rubber boots) had spent his life in ranching and Blue Jowls (by his insight into the goings on at the courthouse) had served in some civil or governmental capacity. "Well, they could give us a few details," Roger said.

"They don't have the toxicology report back yet," Suspenders said. "They usually send the organs to North Platte."

"Heard he was tortured," said Blue Jowls.

"Heard he was wrapped in barbed wire," Roger added.

"Ended up with the wrong people it looks to me," said Suspenders, leaning forward for a moment as if his garter had bunched. "Said he was gay."

"What I heard too," Roger said.

Blue Jowls turned to me. "You ever see him?"

"A few times," I said. "Very nice guy. Brilliant mind."

"Math nerd."

"Hmmm."

"He never came in here," said Roger.

"He was bald," I said. "Mostly."

"Half my clients are bald, mostly," said Roger, who was bald, too, mostly.

"That Haug is a moe-ron," Suspenders announced. He referred to our county attorney, called a district attorney in some places, a moe-ron or a pinhead (as the sheriff preferred) in others. I hadn't met Vance Haug (pronounced Howg) yet myself. I'd see him around town, riding his Kawasaki KLR650, and I'd see him at Wrecker's having dinner with his family, and I'd see him at the public swimming pool sprawled skinny and pale out on the cement in his black-and-white swimming trunks, as he watched his son, Zach, who was enrolled in the same kindergarten class as my son. He came in to eat at the Olde Main as well. An avid fisherman, a Colorado native, he seemed a nice enough person, not a pinhead or a moe-ron, a guy just doing his job. No one expected him to be Vincent Bugliosi. You don't get that kind of talent as a rule this far out in the sticks.

"I don't know about that," replied Roger, who was now vacuuming the Indian boy's neck.

"That press release was a nightmare," said Suspenders. "Got everyone in a panic. Got everyone thinking there's a three-headed monster loose in the hills."

"Got everyone in a panic," said Blue Jowls. "Once you do that you can spend the county's money."

"Probably was a homicide, though," said Roger. "I'll put my money there."

There happened to be a copy of this week's *Chadron Record*, still opened to the press release, which read in part: "Due to unusual circumstances and the condition in which the body was found, law enforcement is treating this case with an abundance of caution and is investigating it as a homicide."

The Indian boy, who hadn't said a word the whole time and managed to avoid all eye contact, stood and paid Roger. "Thank ye kindly," said Roger, a big proponent of the existence of our town being dependent on the vast federal sums that poured into the reservation just a few miles north. Roger treated all his Native customers with the utmost respect, thereby insuring his future. The bell on the door jingled. I thought one of the men might be next but they'd only come in to chew the fat. Roger set a booster seat in his chrome and vinyl chair and Tom hopped happily aboard. "What are we doing today?" he asked me.

"Mohawk, green stripes," I said. "The usual."

Roger nodded and flashed his scissors through the air.

I opened up *The Chadron Record* and shuffled back to the obits:

Steve was born July 20, 1960 in Minneapolis, Minn., the son of Esaja and Doris (Miner) Haataja. He lived in Bloomington until the summer of 1970 when his parents purchased Rim Rock Lodge in Spearfish Canyon in South Dakota.

Steve graduated from Spearfish High School in 1978. In high school he won the West River Math contest three years in a row. During this time he also became an avid chess player, competing in tournaments and at one point becoming one of the top ranked chess players in South Dakota.

He attended Black Hills State College, graduating *Summa Cum Laude* with a bachelor of science in 1985. Mathematics was his major, but he also had minors in theater, psychology, and political science. He participated in many theatrical productions while at Black Hills State.

In the fall of 1985, Steve attended graduate school at the University of Nebraska-Lincoln, where he received his master of science in mathematics in 1987. He was a mathematics professor for two years at Augustana College in Sioux Falls and worked for many years at Gateway Inc. While employed there he became an A+ service technician and a Microsoft Windows 95 certified technician.

In 2000, Steve returned to the University of Nebraska-Lincoln to obtain his PhD, graduating on Aug. 12, 2006. His dissertation was on "Amalgamation of Inverse Semigroups and Operator Algebras." He began teaching as a professor at Chadron State College in Nebraska in the fall of 2006.

Steve was sociable and made lasting friendships. He was a member of the Mathematical Association of America, the U.S. Chess Federation, and the Chadron Community Chorus. Playing the piano, reading, walking, and watching baseball games were some of his hobbies. Like his mother and nephew Zach, he was a huge fan of the Minnesota Twins. He was excited about the good football season the Chadron Eagles had. He especially enjoyed spending time in the Black Hills and talking on the phone with family and friends.

Roger spun Tom around in the chair so he could see himself in the mirror. Tom smiled. "Lookin' good there, partner," Roger said, handing over the most important part of the contract, the two pieces of bubble gum, one of which was promptly unwrapped and installed between Tom's lips.

52.

Everyone (except Hazel Devine) is a suspect

THE RUMOR MILL, A CHROMIUM-DIPPED, TRIPLE-DECKED, steam-powered flibbertigibbet with wrought iron shafts, tied-down escape valves, and overstoked boilers, continued to chug out the rumors. Haataja had been killed by aliens, rednecks, drifters, Indians. He'd become the sacrifice in a satanic ritual. He'd been killed by a lover, a drug dealer, a pimp, a student. He'd been picked up by a stranger, offed by a bookie or an academic rival. He'd angered someone in a bar. He'd fallen into the arms of "Black Betty," in whose amorous embrace my neighbor, Lord Byron, had succumbed.

It was said that Haataja was bound in barbed wire, that he was wrapped with duct tape to a fence, that he was sitting in a lawn chair, an armchair, a chaise longue, a davenport with his legs crossed, that he was lying in a ditch with his wrists and ankles bound or tied to a tree like Captain Cook among the Aborigines. Because of the wildfires that had torn through the area the previous summer, many noted that his blackened body would've been perfectly camouflaged, the deliberate design of an artful killer.

Since there was no official account, and presiding law enforcement made the Soviets at the height of the Cold War look like a herd of harbor seals during mating season, you could've said whatever you liked and entered it in the contest, painted your own macabre portrait, set him at a piano with a burning drink or dressed him as Jean Cocteau in coat and tails, cobbled it together with Bohemian fairy tales, and no one could've disputed it. Super-secret-James-Bond-if-I-tellya-I-gotta-killya culture gave no indication of relenting. The late-arriving investigators understandably refused to comment on any aspect of the case, including about whether the professor's body was decomposed, or, worse, if it might have been moved to where it was discovered, a prospect that invited a dizzying set of deviously unsettling possibilities.

The two essential communication networks in the Haataja case, one controlled by grapevine substation and composed of hearsay, rumor, barber-shop gossip, invention, hysteria, half-baked clues, and other Misty Boat Rides into Whimsy and Willful Misconception, and the other supposedly grounded in objective fact and proceeding through empirical method, worked independently, even competitively, one would hope divergently, but they were pretty much on the same trail, the one, in so many words, that led nowhere.

That he was burned was the most troubling aspect for most. The idea he'd torched himself didn't make sense. The idea that someone else had torched him was even harder to accept. It was therefore proposed that he might've been killed in another fashion, that he was the victim of a botched robbery attempt, random violence, an ill-fated liaison, that the killer was only trying to cover his tracks, that the body had been moved. Perhaps Steve had been accidentally burned, by dry lightning, a meteor, a space ray, or some ninth century dragon escaped from the literature department.

Spontaneous combustion was also proposed. Spontaneous combustion would've explained at least the burning and possibly why the ground around him and the tree to which he was tied had not been appreciably burned. Unfortunately, spontaneous combustion only occurs in speculative fiction. The human body contains no substances that ignite spontaneously. Neither does human flesh contain any oxidizing agents. Spontaneous combustion believers insist on some unidentifiable internal source

of combustion, some pyrotechnical virus or tiny maniacal inhab-
itant of the pancreas with a Bic lighter, but all factual accounts
show that for a human body to burn an external source of ignition
is required.

If this were a trial by media, the police would've immediately turned all their attention to hate criminals (ignoring the
vast populace of love criminals entirely). Because the professor
was assumed by some to be homosexual, many amateur crimin-
ologists, including a number of bloggers, went after the Chadron
Police Force hammer and tongs. They were "rubes," "apple-
knockers," and "jerk-off pigs." According to the objective and
careful observation of these bloggers, Haataja had been "missing
for eight months," had been "gagged," and was "foreign." The
crime would never be solved because Chadron was a "shithole
town" in the "Bible Belt" where the "message to the queers"
was "leave, stay in the closet, or die." The only way to solve this
case, many of the fishwives thought, was to pass a federal Hate
Crimes Law and call in the FBI.

From a distance, perhaps from the cozy living room of a
trembling urbanite who'd never set foot in the "Bible Belt"
(which is about 700 miles from here) it might've seemed a tenable
position. We were a community of stiff-necked agricultural
clods, with pigs dozing in the shade of pro-life billboards and
more churches than bars and droves of inbreeds draped in
sheets chasing off homos and Democrats and lynching darkies
by the dozens by bonfire at midnight. We all wore dirty Wranglers,
chewed on weeds and Copenhagen, and branded queers when
we ran out of cows. We were perplexed as to how this fella ended
up all roasted so close to our shithole town, but we'd probably
been at a rodeo or a hoedown, and since we didn't have no use for
mathee-matics anyways it was no great loss. We were no different value-wise than our hayseed neighbors in Laramie, Wyoming,
where Matthew Shepard had been robbed, beaten, and tortured to death for being gay 10 years earlier. And if it pleases you
to draw these conclusions, if you enjoy this sort of whipped-up,

bigoted, baseless, cartoon frenzy of a no-different breed of rotten bone-sucking hatred than the one you are making accusations about, then don't ask me why there's always a war.

But there are many gay men with "effeminate mannerisms" in this college town full of artists and bohemians, a Hindu newspaper editor, a New York sheriff, a longhaired public defender, a surf-bum philosophy professor, a retired-NASA-engineer radio station owner, and a Cowboy-Indian-Biker-Police-Gay bar, a town where an iconoclast like myself finds it easy to move about. If someone had so despised the affectations or the supposed orientation of this private, professional man newly arrived (is this what you mean by "foreign"?) in our town, why was Steven Haataja the only one singled out?

Unless of course it was someone new in town himself, a lusty old soul, bold of appetite, a John Wayne cutout, a *chingon* with a pickup truck bannered with deadly proclamations, a man with experience, pride, and an expertise in all aspects of killing, a "bad-tempered," reckless man whose lifelong professional interest and even his extracurricular activities tended to gravitate toward death and calamity. A man who'd led searches, especially into the hills south of campus, where he suggested from the beginning Haataja might be found, even if he believed that Haataja wasn't capable of going there. Someone with a sharp self-interest and a habitual disregard for consequences. A man who, because he wanted to be the next police chief, needed a way to ingratiate himself to the town and demonstrate his superior criminological talents. Except to lead a major investigation, you need a major crime.

One day I confided to Sheriff Conaghan my suspicions about Loren Zimmerman, who courted other men's wives and laughed about shooting and killing people and who was the only person I could think of in town with the temperament and expertise to do what had been done to Haataja. Call me vengeful or jealous, but Conaghan surprised me by agreeing: "He was my number one suspect, too," he said.

I had to ask Cristina if while she was in Zimmerman's employment had she ever seen anything unusual in his house?

Like what?

A spool of baling wire? A case of peppermint schnapps? Accelerant? Burn photos? Shrunken heads? A charred copy of *Principia Mathematica*?

53.
Truce

1:06 P.M. Caller from the 400 block of West Second St. advised that she came home for lunch and had noticed that someone has put a tiki light in her front yard by her trees. Caller stated that they are afraid to move it and is requesting an officer.

IN THE BEGINNING TOM WAS THE GREATEST BENEFI-ciary of our matrimonial cease-fire. Rocking in his chair or scribing on his dry-erase board, he admired with one wary eye the unnaturally tranquil landscape, stating regularly his hope that we wouldn't fight anymore. He remembered all the fights, the one when Momma balled up her glasses and threw them across the room, the one where I broke the CD in half, the one where I sprayed his momma's PJs with Baileys, the one where she walked out and drove away after I'd called her blackhearted and we tried to find her for hours hoping she hadn't gone off a cliff or smashed into a tree, the one where we slapped each other like two Hungarian cab drivers, the one where I stomped out and didn't come back until the next morning.

I told him that married people fought sometimes because people were weak and they fought also in the interest of what they thought was right and what they thought was best for their children. Women and men were opposed in nature like cats and dogs, or like hot and cold air that when mixed made storms. It wouldn't be long, I told him, until he came across that passage in the Bible about the enmity between the sexes, which came after Adam and Eve disobeyed God and moved from the forest into a condominium in the Big Apple. I told him that because we loved him we were going to find a way to get along. I told him that we were going to be a good Mom and Dad from now on.

The war had subsided, but there was a lot of wreckage to

clean up, bridges to rebuild, wounds to be dressed, communication lines in need of repair. Cristina was also still an unhappy person in my eyes, little changed essentially from the first days of her arrival upon the golden shores of her three big dreams. The only time she ever truly glowed and smiled and laughed and her eyes sparkled, besides a shopping or gambling trip, was when she was on the phone to her family in Mexico. She would buy the five-dollar international phone cards and use up a whole card in one call. Occasionally I also talked to her parents, which was awkward since no one in her family spoke English and I had trouble on the phone with Spanish speakers, but I could usually get through identifying key words and putting them into normal phone-dialogue context (So, how are you? How is your health? Is the boy doing well? Are you working on a book?).

Once when Cristina had stepped out of the room I was emboldened to ask her mother, "*Porque es tan infeliz tu hija, es mi culpa?*" Why is your daughter so unhappy? Is it my fault?

"No, no." Her mother, a broad warm woman, laughed. "She is happy with you. She is the happiest she has ever been. She just worries. She has always been like that. Her father is like that too."

54.
Difficult air

IN MID-APRIL, A WARM, DRY DAY, WIND OUT OF THE SOUTH, my son and I went off in my hail-pocked wreck of a '93 Subaru to have a look at the tangled gully where Steve Haataja was found. Ridgeview Road turns to dirt just past 10th Street and we followed it until we came to a wooden sign that reads "May Queen Ranch," Sandy Burd's property that overlooks the Chadron State College campus, most of the town, and South Dakota on a clear day. The entire ranch is surrounded by barbed wire fence, some of it burned and not yet repaired. The fence that runs the length of the entrance side is not only intact but electrified and tight, and the only place to pass here, unless you climb or crawl through the fence, is through the gates under the sign. The dirt road continues from there past a small trailer owned by Sandy Burd. I didn't know who lived in this trailer for a long time, but I assumed because it was next to a large corral that the occupant was associated somehow with the ranch. I presumed that Slim Buttes or another cowhand lived here. Ranch employees often live on the ranches where they are employed; few others would choose to live right next to a corral. The dirt road that passes this trailer, which sits at the entrance like a tollbooth with full view of all those who come and go, ends a quarter mile or so at Sandy's two-level house, its second floor encircled by a redwood deck. Sandy, I'm told, was once an executive in a development company that built the Staples Center in L.A. and two Las Vegas megaresorts, the MGM Grand and the Stratosphere, though he doesn't like to talk about it. Con Marshall, who's been the information director at Chadron State College for close to 40 years, thought that Burd's accomplishments warranted a human-interest piece in the school paper, *The Eagle*, but Burd would not participate. Neither would he concede to an interview with George Ledbetter for *The Chadron Record*.

I'd never met Sandy Burd, but I knew his brother Brown, a surveyor, and I was acquainted with another Burd brother, Collin, who had a reputation as a roaring drunk and was also a surveyor. Although I'd never talked to Collin, I had seen him on several occasions swiggered off his *pons Varolii* at the Red Zone, which is just across the street from where he lived, four buildings south of Haataja's apartment, on Bordeaux.

Tom and I drove past the trailer onto the Burd ranch. Along the dusty, bumpy dirt road about halfway along to Sandy's house, we came upon a man pitching hay into the back of a pickup truck. He was a very stiff chap with a Wild Bill Hickok mustache, sunburned neck, and crooked spine, the type that would send Jeanne into ecstasy. I stopped the car, rolled down my window, and said hello. He lowered his fork, tipped up the brim of his black cowboy hat, and sauntered over. I introduced myself and my son.

"I'm Slim Buttes," he said.

"I've heard of you," I said.

"Oh, you have," he said

"You're the one who found Haataja."

His expression soured and he looked away.

I asked him if he might tell me where to find his boss, Mr. Sandy Burd.

"Just saw him go by on his Rhino," he replied. "Might be home by now. Anything I can help you with?"

"I wanted to look at the site where Haataja was found. I'm writing a book," I said.

He scowled. "What for?"

"Well, it's an interesting case."

"You keep my name the fuck out of it."

Now Slim was stalking away, his body contracted to the left, stiff as a stereotype or a man made of wire, the pitchfork on his shoulder pointed at the sky.

"I know it must have been hard," I called to him, "finding the body."

"It wasn't hard," he replied, turning back once more with a sneer. "I'm just tired of people asking me what I think."

We left him with a "thanks" and drove the rest of the way to Sandy Burd's house, and though there were a number of vehicles outside parked under the shade of the deck, including Sandy's Yamaha Rhino, no one answered the door.

The next day we went over again and again no one answered the door.

A few days later Dawes County Sheriff Shawn Conaghan showed me on a map where Haataja had been found, then drove me up the road to Sandy Burd's place, and pointed down into the culvert where the deed had been done. It was possible but not practical to drive down there if you had a four-wheel drive unit. The sheriff, who had a four-wheel drive unit, chose not to. He said he was good friends with Sandy Burd and would get me permission to walk on Burd's property if I liked. I thought I would eventually, I said, but privately I didn't want to take the risk of having him say no. I wanted to have at least one good look at the site before putting everyone on alert. Sheriff Conaghan drove me back down into town, dropped me off at the courthouse, and wished me luck.

The next day, Tom and I decided to walk from CSC trying to retrace Haataja's steps. I surmised that his possible route that night would have begun at Math and Science so I parked in the lot and we crossed the football field and hiked up the only marked trail. If Haataja, who had no car and whose bicycle was behind his couch, walked from campus, this had to be the route, the Long Way Around, he would have taken, I kept insisting to myself.

Our dusty golden retriever trotted up ahead, chasing

grasshoppers and snacking on "bean poop," as my son has labeled the wildlife scat along the way. There was a sign up ahead along the steep, narrow, and sinuous trail: DANGER FALLING TREES KEEP OUT. The fire was so hot in this area that telephone poles burned to stumps and the scorched ponderosas are snapped in half or lying on their sides, their muddy roots in the air.

My tireless son, even though he didn't know where he was going, took the lead as always and I had to direct him and point. Today Tom carried with him an old metal toy police helicopter. He marched ahead, unafraid of anything that might be lying in wait: coyotes, snakes, strangers in black hats, surly ranch hands, old age, prairie dragons, or falling trees.

"I'm so hungry I could eat the whole earth," he said, toeing a stinkbug struggling through the dust.

"Just don't eat that stinkbug."

"That's a girl stinkbug."

"How can you tell?"

"It has a long head."

"When we get back, we'll have lunch. What do you want?"

"Old MacDonald's."

"We went to McDonald's yesterday. You can't eat that stuff every day. It isn't good for your heart."

"I don't have a heart," he replied. "I have a square."

"Why do you have a square?"

"Girls have hearts," he said, "boys have squares."

"It isn't good for your square then."

"OK, french toast," he said, with a sigh. "And orange juice."

We made our way up through the waving sunflowers, the snowberry, buffalo grass, and the dead, falling black trees ("widowmakers" as they are sometimes called, for their tendency to break and fall without warning). To the undiscriminating eye all this prairie grass looks the same, swaying golden all about like the underwater hair of Shelley Winters in *Night of the Hunter*, but look more closely and you'll see dozens of varieties: thread leaf sage, little bluestem, blue grama, needle and thread. The terrible grass fires had burned much of this area and we found several easy places where the fences were down to cross on to Sandy Burd's property. Tom and I surprised five mule deer that bounced away like spring toys without looking back. This was the herd of five. There were two other regular herds in this area, their numbers fluctuating from season to season, but at present there was also a herd of seven, another of 13. Tom was delighted. Off to the east was the water tower written with the name of the town, its "C" a crescent moon. At the top of the crumbling limestone bluff I could see Sandy Burd's house.

We now stood at the highest point in these hills, much higher than C-Hill behind us. Down below to the left was the trailer and the large corral. From this vantage point I saw that the only way Haataja could get to where he was found that night, unless he walked all the way up the road that led to Sandy Burd's house, was to cross the large corral that led to a trail that ran along the electrified fence. I understood that the trailer had been occupied on December 4, 2006, but at that point I had not yet learned who the occupant was. Taking into account Steve's reticent and cautious nature, I doubted very strongly that he would've hiked passed that trailer and gone up the winding, private dirt road that leads to Sandy Burd's house. I doubted even more strongly that he would've tried to climb or squeeze through the wires of that electric fence. To walk where he ended up he would've also had to cross the large corral adjacent to the trailer, facing not only the possibility of livestock, but the certainty of their excrement.

If Haataja had gone the way Tom and I had just come, the Long Way Around, sacrificing utility for stealth, it seemed likely that he'd traveled alone. If he'd gone past the occupied trailer, and up the road toward the Burd house, it supported the possibility that he'd had an escort who knew the area and would not arouse suspicion or draw attention. With someone driving him up the road he could've also avoided the corral. Perhaps Haataja was an unwilling (or unconscious) passenger in that person's vehicle. Of the many questions I had at this point, determining Haataja's route that night was the most important.

As I stood looking down on Burd's ranch I thought about Haataja taking this route that Tom and I just walked, and how it was just too long, more than a mile, rough, and roundabout for him to navigate on such a cold and inhospitable night. Nevertheless we pressed eastward, staying as best as we could out of view of Sandy's place.

About a quarter of a mile down a steep embankment from the main road we arrived at the hollow where Professor Haataja had spent the majority of a winter. There were a few trees, elms and cottonwoods, and I couldn't think of one reason he'd set up camp in a thicket of buffaloberry, whose thorny treelike shrubs grew no more than eight feet high at any point. This area, like much of Burd's land, had been spared the fire. It was more "secluded" than I expected, walled in, the ground fertile and damp enough that I suspected we were standing at the bottom of an old dried-up pond. In spite of the brush and trees, the wind through the western aperture rushed down upon us.

I couldn't picture Haataja hiking all the way out here by himself, whether he came up the dirt road or took the Long Way Around, at midnight, in pitch darkness, onto private property, the air temperature approaching zero, carrying charcoal, accelerant, booze, and who knows what else, then starting a campfire and tying himself to a tree.

Then again, the bottle of schnapps that he'd bought at the Highway Express around 10 p.m. of his last day among the living indicated that he'd very probably been drinking that night. I've performed some amazingly regrettable feats under the influence, including suicide attempts. Not that I'm strong in math, but there are certain reliable time-tested formulae: Alcohol plus X equals No Why. He was also of Finnish descent. I'm told depression is the national disease of Finland.

This is just a place, I reminded myself, but I couldn't resist a wave of grief, a pang of mortal awe. I knelt for a moment. A grasshopper on wings clattered clumsily past. A nervous white bird, the type you often see down along the railroad tracks or crushed out on the highway, flashed past and gave out a warning scream.

Tom did not know why we were here. I didn't try to explain. "The air smells very *difficult* here," he said.

55.

The exhumation party

ONE FRIDAY NIGHT AFTER MY AND TOM'S EXCURSION
to the Burd property, the whole family went as usual to the Olde
Main. Among others at the President's Table were Deane, Kathy
Bahr, JW, and her husband from Mexico City. Abner Violette
ambled up grinning with a pitcher of beer in his fist. I hadn't seen
him since the time we'd gone looking for electromagnetic evidence of Haataja a few months before. He was just back from Huntsville, he said, and though he'd been unable to sell either of his
homes there (the real estate market was down in Alabama in
2007), he'd found an old run-down house in Chadron, finally, on
Bordeaux Street, only four buildings up from where Professor
Haataja had lived.

"Which one is it?" I said, trying to picture that block, which
was mostly commercial property.

"It's Collin Burd's old place," he said, "right across from the
Red Zone."

"Collin Burd?" Deane said. "Where'd that old barfly run
off to?"

"East," said Jeanne, mysteriously, who had appeared with
a tray of drinks. She set down a glass of Cabernet in front of me
and a Windsor and soda (no ice) for Cristina.

"East where?" I said.

"That's as much as we know," Jeanne said, doing hyperbolic
fortuneteller calisthenics with her eyebrows. "The secret cannot be divulged. Supposedly it's for his alcoholism. His family's

afraid he's going to drink himself to death so they sent him away, and they can't say where."

"I remember when Collin bought that house a few years ago," said Jana Binger, who was teaching second grade in Hay Springs and hoping to move to Chadron soon. "He was happy because he could walk home from the bar – he didn't have far to go."

"Do you know where he went?"

"I don't," she said. "He never even told me. He's definitely been different the last few months."

There were sundry recollections of Collin's prodigious drinking achievements, hard falls, foolhardiness hitting on the college chicks (and apparently never having any success for no one could ever recall him taking one home), losing his job for a time as the county surveyor, raging and staggering about like a potbellied bullfighter amid traffic as he tried to negotiate the 20 feet home from the Red Zone. The Red Zone was my least favorite bar in town, a dingy Devonian dungeon with mulchy, beer-sodden floors, where through the loathly murk you might see lobe-finned fish with vestigial legs crawling ashore for the first time. Popular among college students, the Red Zone had been repeatedly cited for serving minors. It was the sort of place an old boozer might go trolling. Jana Binger remembered one night there buying Collin a drink, handing it to him, and watching it slip through his fingers and crash to the floor.

Lisa Aschwege, a ghost-hunting buddy of Violette's and the account executive at KCSR, the radio station located on the same street between Collin and Haataja's homes, was convinced that Collin had killed Steve Haataja. She said that Collin was a mean drunk, that he and Steve had probably been together that night, how else would Haataja have ended up on Collin's brother's land? Collin owned a pickup truck so he could have driven him there. He'd taken off during that time, she said, just packed up his motorcycle and rode it east – it seemed odd to her because it was too cold to ride a motorcycle at that time. Missouri was where she thought he went. Couple weeks later he came back, sold the house with the basement still full of beer cans and dog crap, and moved, lock, stock, and barrel. I wondered where his pickup truck was?

Jeanne, recalling the time that a drunken Collin had knocked someone's tooth out, thought that Collin had probably killed Steve Haataja too. I had no trouble finding others with the same conviction. Some remembered Collin as a bully. Violette said there was no doubt there had been violence in that house. There were many reports of vehement late-night arguments while Collin was living there, and Violette said there were holes kicked in the walls everywhere and he'd found what he thought was drug paraphernalia and that nervous men kept coming to the door, promptly leaving after learning Collin no longer lived there. And though Violette was the only one who thought Collin was a nice fellow, he hadn't seen him yet when he wasn't fried to the hat. It was a strange old house, he added, built in the late 1800s. A number of tenants and families had lived there over the years, among them Doctor Milton Berlin McDowell, a prominent surgeon who sawed off diabetic limbs and dispensed laudanum and peppermint placebos on the main floor in the early third of the 20th century. The house was full of quirks, crawl spaces, funky closets, sealed-off vaults and chambers. The place teemed with spirits, naturally. Violette had contacted three of them so far, including the surgeon. Much of the dirt in the backyard was loose, he told us, as if someone had recently filled it in, perhaps buried something. Curious, Abner had begun digging into the disturbed area until he'd found some large animal bones, which he'd shown around to a few people who thought they were probably deer or cow bones. "And there's a crawl space in the basement, too, with a panel over it fastened down with about 30 screws," he said.

"The basement?" I said, recalling with a tingle the original premonition of Kat the Swami Queen.

"That's too many screws to simply hold down a panel," Violette said, "and I've been meaning to pry the thing up and see what's inside." He took a gulp of beer, hiked his brows, and said with that lopsided grin of his, "Who knows, might be a body in there."

"I knew it," said Lisa.

"Let's open it," said Deane.

"Oh, an exhumation party," said Kathy dryly, who despite her detachment and high-grade literary reputation ate up this sort of stuff.

Cristina was having an in-depth conversation *en español* with her friend JW. A social transformation and restoration of "identity" came about whenever she got to speak her native tongue with someone fluent, which made me feel as if we must soon return to Mexico or perhaps Peru or L.A. where she could be a talented bilingual dentist. Tom was off exploring (I saw him once down in the kitchen hustling french fries, and once again "helping" Jeanne behind the bar) and Cristina had no desire to see moldering cadavers in the sealed chambers of haunted houses, so I said we wouldn't be long and not to worry.

Violette, Lisa, Deane, Kathy, and I left our drinks on the table and stepped out the east door into the spring night.

The wind from the south was sharp. We zipped our coats to our chins. Two blocks later we were there. Across the street from Violette's house, the Red Zone was booming with college kids and gyrating humpty-backed swamp varmints. Violette fished for a key. His two-story house with its dirty gingerbread shingles and sagging wraparound porch was a real fixer-upper, its paint peeling, its trees overgrown and tangled into the power lines, and I wondered if the stairs wouldn't give as we climbed them.

"First thing I do is put in a new porch," Violette said, working open the front door. "Then windows, then a new roof, then paint. About $30,000 worth of renovations if I do it myself. Roof leaks a little but only in one upstairs bedroom. Come on in."

The dank dog-beer stench and air freshener reminded me of the Red Zone. Violette flicked on the light in the living room, which looked like a sort of a laboratory or diagnostic center with four long tables covered with computers, tape recorders, CDs. One computer monitor showed the playlist and the song that was currently cued, "Dust My Blues" by Elmore James. Across one wall was the sort of long-paneled lamp that you might stand in front of to have the doctor explain your X-rays. Clipped to the lamp were negatives of mist photos he'd recently developed from a paranormal expedition to Anderson Pass.

"You ever find anything on those photos you took the night we went to look for Haataja's ghost?" I asked him.

"Nothing on them," he said. "That's what usually happens. My best shots are accidents. Like this one here." He turned on his laptop and showed us a photo of Fort Robinson a few miles west, the windows plagued with vapors. There were many other photos in the file, including one Violette was very excited about that showed an orb hovering in front of an inventor's plaque he'd received for the invention of an Automated Rendezvous Docking System.

"Orb schmorb," said Deane. "Let's pry that panel off."

There were holes in the plaster everywhere, mostly at foot level. We followed Violette to the basement. Most of the doorways were built for hatless Mennonites and both Violette and I had to duck as we went through.

"Watch your head," said Violette as he led us down the narrow staircase into the dark basement, screwdriver in hand.

Violette switched on the lights. The basement was deteriorating, the walls bulging, and sheered bricks lay in heaps. "Just think pure thoughts and you'll be fine," said Deane, who found the panel and began to rap on it as if he expected someone to answer from the other side. Thirty screws appeared to hold the piece of plywood in place, but Violette only had to remove eight before it came away. I climbed inside and poked around to find nothing but heaps of sterile reddish earth hard as brick and a mauve scrap of cardboard packaging that read: Enoz Solid

Sachet. "Don't think this dirt has been moved," I said, "since the doctor lived here."

"The sort of person who'd burn someone outdoors, would not typically be the type to stow a body in a crawl space," said Kathy.

"Where's Geraldo?" said Deane.

Back we went to the warm glow of the Olde Main Street Inn.

56.

Sergeant Chuck offers a theory, or is it a wag?

1:14 P.M. Caller from the 200 block of Morehead St. advised he bought a bear claw from the above location and it had a capsule inside of it. Caller stated he took it back to the store and they acted like it was no big deal. Caller requesting to talk to an officer.

NOT MANY NIGHTS LATER I WAS AGAIN AT THE OLDE MAIN, and an off-duty Sergeant Chuck strolled in, mounted a stool, and ordered a Bud Light. He wore stiff blue jeans, a shiny purple checkered western shirt, and his hair was neatly slicked back. He was about six months from retirement, and a year away from a massive heart attack, a helicopter ride to Rapid City, a quadruple bypass, bankruptcy, and religion.

I was sitting at the north corner of the bar with Jeanne, where she kept all her old newspapers and there is that Will Rogers quote hanging by the safe: "There are two ways to argue with a woman: Neither one works."

The Rapid City *Journal* article that contained the AP story criticizing the police department for its lack of effort in the Haataja case had arrived that morning and had already been pretty well thumbed over:

> By its own admission, the Chadron Police Department didn't conduct any organized searches for Haataja and, "the searches we did were to put the word out," said police Sergeant Charles Chaffwick. A couple Chadron residents conducted about five searches, including two men on horseback who searched, and a man and his son who poked around the college campus.
>
> The acting police chief said the department didn't search because officials didn't know where to start.
>
> "We could've searched these remote areas for days and days and days, but where do you start?" said acting Chadron Police Chief Margaret Keiper.

Two weeks after Haataja was found, Keiper now says looking back, "we'd do things different."

"Surprised isn't the right word," Charles Chaffwick, the police sergeant, said of Haataja being found so close to Chadron. "We were disappointed we hadn't searched that area, but we didn't know where to go. It was frustrating as can be."

Officials didn't conduct a search because they didn't know where to *start*? This requires some exploration into the meaning of the word "search," perhaps a review of *Sound of Music* criminal justice primer "Do-Re-Mi," where we learn that the *beginning* is a very good place to start. In defense of the Chadron PD, and anyone else who did not know Steven Haataja but had read the papers, an assumption had been made that Haataja had made no friends here, that he was lame, remote, and socially awkward, that he was a troubled and volatile genius, probably gay, with a history of sorrow and self-infliction, all due to some abstruse and incurable psychological affliction, and so there was no real point in pursuing what was already a fait accompli.

Chuck looked out of sorts, as if someone had just spanked him or tossed a firecracker into his pants. A tic had developed in his left eye and his head whipped about now and again to the left as if responding to the inquiries of an invisible companion.

"Tough piece in the *Journal*," Jeanne told him.

Chuck winced, drained his bottle. Jeanne rose to get him another. "On the house," she said.

The second bottle was nearly finished before Chuck warmed to speech. He defended his purported lack of involvement by saying that he *had* conducted searches. "We searched the whole city," he said. "We did not search those hills behind the campus because they were not in our jurisdiction. That was Sheriff Conaghan's jurisdiction. Margaret Keiper was out of town when this happened so the case was thrown in my lap." He glanced up resentfully at the sign that read: "Bitch Parking Only. All Others Will Be Slapped."

"So what do you think happened to Haataja?" Jeanne asked.

"No doubt," he said, "it was a suicide."

Jeanne, a member of that 99% who were convinced that Haataja would've never burned himself to death, planted palm on hip and said, "How?"

Chuck admitted that Haataja probably did not intend at first to take his life, things just got a little out of hand. He couldn't explain why Haataja might've been tied as he was, how he'd picked that difficult area, the extraordinary way he'd been burned, the lack of a suicide note, or what he might have been doing when "things just got a little out of hand." He stated, in his defense, though he was not there that day, that everyone at the site, including Mobile Forensics, had concluded by sunset that it was a suicide. The exception was Haug and "two lieutenants," who only claimed it was a murder so they might "get a promotion." The medical examiner in Rapid City had also thrown in his opinion that because of missing genitals and teeth marks in the thigh bones that Haataja had been tortured before being murdered, though even those who believed it was murder had to concede that Haataja's corpse had been desecrated by wild animals.

Officer Joni Behrends, who was there that day, described the scene to me much the same way Sheriff Conaghan had, and strongly believes that Steve was not alone when he died that night. She does not think Haataja committed suicide because it did not make sense to her that he would choose Burd's property to wire himself to a tree and set himself on fire.

I had a slew of questions for Chuck, what type of accelerant had been used, where the accelerant had come from since he hadn't purchased any that night and had no grill, what the police had found on his work computer, and what they expected to learn from a body exposed 95 days to the elements. Even the least forensically sophisticated citizen (trained on *CSI: Miami*) understood that it would be difficult to ascertain clues from a fire-ravaged, three-month-old corpse. CSC business professor and veteran deer hunter Tim Donahue, who started at CSC the same year as Haataja, told me that after four or five days in such

terrain under such conditions, all traces of the deer you're track-
ing would be obliterated. "Too bad," he added, "they didn't
leave Loren Zimmerman on. It seemed like the police could have
used his experience."

But Chuck said he couldn't talk about the case anymore.
He'd already said too much. He pulled at his ear as if it might
come off. I wanted to tell him about waves, how you could sit out
on the ocean all day on your board and never see one, then all
at once here came this giant rising like Fate to the sun, sucking
the tide from beneath you, and it was all you could do to get
out of the way of the very thing you'd waited for all day. Instead I
bought him another beer.

57.

Burned alive

3:38 A.M. Caller from the 2000 block of North 70th Avenue in Omaha advised that he's been talking to some people that live in Chadron and they were telling him that Steven Haataja was really close to an office assistant that worked at the college.

WHEN A FEW SPARE DETAILS FROM THE AUTOPSY RESULTS were released we finally learned that Steven Haataja had died of "smoke and soot inhalation combined with thermal injuries." All invitations to law enforcement for elaboration, according to the James Bond Code, were declined though we were free to discard any notions that Steve had been murdered and *then* burned as some sort of attempt to destroy or conceal evidence. Haataja's sisters (Sheila in Rapid City and Emily in Plymouth, Michigan) were not allowed to talk about the case. Neither were the ranchers, Sandy Burd and Slim Buttes, who had been first on the scene. But the Rumor Mill didn't need family members, first-hand witnesses, or outside forensic experts to understand that the autopsy showed that Steve had been burned alive.

And that's all the information we really needed to fly into hysterics. Burned *alive*? What demon lived among us? Where did he come from? Where had he struck before? When would he strike again? We had to know. Our own survival depended on it. A killing was one thing, hard to accept, yes, but a man burned alive was an abomination. "Highly unusual, probably the first time in the history of the town, certainly in the last 50 years, that we've had anything like this," said *Chadron Record* editor George Ledbetter.

The carnival was now fully underway.

With no shortage of creaky rides and flickering bulbs, of jugglers and freaks and creepy clowns and calliopes, of mocking shadow laughter and muttering glum policemen roaming the hay-speckled aisles.

The midway was packed. A multitude was entertained.

The "disgruntled student theory" was the most popular with police and public alike and yielded a number of prospects. Inflammatory remarks by local students were suddenly uncovered by the dozens, these two by conversing authors on MySpace: 1) "the next time we go to math we should kick some sense into that teacher"; 2) "hey bro you would have never guessed, are [sic] math teacher is missing." Jared Wilson, who hadn't done well in Haataja's algebra class, was interviewed by the police and summarized the experience in three words: "It was ridiculous."

Another "jealous lover angle" was also explored. A classmate of Haataja's in Lincoln wrote a long letter to the police explaining how he thought Math and Science office assistant Karly Schmitt and college food service employee Ted Goldy might've been involved since Karly and Haataja were good friends and possibly having an affair, and Ted and Karly were lovers. Karly and Ted, the classmate thought, had left Chadron around the same time as the math professor had disappeared. This letter-writing classmate also thought it possible that someone besides the professor had accessed the password-protected account, perhaps to change grades.

Sandy Burd and Slim Buttes were both questioned, which is standard police procedure for those who discover dead bodies and on whose land corpses are found.

Several people (including Loren Zimmerman and Dennis Lyons of Crawford) told me they thought Mike Vogl, the math teacher who subbed regularly in the math department and would eventually take Haataja's office on a permanent basis (and therefore had something to gain), must be involved.

Loren Zimmerman, the erstwhile investigator, found himself on the other side of the interrogation table.

Noted Epistler Jonas Greenwheat fell under the unusually comprehensive rubric of "unstable, disgruntled student, who had implied threats against the college and who issued open remarks about his dislike for the 'homosexual agenda.'"

Phoebe Krakatoa, the wandering bipolar coquette, whose fiancé had died under mysterious circumstances, and who'd claimed to have seen Steve "headed for Lincoln with a bunch of grocery bags" the day *after* he disappeared, was considered.

As was her brother, her alleged accuser, Sam Killinoy, who knew so much about killing (the murderer of Haataja, you'll recall him telling Mr. Mad Dog, before any evidence of such a thing had come to light, would have had to *know* him very well and *observe* him for long periods) and what happened to bodies before they were found.

Vagabonds and itinerants, naturally, were sought, and anyone who wore a costume and had taken a vow of superiority (read: contempt). Small towns in the Bible Belt, as everyone knows, are havens for KKK members, retired Nazis, SLA members, Weather Underground, Hell's Angels, Unabomber groupies, ballet-phobes, anti-abortionists, marching band outcasts, and other long-horned brigands and country western anarchists.

Just about every person who knew or had had dealings with Steve was interviewed.

We kept our weather eye out for serial killers and sea pirates.

No one was held.

Few relevant facts were added to the case.

Despite the daily legends told in the corners of living room picture boxes throughout the land, it's not often that you run across a person capable of tying up and burning another human being alive.

We, the Gullible Public, were assured that progress was being made daily, that the slow-footed, clandestine, and theatrically incubated investigation was actually a "meticulous process." The State Patrol taking the investigation over from the Chadron Police Department offered some relief, but most of us wondered if it wasn't already too late.

58.
La gringa

TO BECOME A U.S. CITIZEN THERE IS A FIVE-YEAR "CON-tinuous residency" requirement, three years if you are married to a citizen. U.S. citizenship was unusually difficult to obtain at this time owing to the September 11th attack on the twin towers in New York City, which happened only a few months after we'd arrived in America, and Immigration and Naturalization was being integrated into the newly established, brawnier, and more militant Department of Homeland Security. Xenophobia was at an all-time high, even a Mexican Catholic female dentist looked like a terrorist to the INS (they surely did not want to be held responsible for letting in a suicide bomber, especially one with dental picks), so our case was postponed, suspended, snagged, handed from desk to desk, and even lost on two occasions.

One day my wife's notification of eligibility arrived.

At this point Cristina was working at a good-paying job that pleased and challenged her. We weren't yet the happiest husband and wife on the planet, but the reasons and motivations behind her moods and behaviors were easier to understand, and with our second phase of mutual respect in place, sprouts of optimism continued to appear: the proud way in which she drove herself to and from work, the proficiency with which she spoke English, the expert way she operated a slot machine or filled out her NCAA tournament bracket to win a few bucks off of me, and her plans for the future, including world travel, another degree, learning to speak French, and a room added to the house. She took intense interest in the hundreds of people she had come to know through her employment and at the President's Table on Friday Nights and the bonfire parties at Wingding Ranch, many of whom she was now staring literally down the throats of, yanking and poking and crowning their pearly whites.

Cristina's disciplinary style with Tom was more authoritarian than mine, but he was bound for Catholicism, an idea I liked for its structural, ritual, and moral elements, and this had brought him closer to her. With her English up to snuff and his reduced likelihood of launching projectiles at her or spontaneously barfing on the furniture, they had long walks and conversations and I often found him cuddled in her lap. Once a day at least, sometimes running into the bedroom to wake her, he announced to her heartfelt delight those words, "I love you, Momma," followed by a kiss on the lips that softened her and made her more accessible by the day.

We were a small family, I liked to tell her, four if you counted the dog, and it was imperative that we support each other and get along, because who else could you really count on each day when you walked out that front door? Cristina had at last shed her fear of losing her identity or being changed into someone she did not recognize. The ideas that made America strong, such as merit based upon performance and everyone with a chance to make it so long as you got off the block when the buzzer went off, insured that the people who lived here were strong, too. Assiduously, night after night, Cristina studied to be an American.

The written portion of her naturalization exam, a hundred possible questions, had her the most concerned.

> How many representatives are there in Congress?
> How many times can a senator be re-elected?
> In what year was the Constitution adopted?
> Name the three branches of government.
> Who signed the Emancipation Proclamation?
> In what month is the president inaugurated?
> Name the two senators from your state.
> How many amendments to the Constitution are there?

Which amendments address voting rights?
Who becomes president of the U.S. if the president and
    vice-president die?
What is the basic belief of the Declaration of Independence?
Where is the White House located?
Can you name the 13 original states?

Take the test, citizens, without peeking at the answers, and see how you do. I did not know the answers to most of these questions without peeking and neither did most of my educated friends. Only my father, who taught government and civics most of his life, could pass this test without peeking.

We drove for the sixth or seventh time the nine hours to Omaha, a deceptively rough, rich, and cosmopolitan city full of transvestites and meatpackers, where early the next morning, after a rare good night's sleep, we looked for the brand-new, glittering Neo-Roman Extravaganza called the Department of Homeland Security. We had the address but I got lost, as is often the case. Normally on our trips my wife navigates, map open on her lap, and announces, sometimes even before we have started: "We are lost."

"You must help me, dear. I am an idiot. This is your country now and you have as much stake in it as I do."

"It is not my country now. I am not going to pass this test."

"You have been studying for years. It is time to be positive so that you do not defeat yourself. You know the material backwards and front, 435 representatives and George biting Martha's buttocks with his wooden teeth. *Eres una gringa*, whether you like it or not."

We arrived and the employees of the Department of Homeland Security were out-of-the-way friendly for the first time since we had begun our campaign. The wounds of 9/11 were healing. The three of us sat in a lobby for a while, chatting with the other hopeful naturalization applicants, some of whom would not make it, until my wife was taken away. It might be three hours, we were told. I gave Cristina a good-luck kiss, though she barely saw me.

Tom and I drove back downtown to find some breakfast for him. It was almost impossible to find a restaurant where he would eat, though now and again unaccountable things would happen, like his acceptance of a blueberry or a smoked oyster, and there was the time I bought a cheeseburger in a bar in Lincoln so he could eat the french fries and he watched me – he was only three – and then decided he wanted the burger, which was a large burger that he held in both hands like a wide-brimmed hat. There were all kinds of trimmings he wouldn't normally eat, cheese, tomatoes, mustard, pickles, and grilled onions, but he contentedly munched away on it while I had his fries, and several people who were charmed by him played (at his request) all the Eels songs on the jukebox they could find. It would be another two years before he'd eat a hamburger, between a bun, with cheese on it, but never again mustard, pickles, tomatoes, grilled onions, or any of that other yucky stuff. I can't explain what happened that day, except that nature she do love a surprise.

Today he wanted bacon and nothing else, so we walked the windy streets of downtown Omaha lucklessly looking for a place that might sell bacon. On the way back I saw a little drive-through diner and pulled in. They sold me a side order of bacon. The boy was happy. Happiness is about contrasts: heat when you're cold, pay when you're broke, the peace that follows war, selling a story that's been rejected 35 times, a jumbo beer after working a double shift at the hospital, speaking your native language after weeks or months of being deprived of it, and finding bacon after fruitless hours of searching for bacon.

Cristina was waiting for us in the parking lot when we returned. She wore a relieved smile. She'd passed her test. They'd only asked her six questions, easy ones like how many stars are there on the flag? That afternoon we returned to Homeland Security for the swearing-in ceremony. Two short patriotic films were shown. The roll was called. The would-be citizens recited their oaths. There were two Sudanese, a redhead from the UK, two Vietnamese, two El Salvadorans, one Russian, two Indians, and four Mexicans. The flag waved. Cameras flashed. There was much hugging and many tears. Cristina, baby, where are you? Who are you now? My wife raised her hand and became an American.

We went out and bought some wine for a celebration in the motel room that evening. There was more happiness, a few moments strung together from six years and thousands of dollars and thousands of miles driven, forms, fretting, fidgeting, fighting, and going off the highway at 60 miles an hour in a high arc through the rain to land in the mud, but happiness is like this, not handed out by the bucket from your television set but measured from a thimble by a stingy but wise old God and so we savored it, while Tom splashed about merrily in the motel pool.

59.

The British inspector

1:01 P.M. Caller from Regency Trailer Court advised of a nest of
birds in a nest.

OVER THE COURSE OF MY EXPLORATION INTO THE CURIOUS
death of Steven Haataja, most of the "criminal experts" I tried to
talk to turned out to be either shams or clams, so I felt lucky when
Jeanne called me one Monday night and said that an inspector
from London, a 30-year veteran of the Metropolitan Police Force,
was staying with her at the Olde Main for two nights. Jeanne
had discussed the Haataja Killing with him and he wondered if I
wouldn't like to come down to elaborate (never met a homicide
cop who was bored with his job or didn't mind the after-hours
discussion of a case). Maybe, she suggested, the inspector could
illuminate the record.

My son was in bed, and my yawning wife, getting more
relaxed now about me not being her Siamese twin, was in her
pajamas and about to turn in herself. I kissed them both good
night and said I'd return shortly. It was a crisp spring evening,
with that peculiar scent of ocean, as Nebraska must have smelled
when ocean covered this part of the world some 90 million
years ago. That giant white owl from the satellite tower leaned
down and hooed at me as I walked past. Jeanne was closed on
Mondays and didn't want anyone else strolling in, so Inspector
David Jenks and I sat at the corner of the counter speakeasy
fashion and had a few with the blinds down and the doors locked
as I recounted to him everything pertinent I knew about
Professor Haataja.

Jenks, gaunt and infinitely calm, with scooped-out cheeks

and dark, alert eyes, kept ordering bottles of Miller, and he'd look down at his bottle from time to time as if wondering what in the devil Americans saw in their beer. Long ago, when I was a bartender in Niagara Falls, New York, I'd watch Canadians, who enjoy superior brewing standards, making similar expressions as they gulped from their bottles of Miller and Bud Light that they'd traveled all the way to another country to sample, which only demonstrated to me the power of advertising.

As I unspooled the mass of evidence, Inspector Jenks listened intently, only interrupting now and again for clarification. He was keen on postmortem results, in situ, but I confessed that few particulars had been released, though a more detailed report was supposedly forthcoming, even if the habit of this gendarmerie was toward keeping the public in the dark.

I outlined a dozen basic scenarios out of which, I explained, six dozen more hybrids might be constructed. I had catalogued each scenario with its criterion for probability calculated as a score. The scenarios with the highest scores, I told him, were those in which Haataja had joined up with someone, a confederate or a deceiver. Unfortunately there was no evidence of his having had company at any time that night.

"Riveting case," he admitted, "and shameful of course the way it's been done, but no surprise there. It's a pattern more than an anomaly," he said, "when the village bills came across something they've not encountered before."

Midnight tolled and Jeanne began to flag. I was accustomed to talking for hours, delving, wandering, freelancing, breaking down the facts and reassembling them in a variety of hypothetical molds – and having little to show for my efforts. This meeting in the main was no different, though Jenks provided two useful observations. The first was that he'd never seen a case of self-immolation in all his days as a man and a police officer, and second, he was appalled that it had taken 96 days for the police to seize Haataja's office computer, upon which Haataja had made his last known contact. This computer in his opinion was the key piece of evidence. Jenks, as Violette had also proposed, said it was possible he'd written a suicide note in puzzle form, or that he'd made final preparations in another fashion. A straightening of accounts, files moved, documents deleted, would suggest this. It was not uncommon, he said, for a suicide to clean his house beforehand. Jenks thought Haataja seemed distinctly the type, in the event that this were a suicide, who would have ordered his affairs. "I'd like to look at the computer BIOS (Basic Input/Output System, the first thing you see when you turn on most IBM computers)" he said. "I think that's where you'll find your answer, if there is one."

I got home around midnight, restless, house dark, everyone asleep, and since it was an hour earlier on the west coast and I knew Kevin would probably be up with Rhonda evaluating a Pinot Noir and watching *The Shield* on DVD, I rang him with all the recent rehash swirling fresh in my mind. After I'd touched all the high points, Kevin responded without hesitation, "lover."

The killer, he thought, might have also been an academically disgruntled student, as the psychic first suggested, but it was much more likely a tryst gone sour. Of his five scenarios, four of them involved sex, Eros and Thanatos walking hand in hand into the churchyard dusk. In the margin of my notebook I jotted: "if death has consciousness, it is manifested through sex." I pressed him for a similar case in his experience and he could only think of one: a wealthy attorney who'd made online arrangements with a prostitute, whose accomplice had killed him in the act of robbery. The gist of this, the idea of Haataja being lured sexually and then being forced to a place against his will, perhaps at gunpoint, with all the equipment necessary to execute his fate being transported in the truck or car in which he was conveyed, seemed much more credible and acceptable to me than the horrendous tableau of self-immolation.

"Do you know for a fact that he was bound with barbed wire?" Kevin wanted to know.

"I know nothing for a fact. It might've been baling wire. Some kind of wire, I'd bet, because that's what everyone says."

"I can't see how you'd wrap someone in barbed wire," he said, "or why."

"The Whys so far are throwing a shutout against the Becauses."

"When is this press conference?" he wanted to know.

"May 8."

"Let me check my calendar," he said, then: "We'll be there."

60.

El Cocodrilo

11:58 A.M. (Tuesday, March 27, 2007) Subject came into PD and requested to talk to an officer refer [sic] some forged checks out of Rapid City and he also gave a statement about seeing Steve Haataja hitchhiking out of town the day he supposedly disappeared.

NEWSPAPER ARTICLES, "PROFESSOR'S GRUESOME DEATH Puzzles Nebraska Town," led to national TV news stories. America, ever scrolling the menu for bigger, lusher, more vividly lurid tales, changed the channel. With cameras in every corner of the globe, television is now a 10-to-1 spectacle over substance so we no longer have to miss a moment of someone else's misery: celebrity killers, plagues, mass shootings, filicidal mothers, deadly tornadoes, quakes, crashes, satanic voodoo pussy snatchers, and cannibalistic maniacs with spiked dildos on a special two-hour edition of Anderson Cooper 360. Steve would make the national news for a week or two, but without any actual footage of his grisly demise, it wasn't much of a spectacle, just another hate crime, a gay math nerd murdered by rednecks in a jerkwater cowboy town.

In the meantime, Loren Zimmerman, rebuffed, kicked off the case, threatened with jail time at one point by Sergeant Chuck, fired from his job for losing his temper, was still prominent enough to be continually quoted as the expert in these nationally syndicated stories. It showed how helpless and afraid, perhaps how desperate, we were. And now wherever I went I saw Zimmerman and his purple pickup truck (*I Kill People*), Telenovela at his side, so short she was barely visible over the dashboard. In the big city, where I've spent plenty of time, your adversary can be avoided or even forgotten for months or years at a time. But in a small town there is no place to hide.

Cristina and I took long walks in the evenings with Tom, who declared if we were going east, we were headed for Iowa, west was Wyoming. His favorite city in Iowa was Iowa City because it had "elvegators and hallways," and his favorite Wyoming city was Casper, Yie-Yoming. Casper, Yie-Yoming, also has excellent french fries, ice machines, and a college-ist, though it is sometimes very windy in Casper, with more hats, toupees, tumbleweeds, and coyote carcasses snagged up in barbed-wire fences than you can count.

Cristina looked forward to these walks that kept her from getting fat since she was already three pounds overweight after living in America for six years, and she liked the ever-changing clouds, the crisp air, trains, sunsets, goldfinches, and talking about the people she knew. We always strolled through Tommy's Car Lot to see what was on sale and to find out which vehicle we might test drive on Friday afternoon. It had taken two years before she'd let me teach her how to drive. For a year afterward she'd refused to drive anywhere while her newly purchased Mazda Millenia collected dust in the garage. One day she gathered up the nerve to take her Mazda for a whirl and before long she was commuting the mile to and from work all on her own.

For Cristina, test driving a car was almost as exciting as spinning the reels on a slot machine or eBay bidding on a Burberry purse; her eyes would shimmer and shine (I remember that first big jackpot she won at the Flamingo in Laughlin, "*Quinientos!*" she cried, her dark childlike eyes ablaze), but she was so shy and reserved and afraid that the salesmen would think she was crazy if she kept test driving cars that I had to insist on it for her own good, explaining that it gave the salesmen a sense of purpose when she drove their cars. It was also important that she buy a car based upon its performance rather than the way it looked.

Test driving became one more way of tripping her out of gloom and preoccupation, and the more she drove, the less nervous she got when I drove. Soon we were going to be a three-car family, which happens naturally, like childbirth, after you test-drive so many cars. This is something I would've never guessed would happen when we first came here to America with nothing but a few suitcases, something I would've objected to strenuously a year or so before (I hadn't owned a car myself in 20 years), but it was her money, she made twice as much as I did, and I had learned to let go of those little things that gave her pleasure.

On the way home from Tommy's Car Lot, we'd head down Main Street and Cristina and I would stare at Zimmerman's truck (*I Kill People*) as we passed his favorite bar, fittingly named "Wreckers." Whenever we drove by his house on 10th Street, Cristina would crane her neck to see if Telenovela's car was in the driveway. I'd be fibbing if I said I never wondered if Cristina was nostalgic over those daring and dangerous times and perhaps even envious of the triumph of her closest friend.

But off to the south, almost directly across the street from where Zimmerman lived, stood the water tower; its looming proximity to the crime scene of Steven Haataja always stirred up pictures of him: singing in his office, walking through the snow with his laptop, smiling goofily with a Corona in his left hand, helping a student outside of class, striding down the Math and Science hallway in his four-buckle overshoes, having martinis with the Minister of Debauchery, and a blink later: trussed and charred in a ravine, slumped in the Cold and Great Alone, the bluebirds and sunshine and snow whirling in a perverted Disney carousel all around him, which would snap me back to what was important, the fragility, brevity, mystery, luck, and sorrow of life, and the duty I had to the two in my care.

All I had to do was look back a year to see my American wife growing sometimes as fast as my son and about to buy her second car and spreading her wings and telling jokes with her hands on her hips after understanding 92.7% of everything you just said. She still worried more than six people combined, but she enjoyed worrying and she was good at it, the same way I was good at "thinking," which never got me anywhere either. We were that elementary exercise in polar coordinates, where once the azimuth is determined you can locate your star. And though I was poor and had never killed anyone, and my servile sincerity often made her cringe, Cristina could still appreciate my puzzling but genuine liking for people, my good standing in the community, and my ability to read people and other wild animals of the jungle. She particularly enjoyed my description of Mr. Zimmerman as *El Cocodrilo*, The Crocodile.

61.
Donut coma

11:07 A.M. Caller from the 100 block of North Morehead St. requested to speak to animal control because caller felt that someone was coming into his yard and cutting the hair on his dogs. Dispatch advised caller to set up video surveillance on his house. Caller said he planned on it.

IN EARLY MAY OF 2007, TWO MONTHS AFTER THE BODY of Steven Haataja was found, my publisher, Rhonda Hughes, and her fiancé, Detective Kevin Warren, came once again to visit us in Chadron. When I picked them up at the airport this time it was raining, our quasi-monsoon season that usually lasts the month of May. Rhonda had a terrible cold and lunged periodically into the wad of tissue in her right hand with a miserable shudder.

Tom was thrilled to see his old friends so soon again. "But don't get too close to me, honey," said Rhonda, "because I don't want to get you sick, OK?"

"You know why it rains?" he asked her, leaned over the seat.

Rhonda's eyes were swollen from sneezing. "Why?"

"Because – because the world needs a baff."

"It does need a bath," Rhonda said.

Kevin laughed and his shrewd eyes gleamed when I pulled up alongside Millie Heiser's wrecked old mansionette and told him about the Iowa psychic. The Portland police had just employed the services of its own psychic in the case of a woman who'd been missing for a year, Kevin said, and the woman was still missing.

"Psychics are like porno stars," I said. "Anybody can be one."

Kevin envisioned psychic porno stars.

Rhonda and Kevin once again checked into Jeanne's best room, the General Miles Suite. Cristina made *chiles rellenos* that night, folding the egg yolks back into the whipped whites at the last minute. We bring all our *poblanos* down to the Olde Main kitchen to blister them on the broiler there, which gives them that sweet, roasted flavor and makes them easier to peel. Rhonda had a black umbrella with polka dots that Tom took a shine to. When you opened it, it went WHUMP and knocked everything off the table. Rhonda let Tom play with the umbrella and promised he could have it when they left in a few days, which forged a lifetime alliance in his mind. It was Rhonda-and-Kevin, Rhonda-and-Kevin for the next year. When were they coming back? When were we going to visit them in Portland, Oregon?

Tom made a tent with Rhonda's umbrella and furnished it with his dry erase board, his SpongeBob piñata, a bag of marshmallows, and a broken alarm clock Jeanne had given him that he called his Thrillion Million clock. The Thrillion Million clock could register any time up to one million o'clock, which was when the sky was a *little* blue. At one thrillion o'clock you had only bacon for breakfast.

Rhonda was so ill she had to turn in early that evening and the next day she stayed in bed, rolling in fever in the General Miles Suite on the second floor of the Olde Main while the rain rolled down the windowpanes and the ghosts frolicked in the halls. Ghost activity was comparably minimal in the General Miles Suite, Jeanne said (once a burner on the stove had lit by itself and another time guests complained they'd closed the windows only to find them open again in the morning), she didn't know why. Maybe because Nelson A. Miles was an Indian killer or a famous war hero, or since he'd headquartered himself here during the campaign against the Lakota (which resulted in the death of Sitting Bull and the first siege at Wounded Knee), some imposing but unmanifested and repellent spiritual residue or accretion of massless photons of his legend remained. Violette had gotten some pronounced EMF readings in that room indicating at the very least a conspicuous magnetic field, though the "energy" never seemed to move, suggesting it might be a force (possibly by its inert nature a police force) other than spooks.

That evening, while Rhonda sneezed and experimented with cold medications, Kevin and I drank downstairs at the bar. Steven Haataja had been buried that day, May 7, 2007, at St. Paul Lutheran Church in his hometown of Spearfish, South Dakota. The conversation turned naturally to him once more. Andrew, a Lakota Indian social worker, Tony, the new police dispatcher, also Lakota, and Martha, whose husband had recently died of cancer, were there. The minute you start talking about the Haataja Case, everyone in the room throws in and most of it is a miss or a half truth or a top-10 gossip hit with personal embellishments so the talk goes long into the night and the drinks keep getting poured and we sail away south until the land falls out of sight.

Because I had become the repository for Steve's story, had interviewed hundreds of people including three law enforcement officials who'd been there that first dreadful day of discovery, had viewed the crime scene myself, and therefore knew as much as any journalist and probably half the investigating officers, I spent most of my time in any discussion of the case swatting back rumors: he hadn't been fired from the college, his hands and arms hadn't been bound, he hadn't had an affair with another professor. Neither had he been as isolated as the newspapers asserted. He hadn't been depressed, not at least from what any of us had judged and especially according to the people who knew him best, his colleagues, his sister, and his best friend. He hadn't been hampered by his hip replacement, since he often walked 10 miles a day on it, including into the hills south of campus, where he was eventually found. The tendency to make the facts fit the circumstances, even in the most respectable journalistic accounts, is the chief obstacle to the world ever making sense. The truth, much as we like to pretend, is just not in us.

Sergeant Chuck strolled taciturnly past the saloon windows, and I explained how he'd been painted a plonker in the papers.

The charges were not altogether fair, though the uninspired investigation and its conspicuous lack of results had required a scapegoat and Chuck's easygoing style had made him a natural. It hadn't helped when the department had admitted conducting no searches for Haataja because they didn't know where to start. Jeanne brought down her hunting rifles and old muskets to show Kevin, and otherwise basked once again in his virile, Dick Tracy spell.

Kevin and I played about a dozen cards of keno, a game one can reputedly win money at, though I've never personally seen the proof. Kevin asked me how the marriage was going and I admitted it was tough sledding some of the time, but that we were slowly working things out. That time she had laughed at one of my jokes I'd felt like Anne Sullivan after Helen Keller had spoken her first word. She was also suddenly lenient about my writing time. She was also routinely letting me out of the house without a cross-examination.

Both Kevin and Rhonda had been victims of previous marriages. Kevin had a seven-year-old daughter from his. "The interesting thing about marriage," he said, "is that it's completely impossible."

"Kind of like winning at keno," I said. "But you're going to marry Rhonda anyway, aren't you?"

"Do you think I could do better?"

"Not unless you went on eHarmony."

About 7:30 that night the rain let up and Kevin decided he wanted to see the place where Haataja had been found. Though Sheriff Conaghan had shown me the spot and I'd promised him I wouldn't conduct freak tours or make a habit of trespassing on private land, I thought it might be useful to make an exception in Kevin's case. I borrowed a flashlight from Jeanne and, half tuned-up as the old saying goes, we headed out the east door.

It is a mile due south from the Olde Main Street Inn to the Chadron State College campus. If there weren't a fence, Main Street after about 12 blocks would lead you straight up C-Hill, which was lit for some event. Many of the houses along the street, as old as Chadron itself, are some of its most magnificent specimens. There was still light in the sky and all the street-lamps had gone on to make the mist glow like clouds in the great trees or some of Abner Violette's more compelling boogeyman photography. We passed under a blossoming linden tree, the heavy fragrance of which reminded me of Adrienne Schultz, who I'd gone steady with in the love-drunk summer of my 14th year. "Tell me a little more about Haataja," said Kevin. "Personal things."

I told Kevin that Haataja liked Russian and Hungarian movies and that he loved baseball, especially its statistical side. When he cracked a joke or explained to someone one of his theories you could hear the crickets chirping, but that was only because he was two stratospheres above everyone else. I explained that Haataja liked little boxes of raisins. He was compulsively meticulous, OCD if you prefer. He was married 10 years, no kids. I'd talked to his ex-wife, a very intelligent and sweet woman, who wouldn't tell me much because she'd been warned by Steve's family that I worked for the circus and would do anything for a buck. I told Kevin that all of Haataja's students I talked to liked him. Some of them, like Amy and Chance, sought him regularly outside of class. I mentioned that I never detected any attitude toward Haataja outside of a platonic affection and mutual respect. Amy had been diagnosed with MDD and took the same antidepressant as Haataja. Amy, it should be noted, didn't understand what Haataja was talking about her first day in his algebra class, so she met him afterward and he very graciously guided her through the term, and she got an A.

I told Kevin the story about Haataja interviewing for his job in Augustana. He'd been waiting for his interview and when the personnel director came out he was helping a student with his homework. I didn't think you'd find anyone who'd say he wasn't dedicated. An argument could be made, by comparing student ratings and his methods of interaction over the years, that he was improving. One time he announced to his algebra class the anniversary of his billionth second on earth.

Kevin wanted to know if Haataja was religious.

"Ostensibly Lutheran," I said. "He taught at Augustana, which is ostensibly Lutheran. He never talked much about God or religion. I know he was on an advocacy roster of the National Center for Science Education for teaching evolution."

"How important was music to him?"

"I spoke just the other night to one of his colleagues, Dr. Beth Wentworth, his office neighbor in 214 (Haataja was in 213) and she told me he'd sing in there at night, close the door and practice for choir. The last night she saw him in his office he was singing, she said, which makes it very hard for me to believe that he decided to take his life."

We passed County Attorney Vance Haug's office and I pointed out the blonde-brick three-story courthouse across the street where he was to release the autopsy details tomorrow, the first press conference since Haataja's disappearance. Kevin said, "Should be quite the show. Is this the way Haataja walked to work?"

"Usually he went straight up Bordeaux or King, which put him closer to where he worked in the Math and Science building." I pointed east. "Both King and Bordeaux are one-way streets. Funny that a psychic from Iowa would know that."

"She probably looked at a map. You say all the policemen concluded this was a suicide before sunset?"

"Most of them."

Kevin kicked a pinecone, soccer style. "Sergeant Chuck believes it's a suicide?"

"Emphatically, though most of the hows evade him." I added that if Haataja had constructed his own funeral pyre, the popular speculation that this was a hate crime would be ironically correct, except the motive would be self-hate. Possible also, I said, that to ease the shame of suicide he did away with himself in a manner that he thought would make it appear as if he'd been murdered, though if he didn't have the guts to hang himself, it was a tough jump to self-ignition.

A white Great Dane barked at us in anxious lunges against a picket fence. "Happy people don't commit suicide, either," Kevin said. "You sure he wasn't gay?"

"Depends on who you talk to."

"And he wasn't fired from his job?"

"I was given a 100% guarantee by the administrator who hired him that his job was not in danger. They liked him."

We arrived at the campus, its lawns jeweled from rain and sloping gently upward like golf greens through the big firs and elms, some of them as high as 40 feet.

"Here's the Math and Science building," I said, and explained about the computer he'd logged onto – his last known contact – which had been stored but not seized until 96 days after his disappearance. I stated the possibility that someone else had logged onto his computer, another rumor that had gotten wings. I also restated what Inspector Jenks from London had said about the BIOS and how it might provide an answer. Recently, Sergeant Chuck had arrested a young man who'd propositioned two underage males, immediately seized his computer and found the incriminating web sites. He obviously knew the criminal procedure, so why hadn't he seized Haataja's computer on the first day in a much more important case?

"Donut coma," Kevin offered. "Happens to the best of us."

I pointed south up the trail. "This is one of two ways he could've gone, though it's possible he walked right up the main road in full view of everyone and through the gates of Sandy Burd's ranch. It's also possible, but much less likely, that he boony-whomped, but you see how rugged the terrain is through this ravine. It's impossible to know his exact route or timeline. I'm convinced his purpose was furtive that night and this is the only place where you can cross barbed wire without having to climb through it or get shocked. The fact that he changed into hiking boots indicates he planned this excursion, but the load he was carrying, seven-pound bag of charcoal, accelerant, a bottle of schnapps, bottled water, ligature, and whatever else, had to be heavy, and the place where he ended up indicates he didn't want to be seen, so I don't think he's just strolling around as a nature lover that night."

"Why schnapps?"

"He wasn't a regular schnapps drinker, far as I can tell."

"Kind of a pansy drink." Kevin stroked his goatee. "Let's have a look."

Some glow spilled over from the college and the greenish moonlight lit the overcast sky like a lamp. It drizzled for a time. Frogs in some wet hollow rattled and twanged below. I flicked on the flashlight. The trail was muddy until we reached the first outcropping of sandstone, where someone had recently inscribed the word MATH. I pointed out the two homes in the area Haataja would've had to avoid. Burd's house on its built-up platform stood above us about 300 yards to the southeast.

"Burd was the developer in Vegas?" Kevin asked.

"They say he built the MGM Grand and the Stratosphere."

"Any mafia ties?"

"He won't talk to me. He's not what you'd call outgoing."

"Haataja is found on his property, burned beyond recognition, and Burd is the second one on the scene after his employee calls him?"

"I'd be more inclined to believe that Buttes, his henchman, did it. I mean, he's the guy who found him. When I talked to him he was belligerent, told me to keep his name the fuck out of it." I also told Kevin about Sandy's brother Collin, who after being a content town drunk for decades in Chadron hastily sold his run-down house and moved to an unspecified point east. Though most who know him will tell you that Collin didn't have what it would take to kill someone, it didn't mean that he wasn't involved in some way accidentally, that something didn't "get out of hand," as Sergeant Chuck put it. A frisson, a bit of funny biz, drunkenness clouding judgment, a big brother helping out. Steven

Haataja and Collin Burd lived on the same street, separated by only four buildings. They were both single, middle-aged men who may or may not have spent some time together. If Collin, "the raging alcoholic," as Jeanne called him, was somehow involved, if he and his close neighbor, Steve, had been together that night for whatever reason, it would be the scenario with the highest score.

"That's a lot of ifs. I'm assuming the police looked into it."

"I have no idea what the police are doing. Except for Sheriff Conaghan, my involvement is resented and thoroughly opposed."

"Maybe you shouldn't write this book."

"That, I expect, would be its appeal. I have not talked to a single person who ever saw Haataja and Collin Burd together, including Dennis Brown, who owns KCSR and saw Haataja go by his door on dozens of occasions."

Detective Warren, in good physical condition, was winded by the time we arrived. "Is it always this windy up here?"

"Every time I've been here." I pointed the flashlight down into the thicket.

"No wonder it took three months to find him," said Kevin.

"Pretty convenient location if someone didn't want him to be found."

"That it is."

I related to Kevin what several people who grew up on ranches and farms (including Herb Peterson of the Ship Shape Shop) had told me: that anyone with livestock (representing large sources of revenue) would immediately investigate unusual animal activity, especially bird activity, which would continue through winter. "And we know there were animals in this area because cowhand Slim Buttes was purportedly wandering down into this culvert looking for a stray steer. You can see the animal droppings everywhere." I directed the flashlight at several heaps of manure. "So there had to be another reason besides ignorance for not noticing a corpse this close to the Burd house for more than three months."

"A lot of ignorance going around," said Kevin. "Which tree was he tied to?"

"That one there," I said, pointing with the beam of my flashlight. "You can see the slight burning at the bottom and the ash circle of his campfire." I explained how when the investigators arrived on the scene they found this tree to which he was bound and all the dry grass around him virtually untouched by flame, an almost impossible set of circumstances for a man incinerated beyond recognition.

"Explainable in some way, I'm sure," Kevin said. "I'd rather know how he made it down here carrying all that stuff," he said. "Pretty tricky hike at night, even for a man on good legs. Is it possible he came another way?"

I shined my light all around until my beam caught the green coin-like gleams of an owl's stare. "Possible. We can walk that route, if you want, but you have to go through a corral, and that horseshit is pretty slippery."

"Was there any horseshit in the tread of his boots?"

"I'd like to know if there was. I'm the only one apparently interested in what route he might've taken. He was not the type to trespass. If he came up the main road he had company."

"Yes." Kevin knelt by the tree and fingered the grass. "I'm betting there was an accessory, too," he said. "Maybe he was already unconscious when he was brought here. Or maybe somebody picked him and gave him a ride. He just didn't know who it was until it was too late."

62.

The deeper you dive

THE NEXT MORNING, MAY 8, 2007, BEFORE THE PRESS conference, Kevin and Rhonda came over for breakfast. We had some Kona beans from the last time we were in California visiting my parents. Rhonda was in rough shape, but her fever was down and she managed a cup of Kona and a buttermilk biscuit I'd made with high-altitude flour. Kevin was now calling the Haataja case "Professor Flambé," according to his cruel sense of humor, a police coping mechanism we'll call it. The case had occupied his dreams (like flames, he said) and he'd tossed and turned so much Rhonda had made him sleep on the couch in the other room with the placid ghost of General Miles. The more he thought about it, the more it looked like murder. If it was a suicide or an accidental death, then there had been an attendant.

In all his years of investigating suspicious deaths, like Inspector Jenks, he'd never seen a single case of any kind of immolation. And though Haataja was a prime candidate for suicide, he didn't think burning would have been his method. Along with talking jumpers down and coaxing shooters out, Detective Warren, owing to his extensive psychological training, also investigated bias-related crimes (a much better name for "hate crimes"). He outlined the profile of auto-immolation, almost unheard of in the West: the actor was usually impulsive, emotionally immature, often angry at himself or his family, often impelled to punish himself or his perceived persecutors.

Most self-igniters were young and uneducated, he said. Haataja didn't fit the profile.

We gave Rhonda a ride back to the hotel. She wanted to go up to Deadwood and Mount Rushmore the following day (winter weather had prevented these jaunts the first time they visited) and thought she might turn the corner with one more day of bed rest. I gave her some books on Crazy Horse, my copy of *The Stranger Beside Me*, and the sequential series of news articles on Haataja, right up to the funeral.

It was a windless morning, slight chill, a high, dry, Aqua Velva sky. Kevin and I stood at the edge of the sidewalk below the courthouse with 60 or so curious and concerned residents. Vance Haug, county attorney and coroner, took the podium at the top of the courthouse steps. On the deck below a gaggle of journalists had gathered – a few from as far away as Michigan – who'd get first crack at questions. The name Haug is Northern European, but Vance looks more Mediterranean to me. He's thin and fidgety, under six feet, mustached, with a quick crooked smile. He gives the impression of having thought things out long in advance. He consults notes but does not often look down. He's accustomed to making statements, since he officially attends most deaths in the county.

Haug confirmed that Haataja was "burned head to toe," and was wrapped to a tree ankles and torso, but that his hands were not bound. He did not say what ligature was used but nixed the rumor that it was barbed wire. Traces of an accelerant were also found on what was left of Steve's clothes. No finger-prints or evidence that others were at the scene had been found. Alone-alone was the palpable beat when you sang the sad song of Steven Haataja. Vance stated that investigators believed that Steve had died at the place he was discovered.

Kevin nodded, as if his own theories had been confirmed. He had a cup of coffee from Daylight Donuts and had already polished off an apple fritter, abating the pulse of that Pavlovian Shiver Electrode cerebrally implanted at the academy in all recruits. He listened with head tilted as Haug enumerated the items found at the scene: an unopened bottle of water, a plastic Tupperware-like container (the kind one might use to carry a sandwich), the charred remains of a flashlight, and an unidentifiable glob of plastic. A 375-milliliter bottle of peppermint schnapps, mostly empty. Steve, known by acquaintances to be a social drinker instead of a problem drinker, had been drinking quite a bit before his death, the autopsy report showed. His blood alcohol level was extremely elevated. No DNA besides Haataja's was found on the bottle.

Haug offered a brief timeline: Steve had a normal workday. He arrived at his office at 8 a.m., greeted his first class at nine that morning. Between 3:30 p.m. and 4 p.m., he and a student scheduled a make-up test for 8:30 a.m. the next day. At 5:00 p.m., he was seen near Pizza Hut on West Third Street. A colleague saw him back at his office around six that evening. A downtown Chadron automatic teller machine showed that a $100 withdrawal was taken from his account at 8:24 p.m., and a woman saw him on the street between 9 p.m. and 10 p.m. (which would also be the time he purchased the schnapps and the charcoal). At 11:41 p.m., his work computer, password protected, was accessed. Haug stated that investigators were continuing to examine Steve's computer, though it appeared its usage was principally related to work.

"Humm," said Kevin.

"He worked for Gateway for six years, though," I whispered. "He could've changed or concealed anything he wanted."

Haug said there was no evidence of a hate crime, no indication that anyone hated Steven Haataja. No suicide note was found and there were no indications he was thinking about suicide, though he'd indeed tried to kill himself the year before. Despite having committed hundreds of man-hours to the case, interviewing more than a hundred people and closely analyzing the evidence, Haug concluded that the investigating team was still baffled.

"All we have for you today folks," I said in mock County Attornese, "is a big box of Nut 'n Honey."

The follow-up questions got us no closer to the nougat, and Kevin's attention began to stray. Pressed on whether or not this was likely a suicide, the county attorney/coroner could only say that the case was unresolved and that the investigation would continue as a possible homicide. Many wanted to know about the bindings, but "unburned" and "not barbed wire" were as far as Haug would take it. The briquettes found at the scene could not be directly linked to those Haataja purchased. All reasons for buying the briquettes (Steve, recall, had no grill), outside of a cozy campfire, were ruled out. The autopsy had shown high levels of carbon monoxide, a toxic gas produced from the incomplete burning of organic material (such as charcoal), in his system.

Haug explained that extensive background information gathered pointed to Steve being heterosexual.

When asked if people in Chadron should be worried, Haug replied that people needed to be cautious. "We don't live in Mayberry," he said.

"Though Sheriff Taylor would've solved this one by now," Kevin muttered off the side of his hand.

"And we already are worried," I said.

Over drinks at the hotel afterward, Rhonda was hungry for the first time since she'd arrived, so we decided to go Chinese: Tsingtao, pot stickers, moo shu pork, kung pao prawns, and salt and pepper squid. Our waiter had what looked like a knife scar on his cheek and barely spoke English. The old truck stop this place had been when I had first come here in 1994 was in good hands. The green bottles of Tsingtao and the pot stickers arrived.

I asked Rhonda if she'd seen any ghosts yet.

"My head is too stuffed up," she said.

"You have to look for them in the daylight," I said. "They especially like to fool with the maids."

"That's what I'd do if I were a ghost," said Kevin.

Rhonda backhanded him playfully and asked if we'd solved the case yet. She'd heard most of the press conference on the radio.

"I actually feel like I know less," I said. "The deeper you dive, the darker it gets."

Kevin clapped his chopsticks at us. "If Haataja intended to do himself in and had amassed all the equipment to do so, why would he stop in at Math and Science to log on to a computer if he wasn't going to write a farewell? Or why, if he had just planned a secret solo picnic or a tryst in the hills, would he stop to check his email at 11:41 p.m. at the risk of being seen?"

I added: "And what apparently content, mild-mannered, middle-aged teacher on an artificial hip would walk deep into rough terrain in the blackness of midnight, find a spot in the freezing night, perch upon a nest of briquettes, wrap himself to a tree, immerse himself in whatever it would take to get the fire blazing, and sit there in the ghastly crackling fat-spattering roar of his own incineration?"

I took a long haul off my Tsingtao. "Not to mention the timing was all wrong. He was a dedicated teacher. Finals were only a few days away. He had an appointment at 8:30 the next morning with a student. He never missed appointments. He'd paid his rent that morning too."

"The sandwich container bothers me," said Kevin.

"Not noticing a corpse on your own land with birds flying all around it all winter bothers me," I said.

Rhonda, who was still getting caught up on the case, dipped her pot sticker and said, "He met with someone. A midnight rendezvous."

"Something was going on," I said. "He was obviously restless that night, roaming all over town. He withdrew a hundred bucks, packed a picnic dinner, and bought a bottle of booze. He seems pretty frisky for someone in a suicidal or depressed state."

"He might've made arrangements to meet someone earlier that evening," Kevin said. "The meeting also might've been set up days in advance. It might have been a regular rendezvous."

"Or maybe whomever he was supposed to meet never showed," Rhonda said, "or he learned when he logged on that his date was no longer interested in him. That might have been enough to send him over the edge."

"What about the possibility of an autoerotic death?" I said. Kevin looked up sharply. "Any history?"

"I never asked."

"Did they find a release mechanism?"

"You'd have to ask them."

"Have you talked to his ex-wife?"

"One of my many weaknesses as a journalist is that I can't ask perfect strangers about the masturbation habits of their ex-spouses, just me being a stuffed shirt again."

"Most AE deaths happen at home," Kevin said, finishing his beer. "I can't think of a single reason why he'd go all the way up into those hills to get his ya-yas out. That's a police term, sorry. What about your ghost hunter, Violette?"

"We're still on the threshold of a paranormal investigator solving a crime. For the record, he thinks it's a suicide or a murder because everyone who investigated this thing had bad luck, Sergeant Chuck, Loren Zimmerman, and Nebraska State Patrol Officer Matt Fitzgerald, who tried to kill himself and is now off the case."

"That is pretty weird," Rhonda said.

"Don't confuse luck for competence," Kevin said, shaking out his napkin and laying it into his lap.

"Why can't you use the Freedom of Information Act?" Rhonda wanted to know.

"As long as the case stays open, my legal access to it is closed."

The squid, the pork, and the prawns arrived. Rhonda blew her nose and said, "Oh, it feels good to be alive."

63.

Detective Warren takes the mantle

AS YOU FLIPPED THROUGH THE SUSPECTS, EACH STOOD out in his or her own way, but the one trip wire was always ability, the cool viciousness it would take to burn another human being alive. If someone had attended or somehow caused or compounded an accident, the population of possible candidates expanded, but assuming this was a deliberate act, premeditated or not, the field was markedly reduced. Kevin wanted to know if I'd talked to Loren Zimmerman yet, who met all the criteria. It was hard not to line up behind Sheriff Conaghan's assessment of Zimmerman as the number one suspect due to his experience and apparent pleasure as an Officer-Involved-in-Shooting and "blowing up stuff" in the jungle, his need to promote his skills for a prominent law enforcement position, his pattern of frequent moves, his uncontrollable temper, his apparent comfort and jollity among the dead, and the fact that he owned a pickup truck (*I Kill People*). "I haven't talked to him yet," I admitted. "I will, when the time is right. I'm not afraid of him."

"Do you want *me* to talk to him?" said Kevin. "I mean just one cop to another. I might be able to get more out of him than you would. I won't say I know you. I'll tell him we came to see the cowboys and Indians."

Kevin would know the right questions, the right method. He'd be able to look into Zimmerman's eyes, even if Zimmerman had a Narcissistic Personality Disorder, and know if he was guilty. I decided it was a good idea and gave Kevin a little background on *El Cocodrilo*, including the fact that Zimmerman might be a little touchy at first since he'd suffered a loss of credibility after his several clashes with local law enforcement. He and Sheriff Conaghan were particularly at odds, especially after Mr. Zimmerman helped Telenovela to enter her ex-husband's house to retrieve some of her belongings and the sheriff cited them both for trespass and aiding and abetting a burglary, both charges dropped by Denny Greenwheat. Conaghan says the next time they try to pull that kind of shit he's going to make sure they go to jail.

Kevin called Zimmerman from the hotel, explaining that he had come from Oregon to Chadron to see the Fur Trade Museum, the Indian Reservation, Deadwood, and so on, and had heard about the fascinating Haataja case. A homicide detective himself, Kevin wondered if Zimmerman, who looked like the only person who might have a real understanding of the case, would like to discuss it. Flattered, Zimmerman agreed. Kevin got the address and said he'd be over within the hour.

It was a cool, overcast day, rain in the forecast. Zimmerman owned that house across from the college, and rented out his two basement apartments to students. I dropped Kevin off down the street, telling him to call me at the hotel when he was done. I needed to pick Tom up from school, right down the street, at 10 minutes past three. I had this strange feeling Kevin, with his confrontational streak, was going to enjoy himself with Mr. Zimmerman. I'd seen him belittle people he didn't like, and in his weekly soccer matches, where he played goalie, he got into regular scuffles with members of the opposing team.

I figured it would be at least an hour, that the two men would swap tales, maybe take target practice in the backyard and leaf through some autopsy photos, and I headed back to the hotel to check up on Rhonda.

Three patrons were assembled at the bar in the Olde Main when I got there, arguing about the greatest guitar player of all time: my good friend Chris, the scholarly bartender from

Wrecker's, who lived in a residential motel, said Leo Kottke; the giant railroad employee they called "Thin" was adamant about Jimi Hendrix; and Tom Morrow, who worked in the uranium mines at Crow Butte and hailed from Mars, Pennsylvania, a true Martian, naturally cast his vote for Frank Zappa.

"Will you be drinking?" Jeanne asked me.

"I'm willing to make an exception in this case," I replied. "Give me five games of keno, too. Random 20. And buy those degenerates down the way a drink."

The three waved at me and hooted.

Jeanne lifted the cap off a Heineken. "What's new?"

"Sold that story about Tom getting baptized in Mexico. Only took me two years to get it right. That's actually fast for me. What about you?"

"Guests from Germany," she said. "And the hotel's full for graduation."

Rhonda appeared at the bottom of the staircase, which emptied at the back of the middle of the bar, so that she stood now pale as an apparition next to the cash register.

"You're feeling better," I said.

"I feel like I just climbed out of *hell*."

"Come have a drink," I said.

"Too early for me." She looked around. "Where's Kevin?"

"Just dropped him off at Zimmerman's."

Her jaw dropped. "Zimmerman's!"

"Yeah, he's going to ask him some questions, detective to detective. Zimmerman's our number one suspect."

"You're kidding," said Jeanne. "Why?"

I shrugged. "Ability, motive, experience, opportunity, temperament."

Jeanne raised her eyebrows, tore a ticket from the keno machine, and squinted at it. "You won a dollar," she said.

"Only game I've ever played where you invest five dollars, get back one, and call it winning."

"All right, I'll have a beer," said Rhonda, taking the stool next to mine. "I could use the vitamins." Rhonda did not usually drink beer. She was on a Weight Watchers program and a beer was like three points out of the 24 she was allotted daily, but this was a vacation, and she'd probably used only 12 points in the last two days. "Give me an Amstel Light," she said.

"Let me get it, Jeanne. I sold a story today."

"Which one?" said Rhonda.

"'Thousand Peso Suit.'"

Jeanne opened the beer and set it before Rhonda, who took a gulp and said, "When will Kevin be back?"

"Hour or so. He said he'd call."

Rhonda shook her head. "You two are crazy."

"You wanted a book."

"I just hope I don't have to finish it for you."

"Be good practice."

"I'd rather have you alive."

"Fate is often like a canoe after you've lost your paddles."

"One day I will understand what you're talking about."

I took a long tilt from my beer. Green glass, I'm told, makes beer skunky, but I like green-bottle beer.

Rhonda, regarding her brown-bottle beer, said, "Where's that consignment store Cristina took me to last time we were here?"

She spoke of Double Exposure, which sold designer clothes worn only 23 times by rich ladies from the East. My wife was addicted to the place, the only store for hundreds of miles where you could buy Armani, Ralph Lauren, and Oscar de la Renta articles for $10 or $20.

"It's on Second, across from the 120 Church, which used to be the 120 Bar. I heard they're turning it back into a bar."

"Original spirits," said Jeanne.

"I'll show you as soon as I've lost all my money here," I said. "How's that beer taste?"

"Like one more."

Jeanne drifted down the bar to pour the guitar historians

another. Rhonda seemed preoccupied. She picked at her beer label. "Does Kevin seem strange to you?"

"In what way?"

She took a sip and stared at herself in the mirror tiles behind the bottles. "Ever since we got here he's just…*different.*"

"He seems all right to me. He's fascinated by this case."

Rubbing the back of her neck, Rhonda confessed that she was concerned Kevin wanted to marry her for her money, that she might end up in the hills somewhere in a year or so like Haataja. "You never really know a person," she said, looking at me sidelong, "do you?"

"*Before* you marry them?" I said. "No. But listen, all this mystery and treachery and reading murder books in a fever has gone to your head. Kevin's a good man. You won't ever do any better. Do you know one time he got us $80 Huskies tickets for $60?"

She laughed without conviction, smoothed her hair, and gazed at her reflection. "I need some sun," she said. "Think I'll take a walk over to that consignment store."

"We'll meet you back here," I said. "Cristina gets off at five."

64.

Grisham versus Turow

KEVIN WAS IN A GOOD MOOD WHEN I PICKED HIM UP.

"How'd it go?" I said.

He climbed into the car and slammed the door. "He's not afraid to talk, that's for sure." He rolled his window down. "I asked him right off how bizarre it must be being a suspect in his own case."

"What'd he say to that?"

"'Was I a suspect?' he said. And then he admitted he would've investigated himself too. He said he had motive and opportunity and a pretty good understanding of how to kill someone in a small town with a local law enforcement agency that couldn't find their keys."

I took a right, found my way up the drop-off ramp, and parked right next to the school building. It would be 10 minutes before Tom was out. Kevin said, "He also said that killing the professor would have fit nicely into his class-ending exercise in homicide investigation. He says he didn't do it."

"Everyone says that, though, don't they?"

"If he killed Haataja to become the new police chief, it would have made more sense if he'd *found* him, yes?"

"When he was taken off the case he probably thought his chances were shot and said screw it."

"That's a stretch."

"What does he think happened up there?"

Kevin laid his elbow into the open window. A lady

carrying a plastic tray of pink-iced cupcakes passed. "He thinks *you* did it."

"What?"

"You were the only one to gain financially from Haataja's death. Admit it, your novels weren't going well, your book sales were poor, you hadn't been able to make a magazine sale in months, and without something truly spectacular to write about, something outside of your own mundane complaints, you were stuck cleaning floors for the rest of your life."

"It's too Scott Turow. Wait a minute, what about *you*? You had as much to gain as I did since your soon-to-be-wife owns the publishing house. He disappeared the day before you left! And Rhonda had those new sleeping pills that knocked her silly so it would've been easy for you to sneak out the east door without her knowing about it. Or maybe it was her idea."

"Too John Grisham," he replied

"Zimmerman didn't really say that, did he?"

"Just wanted to see what you'd say. You know us homicide cops think like killers." He winked.

I caught a flash of Rhonda lying dead in the grass and remarked to myself how alike policemen and the criminals they chase are: creatures of adrenaline and wile, they cannot exist without each other. Like matter and antimatter or the ridiculous and the sublime, they are often interchangeable. In other words, they are both looking for trouble. I suppose you could say the same thing about writers.

"He thinks it's a suicide," said Kevin, "but he's not really sold. Too many questions unanswered. He's never seen a case of self-immolation either, especially someone wired to a tree. He believes someone was with Haataja that night, too."

"Who?"

"That's the $10,000 question. Interesting that he tried to go up to the scene on a couple of occasions. He said the police stopped him. That kind of curiosity says something. Maybe he's reveling in the deed, picking up the heat of the excitement, or maybe he's just trying to see how much the cops know." He scraped a leaf off my side mirror with his thumbnail.

"Did he show you his crime-scene scrapbook?"

"Does he have one?"

"That's what I've heard."

Two children passed, singing, "Roll roll roll your boat, gently down the stream. If you see a crocodile don't forget to scream..."

"He's pretty bitter about losing his job," Kevin said. "He blames the college. He thinks the police deliberately botched the investigation and conspired with the college so the case would be forgotten, but if the cops are as incompetent here as everyone says, they wouldn't have been smart enough to arrange all that. His teeth aren't yellow, by the way. He wears dentures."

I slapped my forehead. "Bad imagination. Bad writer."

"Where's Rhonda?"

"Shopping. I told her we'd meet her back at the hotel. Here comes Tom..."

65.

The glorious panoply

4:46 A.M. Caller from the 300 block of Lake St. advised that he was at a party down the street and a guy there [caller gave subject's name] poured some beer on his head and punched him in the nose. Caller requesting an officer right away. Caller refused rescue unit for his nose.

WHENEVER TOM WITHDREW, OR WENT INTO ONE OF HIS spaz-trances rattling a juniper bush or stroking the tassels on a couch cushion, I'd never let him go for long. Fixed in my mind was that archetypal image of autism: the rocking, drooling child who receded one day and never returned. There was nothing known to counteract autism, not psychology nor drugs nor prayer (I will not ask God to pick my child over someone else's), not even buying an old school bus, hitting the road, and becoming a three-chord tambourine band like the Partridge Family.

Finger spiders, Spidey and Whitey, were my primary tool for retrieving him, and every day at least once he was attacked by the Kissing Monster or crushed in my arms with love, and I'd tell him a dozen times at least that he was the most fantastic boy in the world, the one I loved the most on earth, the one who made all the difference, and I'd nuzzle his ears until he giggled and he was once again mine. Darkness holds title to half of Creation, children are afraid of it for good reason. One day you are walking along the railroad tracks or up a trail into the wilderness or down the soup aisle at Safeway and wham there it is, nothing really that you can say except a feeble, "Where's the clam chowder?" Love might seem a sentimental defense, but it was all I had, it was my only light in the great dark forest below the star-crowned trees.

Cristina sometimes went away too, her eyes dazed blots as she floated mysteriously off like a wizard balloonist into Cristinaland, ice-cream dish of potato chips in her left hand, or worried or wearied or ailed herself to a frazzle over the future and money. But Cristina was easy to retrieve. All it took was a Chinese restaurant, an Indian casino, a cheeseburger with olive-oil fries, a shopping trip to Rapid City, or the suggestion that we test-drive a car.

More importantly, Cristina had returned to church. This tethered her, revived her, countered her worldliness, gave her nourishment and support. She'd overcome her biases against American Catholicism (which in theory should've been identical to Mexican Catholicism but didn't really come close) and understood what the Padre was saying and knew many of the parishioners and their stories and some of their dental histories and many of their indiscretions (oh the world seems like a slimy place when you know everyone in town and each of us takes our turn in the newspaper or the Police Beat or upon the lips of the gossipers for whatever rash or selfish thing we have done).

The boy accompanied her to every Saturday mass. Liturgy invigorated them both and they'd come home aglow and Tom usually brought me a cup of Catholic lemonade. Eventually we'd have our marriage blessed by the Father so she could take communion. Not far away was the boy's communion, too, and full entrance into that Glorious Panoply that covers everything you need to know (but were afraid to ask) from the beginning to eternity.

From the beginning (and to eternity) Cristina must've known I was on her side, that it gratified me to help and teach her, that my weakness (and my strength) was people, but she was just too preoccupied to notice me much of the time. For a long spell I was more like a tour guide or a personal bilingual attendant who also served as cook and chauffeur as she gained her footing in the new land. She assumed my life was easy, perhaps it was. On top of this she didn't believe anyone could truly love her. Like me, she didn't believe she deserved to be loved. I was permitted to love, however, even if I was not allowed to *be* loved, that had always been my role, "Friend of Man," as Les in Mexico used to call me. I was like a motivational psychologist or a senile Danish grandmother always saying, "It's going to be just fine," or, "Everything will work out for the best," or, "Don't you worry, you'll grow up to be a wonderful gynecologist someday," or, "How about a catfish sandwich with hot pickled zucchini and romaine lettuce or an iron skillet of cornbread and a cassoulet of white beans and Italian sausage?"

But everyone needs to be loved (as I cue up that Smiths song "How Soon is Now?") and the way some of us make inroads into each other's fugitive secrets, furtive beliefs, and festering denials, is to knock down their walls. That's a funny way to describe love, which is less like a map or a type of caramel-flavored opium than it is a hard-won fight, and another reason there will always be war.

So it is our seventh year together, our sixth married, and Cristina is a little down, a little tired after a long and hectic day and a little worried because who knows what will happen tomorrow and what if I lose my job (don't worry, I always lose my job, dear, and I have never failed to find another one just as crappy as the last; I really do need an arrangement where I can have a day off now and then anyway). I pour us a glass of wine (she liked Boone's Farm when I brought her to America, now she likes the dry deep reds) and I put my arm around her. "Oh come now, Flooper Booper, let's laugh. Life's too short. There is no happiness tomorrow, only happiness today. You know I love you, and that will never change."

Cristina and I stayed up late, even if I had to get up at three, and we drank too much deep red wine. After a while she sat on my lap and said she was happy and that she appreciated all the things I'd done. Those were rare words for her, but she was just waking up and folding out into three-dimensional form. I said pshaw, I'd done nothing. Without her I'd be walking through a blizzard all alone to the liquor store. We listened to her new CD and danced extravagantly and one thing led to another and so I leave you there.

66.

The wick effect

ABOUT A WEEK AFTER KEVIN AND RHONDA LEFT, I MADE arrangements to see Sheriff Conaghan once again on the third floor of the courthouse. The jail elevator and the courtroom are also on this floor and whenever I go up there I listen for the wail of inmates and the strum of their tin cups across the bars as they croon their rough buccaneer ditties.

I found Conaghan in his small office overlooking the park. He greeted me congenially as always. I said I only had a few follow-up questions. "Sit on down," he said. "What's on your mind?"

I wanted to know why the majority of those qualified to judge the Haataja case insisted it was a suicide.

Conaghan nodded and explained that if Haataja had doused himself or if someone else had doused him with the amount of starter necessary to get him burning the way he was burned, the tree to which he was tied and the grass all around him would've been burned to some extent.

"Well then," I said, "he must've been moved."

Conaghan shook his head. "No evidence of it."

Tell me more, Sheriff.

Haataja was bound with extension cords, those around his ankles *plugged* in, those around his midsection fastening him to the tree plugged in behind him. They weren't long extension cords, just those cheap brown five- or six-footers. And he didn't bring a lot of charcoal with him either, like everyone says, just enough for a small campfire. Probably everything he brought that night he could've fit into a plastic Walmart bag.

"Where did everyone get the idea he was wrapped in barbed wire?" I asked.

"There was a piece of barbed wire not far from Haataja's body that Fitzgerald picked up as possible evidence, but this was on a ranch where there are miles of the stuff, and there was never any connection made to that piece of barbed wire and how Haataja was tied."

"So you don't think anyone caught up to Haataja, met him on arrangement, or came upon him down in that hollow?"

The sheriff continued to shake his head. No drag marks, no footprints (except Haataja's), no tire tracks, nothing on computer logs, no sign of struggle. No DNA on site, including saliva from the neck of the bottle, belonged to anyone else but Steven Haataja. Neither was it a place where a body might've readily been moved without the help of several men. Not once that night had he been seen with anyone else. Alone-alone.

And how, the sheriff iterated, could the body be so thoroughly charred without the area around him being burned in similar fashion?

And if you were going to murder someone and you tied them up with extension cords, even if your victim was drunk, would you plug the *ends* together?

And would you leave his hands free?

And if someone murdered Steve, burned him alive, where were they? If it was someone who lived in our town, why wouldn't we have seen some pattern or sign of their maliciousness at some point before or after the killing? Or if he'd run into a perfect stranger at midnight, how had the stranger been so well equipped and thoroughly undetectable? And what could Steve have possibly done to deserve such treatment?

I submitted the considerable evidence that contradicted suicide, the just-bought groceries in his fridge, the absence of note or preparation, the student appointment in the morning, his sister's birthday, the fact that he'd paid his rent that morning, the $100 withdrawal, his complete incompatibility with the profile of self-immolation. The singing in his office his last night, the good-mood-new-life testimonies of friends.

Conaghan leaned back in his chair and folded his hands over his chest. "He was *happy* about his new life? He was way up because things were going great? He had a history of psychiatric problems? That's a classic suicide profile." He shook his head and rummaged around in his desk (glimpse of a small black pistol) until he'd retrieved a packet of fish-shaped fruit-flavored gelatin snacks. I declined his offer of a packet. He opened his. "You know, when Matt Fitzgerald from State Patrol became the lead officer in this case he went all over the country, east and west, high and low, spent probably hundreds of thousands of dollars investigating this as a murder. He drove himself to exhaustion, then depression, attempted suicide, and finally quit the force." He shook three yellow fruit fish into his palm. "The *reason* he could find nothing is that there was nothing to find. He was hunting *ghosts*."

I'd known and even worried that Haataja might've believed that in Chadron he'd finally found his Shangri-la. I'd found it a dozen times myself, always leaving disappointed (instead of killing myself) a few months later. By age 46, Steve's age, I didn't care if I lived or died, until marriage and Tom made me feel like living again. Haataja hadn't been so lucky, that was the difference between us. But I still couldn't comprehend how you could work for years and years to earn your doctorate and then a few months later throw it all away. And would you kill yourself if your father was dying, if you were the last man left in your family?

"As far as I'm concerned," Sheriff Conaghan said, chewing up the last of his gelatin fish, then wadding the wrapper and tossing it in the can, "the case is closed. There is no new evidence and there has never been any evidence to suggest that there was anyone with Haataja at any time that night. You'd have to show me something really extraordinary to change my position."

"Could his death have been an accident?" I asked.

"Possible," he said. "He might've gone up there to freeze to death, I could see that. That would've been more his style. He picked a very cold night, five below zero. He made a small fire for comfort, tossed off that booze, which as you know in large doses is a vasoconstrictor, tied himself up for courage or to keep himself from falling on his own fire, started to get drowsy from hypothermia, then, because he was tied loosely, fell over in a stupor on his fire anyway. But that's still a suicide."

"What about an autoerotic death?"

"Again, possible. He could have been murdered, too. God could come back tomorrow. But I'll go to my grave believing this is a suicide."

"How do you explain the remarkable way he was burned?"

He squinted, paused, glanced to the door. "Do you know about the wick effect?"

"No."

"Everyone thinks I'm talking about spontaneous combustion when I bring this up, but the wick effect is documented." He shuffled through a stack of papers on his desk until he produced an article. "Read this and tell me what you think. No one has to believe me if they don't want to. It's not my investigation."

I read the piece that Conaghan gave me when I got home. In summary, it explained how a body could burn inside out like a candle in its own fat. It related baffling cases of people found in their houses deeply, skeletally burned, yet their legs would still be intact and nearby items such as furniture and rugs would be unaffected by heat. Such cases had been heretofore mistaken by some to be examples of spontaneous combustion. Experiments with dead pigs (which have similar body-fat ratios as humans) wrapped in cloth containing a small amount of accelerant and ignited with the coal of a cigarette, caused a fire so hot that after five hours, bone destruction was taking place. These experiments proved that the rare phenomenon called "the wick effect" was valid, and for a long time I thought them relevant to the case of Steven Haataja.

67.

Testimony from a friend

AS THE MONTHS PASSED I WATCHED THE FEW KNOWN facts (mingled liberally with gallons of free-flowing gossip) about Steve Haataja coalesce and harden into several exciting and highly palatable but totally bogus stories of a friendless mathematician with a history of sorrow and self-infliction who died in a bizarre fashion for reasons no one would ever understand. All good stories passed down through generations tend to shed their facts in favor of an aphorism or moral lesson. The lesson in the more recent case of another missing math professor in Sidney, Montana, who was eventually found dead and determined to have been hunted down for sport by drifters attracted by the local oil boom, was that if the economy of your safe and friendly small town booms, you are going to have to say good-bye to your safe and friendly small town.

The lesson in the more nebulous case of Steven Haataja was harder to ascertain. Basically, opinions diverged into three camps. Those who did not know Haataja or the circumstances under which he was found more often than not voted vehemently for foul play. Those who were well acquainted with the facts and the history of Steve but did not know him personally (and who almost universally assumed that he was friendless and isolated and therefore any examination into his social life in Chadron was pointless), law enforcement in particular, consistently declared suicide. Those who knew Steve well with few exceptions did not accept suicide or understand how he might've entered so rapidly such an appalling state of mind.

Phil Cary, a very popular associate professor of mathematics at Chadron State, who had long weekly conversations with Steve, described his colleague as a treasure and a well-spoken and engaging man with an unusual sense of humor. Steve had a tremendous memory, bordering on the photographic. Cary felt that a rural college with low admission standards that didn't pay its professors much was tremendously fortunate to win the services of this mathematician who was so conceptually advanced that his colleagues didn't understand what he was talking about much of the time (though Steve was always happy to try and explain).

Professor Cary wanted to honor the family's wishes by not submitting to an interview. They had suffered through a series of vain and uninspiring investigations, the rabid and deliberate distortion of bloggers and gossipmongers, professional reporting that too often catered to titillation and hyperbole, and a college that resisted inquiry and wanted to have the incident forgotten as soon as possible to keep their matriculation on track. But Cary spoke out instead his resolute belief that Steve did not take his own life. Phil had known many people who had committed suicide, and looking back, he said, there was always that warning sign, but he never discerned such a warning sign in Steven Haataja. Cary thought also that there had been a profound misunderstanding about Haataja's turmoiled mental state the year before and resented the way it had been recycled to explain his situation in Chadron. This equation of the two mind-sets had clouded and colored everyone's perception of Steve, and along with the way the papers had emphasized his effeminacy and isolation, had provided a faulty rationale for his presumed actions, and had made it easier to discount him as a human being and dismiss him once he was gone.

Professor Cary had been in lengthy correspondence with Steve's best friend, Tim Sorenson, and both had agreed that there were numerous reasons Steve hadn't committed suicide. Haataja was happy, acclimated, and looking forward to the next semester. Though he was not intellectually challenged by any of his classes, for example, college algebra, becoming a better teacher and helping his students was a challenge he embraced. The stress and strain that had befallen him and caused his suicide attempt the year before (broken hip, PhD struggles), the subsequent depressive disorder diagnosis, and the prescriptive regimen for depression, had all been mitigated to the point, in Cary's opinion, that they were no longer factors. Moreover, Cary did not believe that Haataja, for any purpose, would have walked onto private property. The entirety of the circumstances under which he was found was not consistent in any way with his nature.

Phil Cary, who knew Steve as well as anyone in the department, was upset that not a single law enforcement officer ever came and talked to him.

68.

A ranch-flavored mystery

I STUDIED THE CRIME-SCENE PHOTOGRAPHS AND FOUND many things that caused me to doubt law enforcement's assessment that Haataja committed suicide or that this was an accidental death. First off, it's odd that his body was tied to the tree on the opposite side of the campfire. Because the front of the body is so deeply, skeletally burned, I would have thought that it would have been found facing what looks to be the ash pit. Perhaps Haataja did start out in front of the fire and when the heat became too intense, he tried to get away, but tied to the tree he could only manage to scoot to the other side. Or was Haataja actually sitting on the fire when it was lit? Or was he bound to the tree after the fire was started?

On the other side of the tree from Haataja's body is what looks like the ash ring left over from the campfire and there are two plastic bottles sitting just outside of it, unweathered and clean, as if they'd been placed there an hour before the photographs were snapped. One is an unopened bottle of Sam's purified water and the other is a near-empty bottle of schnapps. Because it has the gold cap and shape of the only brand of schnapps Highway Express sold at the time, I think it's Phillips Peppermint, but I can't say if it's 60 or 80 proof. Both bottles are about five feet from the body, and I didn't understand how they were not melted or at all affected by what must have been a hell-hot fire.

Another item neither melted nor showing heat damage is

a sandwich container, which looks to be Rubbermaid, a Walmart staple, and I would like to know if it is consistent with what he owned at home, but his sister is the only one who could tell me, and she wouldn't talk to me. This "sandwich container" on the other side of the campfire in front of the body, seems out of place in relation to the bottles of water and schnapps. From my understanding of the wick effect, it doesn't seem to be in play here because he is not burned inside out like a candle on his own fat. He is burned head to toe as if someone took a flame thrower to him or maybe a propane torch, which is the only other way besides the wick effect to explain how grossly burned he is, but not the tree to which he was tied and the nearby plastic items and most of the vegetation around him.

In addition to the position of Haataja's body and the plastic items unaffected by the heat, the way he is tied up with one extension cord around his ankles and another around his torso is not compatible in my mind with suicide or an accident. His ankles were crossed and bound tightly, like a calf in a tie-down roping event, but his upper body was loosely secured with a heavier gauge extension cord. Where the extension cords around Haataja's middle have burned, the insulation has melted, and the strands of bare copper wires have oxidized a bright green. It is possible that he tied himself to that tree, but considering his weight and size, could he have wrapped his ankles in such a fashion?

It troubles me to see the glasses still on his head. I simply don't believe he would've left them on if he intended to burn himself alive. Throwing even more doubt on accidental and suicidal scenarios was that there were many unburned briquettes lying around the area, as if whoever started that fire was in a rush. It struck me as awfully sloppy, especially given Haataja's obsessive-compulsive tendencies and the excessive order and neatness of his office and apartment.

To determine whether Haataja walked up the dirt road that led to Sandy Burd's house or took the Long Way Around over burned and fallen barbed wire fences, I looked at the photographs to see if there was manure in the treads of his boots. Unless someone drove or otherwise escorted him up the road to Sandy Burd's house, and they walked down a steep, rough grade from there, he would have had to walk through that corral by the trailer to get where he was going. I've gone through that corral and ended up with manure in the treads of my shoes. There was no manure visible in the treads of his boots. For a long time I'd been wondering what happened to the heavy blue and gray Columbia jacket that many told me he wore when it was cold and that Chuck did not recollect seeing in Haataja's apartment, but there was no sign of it in the photos, indicating the possibility of his desire to freeze to death, as the sheriff (and the psychic) suggested. More likely it vaporized in flames, like the rest of the clothes he was wearing.

As I study these photographs, I find myself saying over and over again, "I'm so sorry, Steve. I am so sorry they did this to you."

I submitted the photos to Detective Warren. He wanted police and autopsy reports, none of which I could supply. He had many questions and comments, among them:

1. Accelerant? The body is very burned, which would have required a lot of flammable material. I'm wondering if some-one didn't dump a shitload of accelerant, touch off a match, and run like hell.
2. No way that Tupperware contained enough accelerant to cause this damage. Unless it was napalm (or any other type of denatured alcohol gel, see: Sterno), which, if it is, makes for an even more interesting story.
3. Interesting his glasses are on his head.
4. If anyone says that you can get a "highly elevated BAC [blood alcohol content]" from that one pint bottle of peppermint schnapps then you're either talking about a five-year-old or you're an idiot.
5. Which means he was drinking beforehand, so who was Steve, a "social drinker," drinking with that night?
6. Does anyone honestly believe that he bound his own ankles

with a cattleman's expertise and then tied himself to a tree so that he couldn't run away?

7. And why, again, if he were trying to prevent himself from escaping, would he tie himself to a tree that looks more like a shrub when he could have chosen one of the larger trees nearby?

8. Lastly, you've told me that the house was just up the hill from the body, not more than a few hundred yards away, so I wonder why the owners of the property would not have noticed or at least smelled a fire of this magnitude, or heard screams or commotion.

The detective's comments gave me much to ponder, and I've gone back out to the site on numerous winter nights trying to figure out what might have happened. It is bleak, desolate territory, the sameness of the landscape making it easy to get lost or turned around, the cold wind without exception rushing down. Once I went out and tried to climb through a break in the electrified fence, but a large herd of snorting, seething black cattle prevented this. Another time, coming back down the road under the wooden May Queen sign, someone shouted at me. I walked toward the figure in the darkness. It was Brown Burd, who had recently surveyed our property. Brown looked just like his brother Collin, though less gnarled from wear. I liked him because he had done good work for us promptly and always remembered my name. He smiled in a relieved way when he recognized me and shook my hand. I'm sure he was as surprised to see me as I was to see him. "What are you doing out here?" he wanted to know.

"Trying to retrace Steve's route the night he died," I replied. "I got permission from your brother through the sheriff. What are *you* doing out here?"

"I *live* here."

"In the trailer by the corral?"

"Yes."

"Were you living here when Haataja was found?"

"Yes, that's right." He got very nervous then and began

answering questions I hadn't asked. "The State Patrol came out and I told them I saw nothing that night," he said.

As we ended our conversation, the words of ranch hand Slim Buttes kept ringing in my head: "I hope they catch the son of a bitch who did it."

69.

Zimmerman for police chief or sheriff?

WED., OCT. 10, 10:20 P.M. Caller from Oelrichs advised the State Line Casino was just robbed. Caller stated he was following suspects in either a silver Dodge Stratus or a white Dodge Dakota pickup. Caller stated they are doing around 100 mph and at this time he does not have a make, model, year, color, or plate. Caller stated they were just crossing the White River Bridge and should be at the three mile corner in about three minutes. Caller requesting officers stop all southbound traffic at North Highway 385 and 20. Caller stated these subjects are armed and dangerous.

AFTER LOREN ZIMMERMAN LOST HIS POSITION AT THE COLlege, he began to openly campaign to become the new police chief. Both he and the interim chief, Margaret Keiper, put in their applications and looked to be top candidates. Zimmerman even asked Jeanne for a letter of recommendation, which Jeanne managed to "squiggle out of." A new chief was found elsewhere, a man named Lordino, a good name for a chief (or a Roman Emperor) and one bound apparently to make us forget the previous regime, for shortly afterward the band of five armed Montana subintellects on an interstate crime spree, including the robbery of the nearby Stateline Casino in South Dakota, came rolling into our town in a stolen car, and were rounded up in swift and inspiring fashion.

Zimmerman, running out of money, and finding himself unable to get a decent-paying job in Chadron because there aren't any, finally landed employment in Georgia teaching criminal justice. After a month he returned to Chadron. Another month later he shipped off to Iraq as a crime investigator. Before he left, he married Suzie Greenwheat and now she has five children to watch and a purple pickup in her driveway. Upon his return, he intends to run for sheriff against his archrival Shawn Conaghan.

The *I Kill People* bumper sticker has been removed.

70.

El fin (The End)

WINTER COMES EARLY AT 3,400 FEET. FREEZES ARE NOT unusual in early September. One November night we had an outdoor fire party in our backyard with Cristina's new friends, George from Valencia, Spain, and his wife, Beth Anderson, who taught high school Spanish in Alliance and Tigers and Bears, Oh My. George, a criminal justice major, and an ex-Valencia policeman, who'd worked for both the Chadron Police Department and as the jailer for the Dawes County Sheriff's Office (he affectionately calls Sheriff Conaghan "Shawnito," and Shawn thinks very highly of George as well), was eager to get his degree and leave Chadron because there weren't many law enforcement opportunities in the area. George was another misplaced surf nut and thought since he was bilingual he'd enlist with the Border Patrol and maybe find his way out to California.

Cristina was completely at ease, laughing and making jokes, her sultry eyes glittering in the firelight. The women drank Dos Equis and Pacifico, talked about cars and cows and living in Portugal and chewed the local *chisme* (gossip), which only gets sweeter as you get to the root, while George and I worked on a bottle of Tempranillo and talked about the admirable innocence of my hero George Orwell (often numbered as a possible autistic, though for his superb wit and decency I don't know why) who fought under the Communist flag in the Spanish Civil War. The reason the Fascist Franco was able to beat both the Anarchists and the Communists is that he let the people have what they wanted, what the Communists and the Anarchists would have prohibited: religion, patriotism, and a monarchy.

With his light skin, aquiline nose, and high brow, George is often mistaken in the States, he says, "for a German, a Russian, an Australian, or someone from New Jersey." The fire full of oak and pine popped and roared so magnificently we had to back up our chairs. I made gringofied guacamole (with chipotle ranch dressing) that passed muster and we ate fire-roasted sausages with onions browned in sherry tucked into slabs of French bread. We listened to Mecano, Los Angeles Azules, Fobia, and Los Heroes de Silencia. Tom, who loves fires, ate two sausages roasted in wine, ran around with a flaming stick, and did for us his "Pompeii Dance," as I have come to call it when he shows us his naked backside (*pompis* being a gracious Spanish word for "butt").

Tom was now six and in his second year of kindergarten (he liked it so much the first time) and we'd stopped taking him to the psychologist in Casper ever since he'd not been able to meet the criteria for Asperger's. If he was autistic, it was an extremely mild form, like a slice of pepperoni on a bell pepper pizza. The psychologist had wanted to continue to see him (at $165 an hour) because Tom had all these other issues, the "focusing" and fine-motor-coordination problems, ritual behaviors, atypical language, asociality, tactile obsessions, hypersensitivity to stimuli, and had scored fairly low on what are now called cognitive performance or assessment tests, what were in my day called intelligence tests. What this meant in so many words was my son wasn't that bright. Or he didn't take tests well. Or his fuse wasn't lit yet. Or he knew exactly what was going on but didn't feel like playing the game.

I'd stopped caring about where he fit along any spectra or the nebulous and poorly understood process that psychology wanted to drag him through in its often arbitrary and drug-happy pursuit of establishing "mental health." Interesting and dynamic people must at an early age reject the relevance and desirability of conforming in an overly mechanized, standardized society. So long as I could talk with Tom, so long as he was robust, growing, bright of eye, and frolicking about the yard with a flaming stick and a sausage, so long as he was curious about electricity, weather, bones, and the properties of metal, that was all I could ask for. Long ago I'd learned to trust my own judgment and instincts, which from the start had told me that come what may, as Bunthram was Bunthram, Tom was Tom.

As we sat in front of the fire George asked, "What's going on with the Haataja case?"

"Nothing. No change. No new evidence."

George knew most everyone involved, including Haataja, and he was acquainted with the basic facts of the case. Though most townsfolk longed for a cowboy serial killer or lava-drooling ogre snorting and slobbering through the hills, George considered this a suicide. He had talked with Haataja once and thought him "nervous and weird."

"When are they going to close it?" he wanted to know.

"Probably never. It would only make them look bad."

He asked me who I'd interviewed, and I said I'd interviewed everyone who would talk to me and many more who would not, but every trail led to God knows where. There would be no satisfactory conclusion, I thought, until that confession or that eyewitness came forward.

I poured George another glass of wine. Tempranillo is a deep Spanish red, highly compatible on cold nights with outdoor fires. He held his glass to the flames, as if to warm it, then took a gulp. "A lot of people are not going to like your book."

"Yes, I'm quite aware of that, which is why I think we'll probably move to Portugal."

The women began to giggle. Cristina liked that idea of Portugal, and so did Beth, though she and George would probably be moving west soon, or south, deeper into America, farther and farther from home, as is the custom here in the New World. Beth was shy, but her Spanish was good and sometimes with another language you get to be someone else, especially after two or three beers. Tom was off inside the house looking for marshmallows and the big meat fork I used to roast them on. The bright black sky was powdered with planets and stars. Far up in the dashed constellations a fast-moving orange blip pulsed in and out of sight.

"Somebody's watching us," said George.

"Let's hope so," I said.

Author's note

IN THE INTEREST OF FLUENCY AND READABILITY I HAVE used fictive techniques, built evidentiary platforms, condensed sequences, swapped out names, and committed other extravagancies, but the facts – and the hearsay pawned off as facts – pertinent to the case have not been altered. Neither have I excluded rumor, hysteria, bias, gossip, and the ignorant rest of whatever tomfoolery has become the basis of this living and heritable testament of the curious and horrible tragedy of Dr. Steven Haataja, the legend if you like, the inevitable fate of all factual accounts.

Acknowledgments

TO THE LEGION WITHOUT WHOSE HELP THIS BOOK WOULD not have been possible, chiefly among them Karl Dailey, Richard Dabney, Kevin Warren, Dave Jannetta, and Rhonda Hughes. And a special thanks to Cheryl Strayed for her generosity and writing the introduction to this book in the midst of her meteoric worldwide tour.

Love & Terror on the Howling Plains of Nowhere

A documentary
directed by Dave Jannetta

*For the latest on the "Love & Terror" documentary
visit: www.LoveAndTerrorTheMovie.com*

I HAD BEEN READING POE BALLANTINE'S WORK FOR A few years. When I found his book of essays, *501 Minutes to Christ*, it was precisely the medicine I needed. After exhausting Poe's œuvre I decided to see if he had a novel or essay collection on the horizon and came across an Internet blurb for his forthcoming *Love & Terror on the Howling Plains of Nowhere*. As a filmmaker I'm always looking for good stories, and this one – about the mysterious disappearance of Dr. Steven Haataja – had me instantly enthralled.

Coincidentally, a friend of mine had written Poe a letter in 2005, which he sent care of *The Sun Magazine*. Poe replied to my friend with a return address in Chadron, Nebraska. Knowing Poe's history, I didn't expect him to live there any longer, but in November 2011 I wrote him anyway, inquiring about the possibility of making a documentary based on *Love & Terror*. A month later I was in Chadron.

It was 5 below when I first pulled into town. After an icy five-hour drive from the Denver airport, I arrived in front of the Olde Main Street Inn just after 1 am. The wide streets were deserted and a light snow was falling. Jeanne, the ex-biker proprietor of the inn, was waiting to greet me with a complimentary welcome-to-Chadron beer. It was exactly as I'd imagined it.

The film is an exploration of many of the same themes and topics described in the book, and because the timeline of their creation overlaps slightly, the film and book inform each other.

The documentary deepens the perspective on Chadron and its inhabitants, the disappearance and death of Dr. Haataja, and the life and philosophies of Poe Ballantine.

Dave Jannetta is an independent filmmaker currently residing in Philadelphia but by the time you read this it's difficult to say where he'll be. His production company is 32-20 Productions and you can contact him at: *info @ 3220productions.com*